Lords of Misrule

Lords of Misrule

Lords of Misrule

❧ Mardi Gras and the ❧
Politics of Race in New Orleans

JAMES GILL

UNIVERSITY PRESS OF
MISSISSIPPI · JACKSON

Copyright © 1997 by the University Press of Mississippi

Manufactured in the United States of America

2nd printing, 1998

The paper in this book meets the guidelines for permanence and durability of the Committee on Production Guidelines for Book Longevity of the Council on Library Resources.

Library of Congress Cataloging-in-Publication Data
Gill, James.
    Lords of misrule : Mardi Gras and the politics of race in
New Orleans / James Gill.
        p.   cm.
    Includes bibliographical references and index.
    ISBN 0-87805-915-6 (alk. paper). —
    ISBN 0-87805-916-4 (pbk. : alk. paper)
    1. Carnival—Louisiana—New Orleans—History.
2. New Orleans (La.)—Race relations.   3. New Orleans
(La.)—Politics and government.   4. New Orleans (La.)—
Social life and customs.   I. Title.
GT4211.N4G55   1997
394.2'5—dc20
                                                    96-32927
                                                        CIP

British Library Cataloging-in-Publication data available

CONTENTS

CONTENTS

CHAPTER ONE

The Old South on Parade

The white men in jackets and ties were obviously out of their element. Normally, at this time of day, they would be preparing to leave home or office for a couple of drinks, lunch and maybe a card game at their clubs. Now, on December 19, 1991, they shifted in their seats, returning hostile glares from a large contingent of black men and women in the packed basement of New Orleans City Hall. The city council was meeting in spartan surroundings while its regular chambers were being renovated, but the physical discomforts were nothing compared to the general psychic unease as everyone waited for the great debate on an ordinance to desegregate Mardi Gras parades and gentlemen's luncheon clubs.

Most of the white men in the audience were members of the city's social elite. They rode in exclusive parades that dated back to antebellum days and made old-world society look like a hotbed of social mobility. They supervised their daughters' debuts, lived amid the privileges of inherited wealth and regarded themselves as the embodiment of the sacred traditions of New Orleans Carnival. They were here to ward off what they saw as an attack on civilization.

The black members of the audience were in high spirits and alive with anticipation. The economic and social power of old New Orleans was about to collide with contemporary political reality, and Councilwoman Dorothy Mae Taylor had made clear her determination to give the white aristocracy its comeuppance. The besuited section looked supercilious, but wary, as Sidney Barthelemy, the black mayor, started proceedings with an address to the seven members of the city council, of whom only three were white.

Although Taylor's principal target was the old-money, white upper class, her ordinance threatened upheaval in every one of the city's twenty-nine organizations, known as "krewes," that staged annual parades through the streets as a prelude to Lent. New Orleans had white krewes and black krewes, men's krewes and women's krewes, highfalutin krewes and demotic krewes, but few, if any, that met all the requirements of the ordinance. If it passed, all clubs and krewes would henceforth be required to accept members regardless of race, gender, handicap or "sexual orientation," or their officers could wind up in jail. In order to receive parade permits, krewes would be required to prove they did not discriminate.

At stake was not just one of the world's great street celebrations. In New Orleans, Mardi Gras is a year-round obsession for many people and inspires the fervor of a pagan religion. Much of the city's social intercourse centers on krewe get-togethers and the endless planning for the next parade. Mardi Gras is a major industry, and helps define the subtle gradations of the city's social and racial caste system. It has also proved a consistent success in a city not otherwise known for efficiency, with parades that have been frequently spectacular and, sometimes, works of art. Never does New Orleans seem more like a foreign city than when the exuberant and bibulous throngs flood its streets at Carnival season, and the masked riders toss trinkets from their perches high on the floats.

But that seemed a million miles away from the city hall basement, where the white krewemen bristled, and most of the black spectators exulted, at the threat of radical reform in Carnival, unchanged and a law unto itself for generations.

Neo-Nazi and former KKK Grand Wizard David Duke campaigning in the Louisiana gubernatorial election of 1991. Photo by G. Andrew Boyd/Times-Picayune.

Relations between the races were already at one of the lowest points in the city's history, thanks to the meteoric political career of David Duke, neo-Nazi and former grand wizard of the Ku Klux Klan. Reporters from all over the world descended on Louisiana as Duke moved from rally to rally, haranguing huge and adoring crowds and causing great anguish in business and tourism circles. It seemed for a while that Louisiana, long self-conscious about its image as a banana republic attached to the United States, was about to make a messiah out of a man who celebrated Hitler's birthday, believed Josef Mengele was one of the world's great scientists, denounced the Holocaust as a myth and once proposed that ethnic homelands be established in the United States for blacks, Jews, Indians and other undesirables.

Duke, after being elected to the state house of representatives from a lily-white suburb of New Orleans in 1989, promptly ran for the U. S. Senate and then for the governorship of Louisiana. The darling of most white voters, he downplayed his past and sounded much like a Reconstruction-era politician when he declared himself "the black man's best friend." He worked hard on his mainstream image, with his conservative suit and a carefully coiffed shock of fair hair crowning a face that was as handsome and manly as the plastic surgeon had been able to make it. He lost both elections, but only because black voters, who make up 30 percent of the state total, decided they didn't need a friend like him in high office.

New Orleans had problems common to much of urban America. White families and businesses had fled to the suburbs, leaving the city chronically short of money. Many of its public schools were in an advanced state of decay; test scores were abysmal. Drug dealers terrorized the housing projects, homicide was commonplace and there were few parts of the city where anyone felt safe walking the streets at night. Yet the city retained its steamy and romantic grace from the narrow streets of the French Quarter to the splendid mansions uptown and in the Garden District, from the ritzy houses along the shore of Lake Pontchartrain to the secluded luxury of Park Island on Bayou St. John. None of the elite settlements was far from mean and ramshackle neighborhoods seething with fury and resentment, however, and a siege mentality descended on the city.

The Old South on Parade

Preachers, politicians and editorialists united in a call for "a time of healing" when Duke lost the gubernatorial election, but, only a month and a day later, Taylor walked into the council chamber to open the public hearing on her Carnival desegregation ordinance. Barthelemy, a former state senator and city councilman, now in the second of the two four-year terms allowed a mayor of New Orleans, cut a distinguished figure, tall and gray-haired, as he faced the council and announced his support for desegregation. The krewes, he said, had resisted all attempts to reach an agreement on reforming their membership policies, which were a threat to the city's reputation and economic prospects. His peroration continued: "We cannot send a signal that we help to foster discrimination in New Orleans. We are a big-league city in terms of conventions, tourism and sports events. Whether we like it or not, this is the modern age." The barb was obviously aimed at the four so-called "old-line" krewes, the preserve of the white male establishment. The most venerable was Comus, which first took to the streets in 1857, followed in 1872 by Rex and Momus and, in 1882, by Proteus. Membership in any one of those krewes carried considerable social cachet. Blacks, women, Jews and anyone of Italian heritage were personae non gratae, although Rex, the largest of the elite organizations, had fallen victim to a creeping liberalism, allowing nouveaux riches and even a few whose Gentile credentials were questionable to infiltrate its ranks. The scions of the old plutocracy in Comus, Momus and Proteus were more persnickety and still capable of rejecting otherwise respectable candidates for membership if their forebears had been "scalawags," as collaborators with federal troops were known during the Civil War and Reconstruction. Comus, Momus and Proteus tended to dismiss Rex as "down the line socially."

To reign over the Rex parade, as king of all Carnival, however, remained the highest honor of Mardi Gras and the only

Sidney Barthelemy, mayor of New Orleans during the Carnival controversy.
*Photo by Ellis Lucia/*Times-Picayune.

public one available to a krewe member. Save for identifying
Rex each year, the old-line krewes adhered to a code of silence.
The queens of Rex, Comus, Momus and Proteus, however, were
featured every Carnival season in the society columns of the
New Orleans *Times-Picayune* along with the rest of the gilded
youth in their make-believe courts. The queen of Comus was
regarded as the top debutante of the year and could dine out on
her distinction for the rest of her life.

The identity of Rex himself was revealed Mardi Gras morning every year when his picture also ran in the *Times-Picayune*.

That evening a Coast Guard cutter, escorted by a flotilla of riverboats, delivered Rex to a quay on the Mississippi, where he disembarked to be greeted by the mayor, members of the consular corps and various other officials. With fireworks exploding over the river, the mayor then declared the next day a holiday and whimsically turned all his powers over to Rex for the next day. After the ceremony (a nineteenth-century custom revived in 1986), everyone paraded informally along the streets, or "second-lined," to meet up with the Proteus parade, which was always held the night before Mardi Gras.

The next morning, with his face exposed for all to see, Rex took New Orleans's ultimate ego trip through the cheering crowds. Otherwise, the men in the krewes kept their masks on throughout the parades and the subsequent balls. To be the monarch of the other krewes, to adopt the identity of a mythological god for a day, was to arrive at the summit of New Orleans society, but only those in the inner sancta knew who had been anointed. The real power in the krewes, however, resided in the captain, whose word was law and who might remain in the position for many years. The old-line krewes regarded themselves as guardians of the true spirit and traditions of New Orleans Carnival, which, to them, meant demonstrating both their civic generosity and their social superiority. To older connoisseurs of Carnival, none of the season's public spectacles compared to the Comus parade, which was always built around some mythological or otherwise learned theme, and which, in the tasteful designs and rich colors of its floats and the striking costumes of its riders, proclaimed itself a gift of the rich and educated classes to the common folk on the street. Its route was illuminated by rows of black men prancing alongside the floats and brandishing flambeaux, which were lit just before the parade in a staging area under the supervision of the krewe captain bestriding a white steed.

The old-line krewes were not, however, universally appreci-

paternalism

*Comus of 1991, the last to parade through the streets of New Orleans, with his queen,
Helen Hardi Martin Nalty. Photo by Norman J. Berteaux/*Times-Picayune.

swaying and shimmering through what seemed a supernatural aura as the light of the flambeaux caught smoke swirling off flares into the night air. Their riders were much more restrained—some said stingy—with throws, as they rumbled past on the same wooden, steel-rimmed wheels that had clattered over cobblestones en route to masked balls in long-vanished theaters and opera halls. The old-line krewes were permament, immutable. They owned their floats and the warehouses, or dens, where they were stored and where members held their meetings. They perceived their parades as moving theater, an attempt to engage the minds and senses of the crowd, and were widely regarded as an anachronism. Yet every participant in even the newest Mardi Gras parade was heir, mostly unwitting, to a ritual devised by the original members of Comus.

Parades were the only organized aspect of public Mardi Gras. For the old-line krewes in particular, running the gantlet of the madding crowd, though a giddy experience, was merely prelude to the private balls and parties that represented the real culmination of a long social season. Most natives and visitors, however, were only dimly aware of the closed world of upper-class Carnival and the debut season. Mardi Gras, so far as the public was concerned, happened on the streets and in licensed premises and amounted to a glorious riot. Every formal parade attracted hordes of "second-liners" performing impromptu dances as they followed the floats. Less formal parades were everywhere, from the marching clubs that proceeded from bar to bar to the "gangs" in the black neighborhoods who dressed up as Red Indians on the warpath, and from the irreverent and frequently scabrous creations of loosely organized wags to the extemporaneous efforts of total strangers caught up in the intoxicating mood or under the influence of intoxicating liquors. Although most people who sallied forth on Shrove Tuesday wore their regular clothes, plenty maintained ancient tradition by strutting around masked and in outlandish garb. In the

French Quarter, one of the nation's most hospitable locales for homosexuals, cross-dressers were everywhere, frequently in clothes of breathtaking, figure-hugging splendor. The quarter was the one part of town where all restraints—never too oppressive in New Orleans at the best of times—were cast aside. People of both sexes sometimes cast all clothes aside too, and it was not unknown for strangers to indulge in acts of congress on the streets. At the stroke of midnight on Shrove Tuesday, the street cleaners appeared behind policemen with bullhorns declaring that the season was over, but few people, whether holed up in bars and stumbling around the streets with "go-cups" full of beer, were ready to embrace the penitential mood of Lent. The religious pretext for the celebrations had always been more or less a fraud in New Orleans, and even in the early days the arrival of Lent was not accompanied by widespread abstemiousness. Until the turn of the century, for instance, a live bull, or Boeuf Gras, appeared in Rex parades, supposedly to provide the last feast before the coming rigors, but it was, in fact, regularly butchered to be eaten on Ash Wednesday. Drunkenness was always common in New Orleans at the best of times; at Carnival late-night promenaders were not infrequently obliged to pick their way through young men passed out in pools of vomit.

Mardi Gras may be best known to the outside world as a public festival, but upper-class New Orleans knew that its real significance lay in the annual reaffirmation of social eminence over merit. The most potent symbol of that creed came on the night of Mardi Gras, when Rex and Comus held their balls in different sections of the municipal auditorium. The evening ended when the mock royalty of the two krewes staged the traditional "meeting of the courts" shortly before midnight. It was not for nothing that the bare-faced Rex, chosen in part for his civic contributions, had to traipse over and pay his respects to the mysterious Comus.

To the aficionados Carnival possessed an almost mystic allure. As Perry Young, quasi-official historian of the old-line krewes put it in 1931, "Carnival is a butterfly of winter, whose last mad flight of Mardi Gras forever ends his glory. Another season is the glory of another butterfly, and the tattered, scattered fragments of rainbow wings are in turn the record of his day." The poetry of the season was, however, lost on a large number of people in New Orleans, who abhorred it as tedious, offensive, or a childish waste of time and money. Dorothy Mae Taylor's ordinance was a sign that those who found Carnival tradition repugnant or believed it to be a drag on the city's economy were no longer content to suffer in silence or leave town. A loose coalition of Jews, blacks, women and disaffected businessmen and professionals had been encouraging her efforts since 1988. They were mostly behind the scenes, but, for them, it was a famous day when Taylor opened debate on the desegregation ordinance and Barthelemy delivered his speech in support.

When Barthelemy was through at the council meeting, all eyes turned toward Taylor, who, with her spectacles and sharp features, bore some resemblance to a bird of prey. In her not-infrequent moments of excitement, Taylor's voice became quite shrill, but she was cool now. "I should like to thank the mayor for diligently trying to strike a compromise with the Mardi Gras krewes. It did not work. There has been no olive branch from the krewes." A murmuring arose from the white krewemen, and Taylor fixed a stern gaze upon them. "Whether you know it or not, we are here for business." This elicited some angry shouts from both sides of the audience, which the burly Joe Giarrusso, one of the council's white minority, promptly quelled. "The police are here to prevent disruption," he announced, motioning a couple of officers from behind the dais to station themselves in the audience. Although Giarrusso was now sixty-eight years old and distinctly jowly, he retained some of the physical presence from his days as the city's barrel-chested police chief during the riots that had accompanied desegregation of the public schools more than thirty years earlier. The battle had not produced schools that were integrated in anything but a legal sense, for white parents abandoned them in such numbers that the system has been 90 percent black ever since. White parents either fled to develop their own suburbs in adjoining parishes, as counties are called in Louisiana, or transferred their children to the city's private schools. Giarrusso therefore knew as well as anyone the futility of trying to impose racial harmony, but his tone made clear that nobody would be allowed to get out of line. The crowd in the chamber quieted down, and Taylor asked Bruce Naccari, the council's legal adviser, how much it cost taxpayers to provide police protection, sanitation and other services for Mardi Gras parades, which go on for a few weeks leading up to Shrove Tuesday.

"The city provides a subsidization of about three and a half million."

"Subsidization, eh? In other areas it's called welfare."

The krewemen groaned, and Councilwoman Peggy Wilson, seated next to Taylor, looked daggers. There was no love lost between Taylor and Wilson, the black Democrat and the white Republican at odds on almost every issue of consequence that came before the council. This one was especially hot, because Wilson's council district included the oak-shaded uptown avenues where the Carnival establishment maintained its mansions, and plenty of blue blood ran in her own veins. Her grandfather, Joseph Henican, president of the New Orleans Cotton Exchange, had been Rex in 1926, and she herself had been one of the well-bred girls chosen as maids of honor to Rex of 1958. Wilson's husband was a grandson of Leonidas Pool, Rex of 1925.

A few months before the Carnival-desegregation hearing, Wilson had irrevocably alienated Taylor and most of her other colleagues, who had rejected her suggestion that they call a referendum on a proposition to change the city charter and limit themselves to two four-year terms. But the charter provided for proposed amendments to be put on the ballot by petition of the voters, and Wilson had gone out and collected the requisite ten thousand signatures to force an election. The limited-terms proposition passed easily, leaving Wilson herself and all other council members, save rookie Jacqueline Clarkson, enjoined from seeking reelection.

Taylor knew what they were saying on the streets: she was introducing this ordinance to teach errant white voters a lesson and to make life miserable for Wilson. Not so, she declared. "I first called public hearings on this issue in 1988, when the ordinance was drafted. What we are considering today has nothing to do with the gubernatorial election or limited terms." Taylor explained that her ordinance would create a municipal Human Relations Commission to investigate "public accommodations" and root out discrimination. Private organizations would be exempt. Carnival krewes would be in the public domain because they paraded on city streets, and several of them held balls in the municipal auditorium. Luncheon clubs would be covered if they had more than seventy-five members, served regular meals and were involved in "the direct or indirect furtherance of trade or business." Bill Quigley, a local lawyer who has worked extensively for the American Civil Liberties Union and drafted the Taylor ordinance, then admonished the council: "This is not just games. This is culture. This is business." The ordinance was modeled on a New York City law banning discrimination in private luncheon clubs, 125 of which had filed suit claiming that government interference in their affairs was unconstitutional on its face. The U. S. Supreme Court disagreed, while noting that "there may be clubs that would be entitled to constitutional protection." Shortly after that ruling, Taylor took her first crack at segregation in New Orleans, but nobody from the old-line krewes or the luncheon clubs showed

The Old South on Parade

New Orleans city council members Dorothy Mae Taylor (left) and Peggy Wilson
in one of their calmer moments during debate over the Carnival desegregation ordinance.
Photo by Jim Sigmon/Times-Picayune.

up for the public hearing she called. In 1988, her focus was
more on the clubs than the krewes. "There are persons meeting, operating under the guise of private clubs, that are conducting business. Business decisions are being made, and yet
there are those of us who are being denied that opportunity for
discussion and input before those decisions are made," she said
at the time. Nothing had come of her efforts, because the council put off a vote until it could set up an agency to enforce any
ordinance it might adopt.

This time, Taylor had the attention of the entire city, and
dozens of people had signed up to address the council on the
desegregation ordinance. First to do so was physician Dwight
McKenna, a member and former president of the New Orleans
school board. Once one of the most respected and eloquent
black politicians in town, Dr. McKenna was now under in-
dictment for tax evasion. "We have in the Mardi Gras krewes
the vestiges of the plantation mentality. African Americans will

no longer accept second-class citizenship," he said and abruptly sat down. A few months later he was sentenced to prison.

The big guns of the defense took their seats at a table facing the council. The leader was Beau Bassich, Rex of 1989 and current captain of Proteus. Bassich, with his amiable disposition, was already recognized as spokesman for the establishment, having for several years chaired the mayor's Mardi Gras committee, which was responsible for promoting order and safety during the parades. At Bassich's side was the 1988 king of Carnival and current captain of Rex, John Charbonnet. Tagging along was James McLain, a professor of economics at the University of New Orleans, who did not belong to any krewes but had spent several years studying the financial aspects of Carnival. Bassich, a stocky figure with silver hair and a florid complexion, read what he said was a statement put together by sixty-four people—"black, white, male, female"—representing Mardi Gras organizations: "There has been no notice of consultation, no opportunity for us to review the ordinance and no evaluation of its economic impact. We should like to point out that no krewe has a charter or bylaws that exclude anyone. Mardi Gras has been organized for 150 years and paid for by private funds. It is wrong for the city to try to dictate what we do. The real losers here will be not the Carnival krewes but the city of New Orleans."

Professor McLain recalled that one of the first things he noticed when relocating to New Orleans after living in northern cities was that "there were no workers with lunch boxes." Generations of political candidates had vowed to rectify that, to bring manufacturing to the city, and "economic diversification" was a standard plank in any election platform. It had, however, never been achieved, and the city was precariously dependent on tourism and shipping after the collapse of the oil industry a decade earlier sent the entire state into an economic tailspin. If the city did not have factories, however, McLain soon concluded that its economy had an admirable substitute in Mardi Gras. He calculated the impact of the 1990 season on the city's economy at close to $500 million, of which 80 percent was money from out of state. Carnival produced tax revenues of $27 million to city government and $15 million to the state. "This is the same as having a company come in with six thousand employees. Mardi Gras is a delicate cultural instrument. It is also what we call a 'cash cow.'"

Charbonnet now weighed in to remind the council that Mardi Gras was "one of the jewels in the crown of the city of New Orleans," and that several thousand people belonged to krewes. "We can't afford to snub our noses at Mardi Gras. Mardi Gras is multicultural and multiethnic. We stand side by side requesting that this ordinance be withdrawn. You do not want to be remembered as the council that killed Mardi Gras." Only a man who equated Mardi Gras with the old-line krewes could have entertained the preposterous notion that the city council, or any agency of government, could kill it. New Orleans was consumed by the Carnival season, which ran from Twelfth Night through Shrove Tuesday and featured so many parades over the final weeks of the season that the loss of a few would hardly have been crippling. To many people, New Orleans was unimaginable without the pageantry and the music of Carnival parades, but, to insiders, the private events, the balls and debuts, were the heart of the season. The city had, in addition to its parading krewes, an approximately equal number of Carnival organizations that shunned the public gaze altogether, some of them just as exclusive as Comus. Indeed, their members in many cases also belonged to the old-line krewes and the gentlemen's clubs, around which the white establishment believed true New Orleans Carnival revolved. No class, however, had an exclusive claim on Carnival, and several parades were staged by men and women who had no social pretension but did have a fierce dedication to their cultural inheritance. Black society had its own cotillions and debutante parties at the Original Illinois and Young Men Illinois clubs. The predominantly black krewe, Zulu, preceded Rex along the parade route every Mardi Gras morning, its riders tossing Carnival's most prized throws—coconuts painted in gold, silver, turquoise or pink. After Rex came the poor man's floats, trucks somewhat perfunctorily decorated, with scores of riders unloading tons of plastic beads and doubloons, not infrequently caught at earlier parades and hoarded for redistribution.

By no means all the residents of New Orleans got caught up in the annual excitement. Many found the huge influx of tourists and the wild abandon of the occasion so distasteful that they left town every Mardi Gras. At that time of the year, New Orleans accents seemed to drown out all others at Disney World in Orlando or on the ski slopes of Colorado. Jewish families traditionally left town to avoid embarrassing the Gentile friends who could not invite them to the leading social events of the season. No municipal ordinance could kill Mardi Gras, but Charbonnet had reason to believe that Councilwoman Taylor would not hesitate to destroy the old-line krewes. Over and over, she complained that membership in them and in the luncheon clubs conferred business opportunities that were being unfairly denied to blacks. She had a point, of course, since the esprit de corps forged among men who lunched and paraded together would inevitably carry over into the outside world, although no member of a krewe or a club would be so gauche as to talk commerce in a social setting. Carnival represents an opportunity to retreat from reality into courtly fantasies that breed a profound hostility to strangers.

Charbonnet nevertheless assured the council that the krewes could be trusted to desegregate themselves. To that end, he explained, with a faint air of irritation, he and other Carnival muck-a-mucks had asked Taylor to defer her ordinance so that "we could work with her," but they had been rebuffed. At that the six-foot-five-inch frame of Councilman James Singleton uncurled in his seat. Singleton, speaking in his distinctive nasal drawl, maintained that the krewes had been given ample time to reach an accommodation and professed himself "disappointed" with the way they had handled discussions with city officials. "I didn't know whether you were serious about resolving this issue or trying to stonewall. This first came up in 1988. I have to conclude there has not been a good-faith effort on your part."

This outburst brought Clarkson, the third member of the council's white minority, rushing to champion the old-line cause. "It would be interesting to hear what y'all do for the city in philanthropic services. Mr. Bassich, don't you manage City Park at a salary of one dollar a year? You could probably afford to pay the police yourselves if you weren't so generous to the city."

Bassich nodded, saying, "There were five captains figuring it out the other day. Between them they were on 113 committees." This was, for the krewemen, the nub of the issue. They had always assumed that the populace was grateful both for their efforts in staging the Mardi Gras spectacle that had made the city world-famous and for their contributions to charitable causes. For the leading lights of Carnival to be pilloried in public was unprecedented and, they thought, entirely undeserved. Bassich's feelings were obviously hurt. "It may cost the city $3 million for services to Mardi Gras, but with the taxes we bring in, there's no subsidy," he glumly observed.

Clarkson was at her most gushing as she extolled the krewes for their contributions to the municipal economy. "We'd be scrambling all over the country, all over the world, looking for such an industry, but we have it right here."

The practical problems likely to result from integration were Bassich's next theme. Discipline would be difficult to maintain if a krewe were not "a compatible group that will listen to its friends." The captain was in charge of the parade, Bassich pointed out, but in the event of an infraction, ranging from dangerous behavior to the removal of a mask, it was sometimes necessary for the float lieutenant or the float sergeant to "call down a rider." One had to be sure all krewe members would take orders. Clarkson found this all so persuasive that she called for the ordinance to be deferred "before we ruin the best thing this city has," but Taylor and the council majority would have none of it. "Bless your heart," Wilson said acidly.

All the talk of economic impact prompted Taylor to ask McLain whether he thought it proper to be "generating these monies through discriminatory practices." McLain said, "I have no opinion on that, but from a cultural/social point of view, I'm fascinated by the whole thing."

Taylor laughed good-humoredly, but her features froze as she turned her attention to Bassich and asked, "Are you a member of any krewes?"

"Yes, ma'am."

"Which ones?"

Bassich, looking as though he were gulping for air, remained silent for several seconds, then said, "One of the things that has made Carnival work is a tongue-in-cheek secrecy."

"You can't say which krewes you belong to?"

"I cannot. I have been a member for forty years of more than one."

"Very well. Tell us how you got into these krewes."

"Well, someone puts you up and then it goes before the committee. If they approve, it's voted on by the general organization. I'll probably get in trouble just for saying that."

"Have you ever recommended anyone for membership?"

"Yes."

"Have you ever recommended blacks, Jews or Italians?"

"I don't know about Italians."

"Blacks?"

"No, ma'am."

"Do you think that generating monies through discriminatory practices is right?" Bassich and Charbonnet stared straight ahead. "Can't answer that?" Taylor was dripping venom.

Wilson, who had been squirming in her seat for a couple of minutes, exploded with anger. "We're not in court here. I object. We have not yet established the inquisition, but we're getting close to it."

It was Taylor's turn to get mad. "What's before us today is discrimination." She pounded the table. "Discrimination! My questions are based on discrimination. That's what my uptight colleagues need to understand. Once we recognize that we discriminate and put an end to it, it'll be better for all of us, not just some of us. If you don't like to hear the word discriminate, then don't do it." The tirade failed to move Wilson, who had over the years perfected the art of driving her colleagues up the wall, Taylor in particular. Whenever Wilson smelled a rat in some pending piece of legislation, her favorite trick was to play dumb and announce, very slowly, "I don't understand." That invariably got them riled up. This time, Wilson sat back and said nothing, cool and, at fifty-five, still possessing some of the pertness common among alumnae of the Rex court.

Singleton pressed Bassich and Charbonnet. "Do you think it right to discriminate on race, religion or what have you?" Each shook his head without a word, and Wilson broke the silence. "But if you're a private organization, you have the right not to go before the grand inquisitor, right?"

A succession of citizens took the microphone to speak for or against the ordinance. The most articulate of the opponents was a nattily dressed lawyer named Harry McCall, who said he was a member of two gentlemen's clubs and two krewes. He was, in fact, one of the principal members and a former captain of Comus.

McCall had achieved a certain amount of notoriety during the election campaign by giving a speech to the chamber of commerce and urging everyone not to vote for Governor Edwin Edwards. The implicit endorsement of David Duke so alarmed the other partners in the firm of Chaffe McCall Phillips Toler and Sarpy that they took out a newspaper advertisement denouncing the white-supremacist cause. The McCalls—like the Chaffes—were socially prominent when the krewes and clubs were first established. Evan Jones McCall had moved to New Orleans from Philadelphia in 1824 and was one of the earliest members of the exclusive Boston Club. The current scion, in no mood to compromise the principles of his ancestors, declared, "Clubs have a right to choose their own members as a matter of principle and law. Freedom of association is a basic constitutional right and we are entitled to ensure that new members are congenial. This ordinance serves no purpose other than to increase racial tension."

Insurance agent Carl Galmon, tireless campaigner for black civil rights, didn't see things that way. "What are they trying to protect? The Confederacy. They are the sons and grandsons of Confederates. Confederate traditions give them a sense of power in a city that is 69 percent black. They are trying to perpetuate a form of slavery."

While all this was going on, Taylor would disappear from time to time to confer in a side room with the krewe representatives and members of the Barthelemy administration. It was obvious that things were not going the krewes' way and that they could count on the votes of only the two white women. Clarkson was a cinch, complaining that "the Ku Klux Klan can parade on Canal Street but not Comus." Wilson too was solidly behind the status quo, but when she observed, "We have a tendency on this council, if someone disagrees with us, to cry racism," it was not one of the black majority but Giarrusso who rebuked her. "I think you're a little uptight," he said. "You need to calm down a little."

*Carl Galmon, implacable foe of the old-line krewes. Photo by Matt Rose/*Times-Picayune.

She was in no mood to do so. "We ought to consider the possibility that the krewes are in good faith. I'm going to vote no. This is a bad ordinance, a terrible ordinance."

Clarkson was of the same mind. "Let's not try to change history and re-create Mardi Gras. Let's not send the affluent to the suburbs. Let's not deprive the poor of the greatest free show on earth."

Giarrusso, who had said little all day, now made it clear why. "This is minor compared to some of the problems facing the community."

He looked profoundly fed up, but Taylor insisted her ordinance addressed principles of profound importance. "We ought to be talking about what is right and aiming for a new generation feeling it can participate in all aspects of Mardi Gras, not talking about money. We ought to hang our heads in shame." Bassich and Charbonnet returned to face the council, announcing that they had reached an agreement with the city. They would drop their opposition to the ordinance, which the council would pass that day. But no action would be taken against the krewes for a year while a "blue ribbon committee on Carnival" reconsidered the issue. The council would then vote on any changes the committee might recommend. The faces of krewemen in the audience dropped, for they felt they had been betrayed by their leaders. Meeting beforehand, several krewe captains had decided that their most effective strategy would be to announce that, if the ordinance passed, all parades would be cancelled. Many in the audience were dumbstruck when Bassich and Charbonnet failed to use the threat of economic havoc to force Taylor to back down.

The desegregation ordinance was unanimously adopted, and the krewemen filed out, grumbling to each other about the capitulation of their leaders and about the offensive remarks made by Galmon in particular. Although Galmon, with his booming, down-from-the-mountain voice, was not guilty of any understatement, there was truth in what he said; the old-line krewes had indeed emerged from the ashes of the old South to preserve its mores in masquerade. Carnival itself, however, went back much further, to the earliest days of Louisiana and beyond.

CHAPTER TWO

The Rise and Fall of French Carnival

On Shrove Tuesday, 1699, two frigates and two ketches of the French navy brought Louisiana's first European settlers into the Mississippi from the Gulf of Mexico and dropped anchor about seventy miles downriver from where New Orleans now stands. Even among the strange flora of the subtropical wilderness, the pioneers had evidently not forgotten that this was a red-letter day back home, for Pierre Le Moyne, Sieur d'Iberville, commander of the expedition, christened their campsite Pointe du Mardi Gras. D'Iberville and his nineteen-year-old brother, Jean-Baptiste Le Moyne, Sieur de Bienville, who was second in command, were Canadian-born, but both had lived long enough in France to be familiar with Parisian Carnival, celebrated in courtly circles with banquets and masked balls and among the lower orders with general debauchery.

The word "carnival" derives from the Latin *carnem levare*, meaning to put away flesh or meat, and was widely used in Europe as early as the fifteenth century to signify a period of feasting and celebration beginning on Twelfth Night, or Epiphany, and ending at midnight on Shrove Tuesday, or Mardi Gras. Mardi Gras, which means "Fat Tuesday," was supposed to leave the faithful in good shape to face the self-denying ordinances of Lent.

Bienville, as commandant general of the Louisiana colony,

founded New Orleans in 1718, and folklore has it that the earliest citizens brought the customs of Mardi Gras with them, although there are no records to prove it. Fears and hostilities bred by a remarkable ethnic diversity dogged the city from its precarious beginnings when settlers were faced with the sticky heat and miasma of the swamps and the constant threat of starvation and deadly disease. They were not all willing adventurers, for their numbers included Indian slaves as well as thieves, cutthroats, prostitutes and beggars removed from Parisian jails and transported to supplement the scant supply of voluntary immigrants from France and Canada. Free black people lived in New Orleans almost from its founding, and land grants enticed German peasants to settle a few miles upriver, some two thousand of them surviving a horrendous transatlantic crossing in 1719, the same year that Louisiana's first two shiploads of slaves arrived from Africa. Jews were officially excluded from Louisiana in 1724, but many were later allowed to settle there nevertheless. If any aspect of early colonial life had a visible impact on latterday Carnival, it was the alliance and interbreeding of the enslaved races. Black runaways could always find sanctuary with nearby Indian tribes, and squaws moved into maroon settlements that sprang up under cover of the forests outside the city. Black fugitives joined an uprising of the Natchez Indians in 1829, which was suppressed with such savagery that few survived. Those who did were exiled to Saint Domingue, and Governor Etienne de Perier wrote, "The greatest misfortune which could befall the colony and which would inevitably lead to its total loss would be a union between the Indian nations and the black slaves."

Carnival, if it was celebrated at all, cannot have been too elaborate an affair at the time. Tradition has it, however, that, after he became governor of Louisiana in 1741, the Marquis de Vaudreuil established elegant society balls that became the model for the upper-class Carnival celebrations of later generations. This, however, may be one of the many myths about colonial life that have arisen to fill the documentary void. None is more beguiling, or utterly at variance with reality, than the image of eighteenth-century Louisiana as an enclave of high European civilization, where a "proud and haughty" Latin race danced away the night in surroundings reminiscent of Versailles, and paragons of chivalry and culture wooed dark-eyed beauties amid the moonlight and magnolias. The golden age of New Orleans society in general, and Carnival in particular, supposedly began when Vaudreuil arrived with a large retinue that included a dancing master called Bebe and commenced to spend the time planning receptions and banquets while his wife rode around town in a carriage drawn by four horses.

This story is not easy to swallow. At the time, New Orleans was a tiny city consisting largely of small wooden buildings, filthy streets, open sewers and a sprinkling of rough taverns, gambling dens and fleshpots where transients and local undesirables disported themselves. A few had prospered from trade and shipping, but whatever social graces were present in Vaudreuil's day must have been discoverable only in a small minority; the pleasures of the salon would have been lost on the brutish and illiterate mass of the population. If Vaudreuil did indeed play the Parisian fop some of the time, he also had plenty of more pressing concerns, including the Chickasaw Indians who raided several plantations on the lower Mississippi and who are reputed to have killed Bebe when he rode out of town one day. Vaudreuil evidently failed to grasp the importance of his role in the development of New Orleans high society, for, though he left fairly voluminous papers, he nowhere mentions Twelfth Night, Mardi Gras or the unfortunate Bebe.

It is nevertheless possible that masked balls were held on Mardi Gras, and other European customs observed. In New Orleans it is an article of faith that, under Louisiana's French and Spanish governors, matriarchs would bake a trinket into a Mardi Gras cake and whoever was served the slice containing it would become monarch of the household festivities. Perry Young asserts that "bals de royaute were an institution of the Creole families from the remotest time of the colonial regime," but all that can be said for sure is that a Carnival season was established by the time of the Revolutionary War. The earliest reference to Carnival in New Orleans appears in a 1781 report to the Spanish colonial governing body, the Cabildo, calling for stricter racial segregation. The magistrate complained that black people were wearing masks and sneaking into Carnival balls. Evidently black people continued to assert their solidarity with Indians, for the magistrate also asked the Cabildo to ban the wearing of feathers. The Cabildo obliged, and prohibited black people from being masked or attending night balls.

By the end of the eighteenth century, it was obvious that New Orleans was on its way to becoming one of the great ports of the world, if not a cultural center. New Orleans's first theater was opened in 1792, and a comic opera, *Silvain*, was performed there four years later, but the city remained for the most part resolutely anti-intellectual, with a leisured class devoted to the frantic round of balls and parties that made up the Carnival season. "They wander from ballroom to cards, from cards to billiards, from billiards to dice and from dice to the ballroom again," one visitor noted of the local gentry. Another observed that there were no bookstores because "the proprietor of such would starve to death in the midst of his books unless they could interest the reader in the art of doubling his capital in a year." The citizens were disdained as "strangers alike to art and science or even to the most ordinary items of knowledge." The manners of the menfolk also left something to be desired, to judge from an 1800 Cabildo resolution urging an end to "the practice of putting wads of chewing tobacco on the chairs where the ladies sit, of chewing vanilla sticks and scattering these wads throughout the building thereby producing an intolerable odor."

Most residents of New Orleans were still incorrigibly French in language, custom and attitude when American troops arrived after the Louisiana Purchase of 1803, and ethnic friction was inevitable. Principal scene of the hostilities, naturally, was the dancehalls where the indigenous population spent so much of its time. Fights broke out at public balls over such vital questions as whose dances were to be played first. Passions flared, for instance, on one occasion when the Americans called for an English country dance while the French stood firm for a waltz. The twenty-eight-year-old William Claiborne, former congressman from Tennessee, just appointed governor of the Territory of Orleans—which was roughly coterminous with the Louisiana of today—somewhat sheepishly reported the terpsichorean troubles to James Madison, then secretary of state: "I fear you will suppose that I am wanting in respect in calling your attention to the Balls of New Orleans, but I do assure you Sir, that they occupy much of the Public mind and from them have proceeded the greatest embarrassments which have heretofore attended my administration." That letter was written January 31, 1804, more than two weeks into the Carnival season, when the threat of dancehall violence was so great that a new ordinance banned weapons from public balls and required two policemen to be present. The Americans became even warier of Carnival two years later, when it was rumored that Aaron Burr, the former vice president who had killed Alexander Hamilton in a duel, was planning to take New Orleans by force as part of a supposed scheme to create his own empire in the west of the United States and Mexico. Carnival masks were therefore prohibited lest they provide cover for spies and, though Burr never did show up, the ban remained in force.

Claiborne agreed with the various visitors who had been

struck by the monumental dumbness of the local population, writing to President Thomas Jefferson that "our new fellow citizens are indeed involved in great ignorance." Others confirmed his opinion. Daniel Clark, for instance, American consul in New Orleans during the colonial era, informed Madison that "not above half the inhabitants can read or write in French and not two hundred in the whole country with correctness." New Orleans had no colleges and only one public school, Clark wrote.

Whatever the intellectual drawbacks of the populace, the port was booming as the focal point for trade in the entire Mississippi River valley when New Orleans became American. A local planter, Etienne de Bore, had perfected a process for the drying and granulation of sugar in 1795, two years after Eli Whitney's invention of the cotton gin. The new technologies enabled upriver planters and city brokers to amass fortunes from a burgeoning export trade, while New Orleans was bursting at its seams. Newcomers kept arriving to seek their share of the bonanza, while suburbs began to spread along the riverfront. Among the so-called *population ancienne* Carnival season was by now an endless round of balls and fêtes, and the ban on masking was widely ignored. The growth of the economy and the increasing opulence in the lives of the merchant elite were measured in an insatiable demand for slaves. It had been illegal since 1804 to import them into Louisiana from abroad, but smugglers continued to arrive with shipments from Africa and to slip undetected through the thick cypress swamps and labyrinthine bayous along the coast. Traders, unable to keep up with demand, also turned to other states for fresh supplies of slaves, although the English-speaking "Virginia negroes," not being used to the steamy local climate, were less reliable workers, and therefore sold for less than homegrown "Creole negroes." The census of 1810 showed that half of Louisiana's seventy-six thousand residents were black, the vast majority of them slaves, which was, to the white population, both a sign of prosperity

The Rise and Fall of French Carnival

and a cause for unease. Plans for a slave uprising had been uncovered by Spanish colonial authorities in 1795, when twenty-
three of the conspirators had been hanged and displayed for several days on gibbets along the river. Slaves in Saint Domingue,
however, had met with better luck, overthrowing the French
colonial government and raising fears in Louisiana that the
contagion of freedom might spread. It did, when some five
hundred field hands walked off the upriver plantations and
began marching toward New Orleans in 1811. Many of them
wore uniforms, although where they came from is unknown,
and their leaders were on horseback. The rebels were poorly
armed, however, and, sandwiched between federal troops moving downriver from Baton Rouge and the municipal militia,
stood no chance. They were quickly overwhelmed, with sixty-
five killed. A firing squad then dispatched sixteen slaves who
had allegedly led the revolt, and Claiborne had their severed
heads mounted on spikes along the river bank. Thus ended the
largest slave uprising in the history of the United States; though
a failure, it at least encouraged somewhat more liberal treatment of slaves as well as free people of color for most of the
antebellum era.

The central ethnic conflict in New Orleans after the Louisiana Purchase was the one that pitted the American newcomers against the Creoles, a versatile word used here to denote
those born in Louisiana of French and Spanish stock. The Creoles were naturally jealous of their European heritage and were
inclined to view their new compatriots as crass opportunists.
The Americans, for their part, found the Creoles idle and backward. Sizing them up shortly after his arrival in Louisiana,
Claiborne informed Madison in the spring of 1804 that "the
principles of a popular Government are utterly beyond their
comprehension." The letter was leaked, causing one of the in-
furiated Creoles, a wealthy planter named Joseph Dubreuil, to
denounce Claiborne as "a stranger here, a stranger as far as the

soil itself is concerned, its local interests, the customs, habits and even the language of the inhabitants and who is therefore without even the most absolutely necessary knowledge." Thus were the battle lines between American and Creole defined from the beginning. The Americans quickly concluded that they had fallen among a dissolute and undisciplined bunch. Creoles celebrated the Sabbath with drinking, dancing, cockfighting and horse racing and were famously averse to manual labor, which generations of credulous local historians in New Orleans have attributed to the fastidiousness of aristocratic lineage. Americans of the era were more inclined to regard it as a defect of character.

The ethnic hodgepodge of New Orleans continued to breed incomprehension and suspicion. Of the city's 27,176 inhabitants in 1820, 6,237 were free people of color, and most spoke a patois known in Louisiana as "Creole French" or, more commonly, "Nigger French." Many were descended from white men who had freed slave concubines and children. Some had bought their freedom, or had it granted for meritorious service, such as helping colonial government keep Indians under control, while others were immigrants who had never been slaves. New Orleans was home to 7,355 slaves, Creole and American, so that the colored population constituted a slight majority over the 13,584 whites. The mayor, Louis Philippe de Roffignac, was one of the so-called *Français de dehors*, or foreign French, who were no more impressed with the Creole intellect than the Americans were. Roffignac was one of the many royalists who had resettled in Louisiana at the time of the French revolution. The Americans were still a minority in a Catholic and Francophone land, but they had already established a new commercial section just upriver from the French Quarter with banks, insurance companies, commodity brokerages, warehouses and stores. The Americans dominated the professions too; the unfortunate Creoles were largely ill equipped, either by temperament or education, to compete in any serious endeavor with the hordes of fortune seekers who flocked to New Orleans from all over the country and Europe.

If Creoles were struggling to hold off the American challenge for economic and political dominance, they still knew how to party, and Mardi Gras was theirs. Tradition has it that a few young Creole gentlemen brought home some Mardi Gras customs from Paris, whence they had just returned from their studies, in 1827. If the story is true—and it did not surface in the New Orleans press until almost fifty years later—these repatriated students, when they donned fancy costumes to dance in the streets, were the last Mardi Gras revellers forbidden to hide their faces. A few months later in 1827 the city council, after receiving a petition signed by two hundred prominent citizens, lifted the ban on masking for the period from January 1 through Mardi Gras. The impetus came largely from the Creole faction, the repressed Anglos suspecting, rightly, that masking would allow people of different classes and even races to mingle in a scandalous fashion. During the debate on the question of resanctioning masked balls, Councilman Maunsel White, stern Episcopalian, noted that masked balls were already held, notwithstanding the law against them, and that "high class" ladies were even to be found on the same floor as quadroons. Councilman J. F. Canonge saw nothing wrong with curiosity in high-class ladies or in their rubbing shoulders with the lower orders, while Councilman Dominique-François Burthe, reminded White that "our population is still French in its tastes and masks are an amusement thoroughly French." White was the sole dissenter when the prohibition on masked balls was removed.

This heralded a brief golden age of Creole Mardi Gras. Organizers of subscription masked balls began to vet their patrons carefully for social graces and refinement, while the public halls catered to patrons of lesser breeding in search of easy women. The streets during Mardi Gras were a sight to startle the visitor. One recorded his impressions of 1835 thus:

> Men and boys, women and girls, bond and free, white and black, yellow and brown, exert themselves to invent and appear in grotesque, quizzical, diabolical, horrible, humorous, strange masks and disguises. Human bodies are seen with heads of beasts and birds; snakes' heads and bodies with arms of apes; man-bats from the moon; mermaids, satyrs, beggars, monks, and robbers, parade and march on foot, on horseback, in wagons, carts, coaches, cars &c, in rich confusion up and down the street, wildly shouting, singing, laughing, drumming, fiddling, fifing, and all throwing flour broadcast as they went their reckless way.

The first contemporary newspaper account of a parade appeared in the just-established *Daily Picayune* on Ash Wednesday, 1837:

> A lot of masqueraders were parading through our streets yesterday, and excited considerable speculation as to who they were, what were their motives and what upon earth could induce them to turn out in such grotesque and outlandish habiliments. Some said they were Seminoles; some that it was the Zoological Institute come to town; some that it was Brown's Circus—while others said nothing and very likely knew nothing at all about it. Boys, negroes, fruit women and what not followed the procession—shouting and bawling and apparently highly delighted with the fun or, what is more probable, anxious to fill their pockets with sugar plums, kisses, oranges &c, which were lavishly bestowed upon them by the so good-hearted jokers, whoever they were.

The only problem was that the din upset "some of the elderly ladies, old maids and such like." One went into "violent hysterics," and another had a "conniption fit," the newspaper reported.

The Rise and Fall of French Carnival

The next year the *Commercial Bulletin*, which cannot have been paying attention, announced on Ash Wednesday:

> The European custom of celebrating the last day of Carnival by a procession of masqued figures through the public streets was introduced here yesterday, very much to the amusement of our citizens. The principal streets were traversed by a masquerade company on horseback and in carriages, from the fantastic Harlequin to the somber Turk and wild Indian. A delightful throng followed on the heels of the cavalcade as it marched through our city suburbs, and wherever it went the procession raised a perfect hubbub and jubilee. The exhibition surpassed anything of the kind ever witnessed here.

The spectacle was planned, the *Commercial Bulletin* reported, by "a large number of young gentlemen, principally Creoles of the first respectability."

The Creoles were by now reduced to a secondary role in almost everything but Carnival. They had enjoyed the whip hand as a majority on the city council until 1836 when the Americans, weary of seeing their section of town neglected while the French Quarter streets were paved and lit, persuaded the state legislature to split New Orleans into three municipalities with separate governments. The result was that the Creoles languished in a district roughly equivalent to the French Quarter, while the Americans prospered mightily uptown, which in New Orleans means the other side of Canal Street, and the largely foreign-born residents of Faubourg Marigny did the best they could.

The feud between Americans and Creoles was small beer compared to the racial confrontations of later years and, though violence was often in the air, there were no pitched battles. Many distinguished Americans, including Claiborne himself, married into Creole families while the old and the new also

came into close contact through friendships and business part-
nerships. But, from 1803 until the Civil War, New Orleans society was riven by the clash of Creole tradition and the forces of
Americanization. For a while, the Creoles, reinforced by the
Foreign French, held their own, retaining their grip on politics, real estate and commerce. But, by 1840, the battle was obviously lost; the Creoles were outnumbered by the boisterous
and ambitious sons of an alien culture.

Americans were no longer the only threat to the Creole way
of life, however, for European immigrants continued to pour
into the city, with huge waves coming from Ireland and Germany, in particular. Untold thousands of Irish laborers died dig-
ging the New Basin Canal, which opened in 1838 and ran from
uptown New Orleans six miles into Lake Pontchartrain, opening up trade routes to the Mississippi, Alabama and Florida
coasts for American merchants. The Creoles, with their Caron-
delet Canal, had more or less monopolized that trade until the
Irish were brought in to dig, at one dollar a day, through the
deadly swamps. They lived in the utmost squalor, died grisly
deaths from yellow fever, cholera and malaria and, as elsewhere,
were despised as a drunken, brawling and immoral subclass.
More respectable and prosperous than the Irish were the Germans, driven to emigrate by political turmoil and revolution in
the 1840s, who arrived in sufficient numbers to make New
Orleans authentically trilingual. The Germans established a
turnverein and an annual volksfest, and brought with them the
national taste for beer, which they liked to indulge after mass.
This seemed unexceptionable to the Creoles, but American
Protestants took a dim view.

Americans, or at least the more successful among them, decided the time had come to flee the crime, poverty and filth of
the city. If the Carnival season found them somewhat lacking
in mercurial qualities, it was because they preferred to devote
their energies to the earnest pursuits of making money and es-

tablishing an opulent garden suburb uptown. Apart from a handful of Creoles and free people of color, the early residents of the New Orleans Garden District were either Americans, Englishmen or Irishmen. They were cotton factors, commission men, steamboat operators, bankers and such, who built Greek Revival mansions, Italianate villas and outsized raised cottages to produce a retreat that left visitors awestruck. Mark Twain in *Life on the Mississippi* described it thus: "Mansions stand in the center of large grounds, and rise, garlanded with roses, out of the midst of swelling masses of shining green foliage and many colored blossoms. No houses could be in better harmony with their surroundings, or more pleasing to the eye, or more homelike and comfortable-looking." Visitors to the Garden District today are still impressed with what seem like the gracious houses of antebellum aristocrats, but they were for the most part built by ruthless businessmen with few interests outside commerce.

The glorious disorder on the streets at Mardi Gras did not meet with everyone's approval, as an English visitor noted in 1846: "The strangeness of the scene was not a little heightened by the blending of the negroes, quadroons and mulattoes in the crowd, and we were amused by observing the ludicrous surprise, mixed with contempt, of several unmasked, stiff, grave Anglo-Americans from the north who were witnessing for the first time what seemed to them so much mummery and tomfoolery." Northerners were not the only ones who did not approve, for, a year earlier, the newspaper *L'Abeille*, voice of the Creoles, had complained that Mardi Gras had gone downhill. This was so "not the less from the abandonment of the old master spirits who led on the merry crowd than from the lewd and miserable crew who, of later years, have been permitted to join in the celebration." Four years later, *L'Abeille* gloomily concluded that "the genuine Mardi Gras of former years has passed forever." The *Daily Picayune* in 1851 wanted no more Mardi

Gras because it had become an occasion for "the vulgarities of lubberly boys."

New Orleans was reunited under a single government in 1852, depriving the Creoles of any hope that they might control their own destiny again. They reacted by looking down their noses at Americans, whom they considered to be crass, money-grubbing destroyers of a delicate colonial civilization. Thus were their mostly benighted forebears first turned by a remarkable feat of the imagination into wealthy paragons of chivalry and culture. That the legendary aristocrats of old Louisiana were largely a figment should have been obvious from the illiteracy rampant in the run-down Creole neighborhoods of the 1840s and 1850s, but the notion of the colonial beau ideal survives today, testimony to the determination of Creole propagandists.

Although the Americans had been able to displace the Creoles partly because they were better educated, the invasion had by no means invested New Orleans with a spirit of intellectual enquiry. As late as 1847, there was "not even a tolerable bookstore in New Orleans," although getting a drink was easy. By the 1850s, when New Orleans was at its economic zenith, two thousand establishments were dispensing liquor, which was available not just in saloons, but in grocery stores, oyster houses and coffee shops. Several travellers noted that nobody was ever seen drinking coffee in a coffee shop, and New Orleans had already established a national reputation for drunkenness. Delirium tremens was commonplace, and 610 people dropped dead in its grip from 1856 to 1860. Confronted with evidence that jurors in a criminal trial had conducted their deliberations in New Orleans over six bottles of claret, a bottle of brandy, a bottle of champagne and a few glasses of absinthe, a justice of the state supreme court concluded that "one or more" were "not in possession of that unclouded intellect which the accused had a right to demand."

The Rise and Fall of French Carnival

One fear united all classes in New Orleans, from the starving immigrants in their shanties at the edge of the swamps to the powerful entrepreneurs behind their suburban porticos, and, in 1853, the worst happened. Yellow fever, which the privileged of the Garden District had hoped to leave behind in the crowded and unsanitary city, descended on New Orleans with unprecedented ferocity, carrying off eight thousand people, rich and poor. Particularly vulnerable were newcomers to the city, and such Garden District yankees as did not flee to healthier regions at the onset of the epidemic dropped like flies. Decomposing bodies were heaped in the cemeteries for want of enough healthy people to entomb them. Nobody in that era suspected that yellow fever was spread by mosquitoes, and it was generally associated in the public mind with unhygienic conditions. New Orleans nevertheless remained unspeakably filthy and noisome. Hogs, goats, dogs, horses and cows roamed the unpaved streets, while garbage and dead animals were left to rot in the open. Human feces ran in uncovered ditches through the city and into the swamp. The public water supply, which came directly from the Mississippi, was often interrupted when some animal carcass blocked the intake and was chronically contaminated by garbage dumped off the quay. Only in 1857 were "nuisance barges" introduced to take garbage out into the middle of the river. The poor and the immigrants suffered through the long, hot nights crowded into dirty, unventilated hovels.

The city was, however, regarded as a pleasant place to visit in the winter, and the Carnival-season influx included professional gamblers, confidence tricksters and a wide range of criminals. The police, although managing to intercept some of the better known of these on arrival, had a large, indigenous population of toughs to deal with and were generally overwhelmed. Immigrants sold fake gold watches and glass jewelry to their newly arrived countrymen on the quay, and hordes of card sharps, with "flashy vests and devil-may-care countenances," were quick to fleece the suckers who came in droves. Classier criminals cashed forged bills of exchange at exclusive establishments, while every gambler could find a game to suit his tastes and his pocket. The high rollers could take their pick of several well-appointed gambling halls, one of them owned by the cultivated John Davis, the city's leading opera impresario for decades.

The riverfront remained a warren of bars, flophouses, brothels and gambling dens, and the women of the area could be formidable adversaries. One, named Mary Egerton, bit off a policeman's ear, while Bridget Fury and Irish Kate Winters became household names from newspaper accounts of their frequent fights and arrests. Bridget was finally arrested for stabbing a man to death. Some prostitutes cursed, smoked cigars and wore male clothes. Two sections, Gallatin Street and an area known as the Swamp, were so violent that the police seldom ventured into them. In areas where police officers were not intimidated, they were bribed to leave well enough alone. Daguerreotype mug shots and the telegraph were introduced to the New Orleans Police Department in the 1850s, but surviving interdepartmental messages do not suggest a sophisticated law-enforcement operation. One of them reads: "J Bentz Keeper of a beer house on Marigny bet Moreau and Casacalco St blowed out his brains." Crime was so rampant, however, that even the amateurish and venal police department recorded 25,417 arrests in twelve months from 1857 to 1858. A British youth named John Rowlands immigrated to New Orleans at this time, where he took the name of the local merchant who adopted him—Henry Morton Stanley. After his "Dr. Livingston, I presume" made him a celebrity, Stanley wrote an autobiography, in which he recalled his youth in the city of "slung shots, doctored liquor, Shanghai-ing and wharf ratting." Low-class hookers took care of their customers in tiny and squalid "cribs," while well-appointed bordellos serviced the upper end of the market. Venereal diseases raged through the city.

When Mardi Gras rolled around, thieves and ruffians spilled out of Gallatin Street and the Swamp, and Irish hooligans went on rampages. Decent citizens remained indoors, while whores rode through the French Quarter in open carriages, gangs of thugs pursued their murderous feuds and the police recorded widespread mugging. The riffraff, no longer satisfied with throwing flour on street maskers, had taken to using lime and bricks instead. By 1856, when Mardi Gras brought cold and wet weather but no diminution of "licentious" behavior, newspapers were calling for an end to the drunken chaos. The *Daily Crescent* dismissed contemporary street maskers as "a Godforsaken and man-forsaken set," and the *Daily Delta* thought that Mardi Gras had become "vulgar, tasteless and spiritless." Creoles, local historians record, were wont to grumble about "swine-eating Saxons," and *L'Abeille* came right out and blamed the newcomers: "In old times, this was the greatest holiday in the whole year round in the Crescent City, but of late years its observance has been gradually falling into desuetude before the march of new people, customs and ideas." The public masked ball by now was a thing of the past, although the more exclusive, subscription variety lingered on. A wave of nativist resentment against German and Irish immigrants, meanwhile, spawned widespread Know-Nothing violence, with the American Party dispatching gangs of thugs to keep voters away from the polls in the city's Democratic precincts.

The sorry state of the city and of Carnival became a favorite topic in John Pope's apothecary at the busy intersection of Jackson and Prytania Streets in the Garden District. Pope's place was nicknamed "The Club" because the rising stars of the American merchant and professional classes loved to gather there of an evening for conversation and cigars either inside or sitting on benches provided in front. A native of Brooklyn,

New York, Pope was not only gregarious but well read and anxious to make a mark on his adopted city.

Pope and his friends resolved to prove *L'Abeille* wrong by making new people and customs the salvation rather than the death of Mardi Gras. Creoles seemed intent on giving up on part of their colonial and Catholic heritage and thereby confirming American suspicions that they were idle and feckless. If Mardi Gras was to be saved, Pope and his drugstore Saxons would have to take the lead. On January 4, 1857, therefore, they sent out an invitation that read: "You are requested to meet a few of your friends at the Club Room over the Gem, Royal Street, on Saturday evening, the 10th instant, at 7 o'clock." The card was signed by Pope, then aged thirty, S. M. Todd from Utica, New York, F. Shaw, Jr., who is variously identified as a native of Alabama or New York City, L. D. Addison from Kentucky and brothers Joseph and William Ellison, born in Louisville, Kentucky, and Pittsburgh, Pennsylvania, respectively. Of the thirteen gentlemen who received the invitation, and duly joined their hosts over the Gem Saloon, only one bore a French name and he was no Creole. Louis Lay was one of the supercilious foreign Frenchmen the Creoles found almost as hard to bear as the Anglos.

The youngish Gem Saloon committee—average age thirty-five—resolved to form a Carnival organization. It did not impose a strict prohibition against Creoles, although only six belonged to what had become the ninety-strong "Mistick Krewe of Comus" by Mardi Gras, February 24, when newspaper notices informed the populace that something special was planned for nine o'clock. The crowd was abuzz with curiosity and anticipation when, at the appointed hour, krewe members emerged from their den and crept through the darkness to the intersection of Julia and Magazine Streets in what is now the New Orleans Central Business District. Suddenly a host of black men materialized waving flambeaux, and two small but exquisite floats set off in a blaze of light, flanked by elaborately costumed maskers on foot and bands playing martial music. For two hours, the krewe of Comus rolled slowly through streets lined with enraptured spectators, disbanding at the Gaiety Theater, which had been "decorated with a profusion of hangings, wreaths and flowers" for theatrics and a bal masque. In the early hours of Ash Wednesday, members departed for an exclusive banquet in rented rooms on St. Charles Street. When they wandered home in the morning light, Mardi Gras had been reborn in a form that has hardly changed since. One of the inaugural members, Thomas Herndon, described what Comus had wrought in these modest terms: "It was reserved for the Crescent City to mold the Carnival festivities into one grand and comprehensive system and plan for the enjoyment of the people, without fee or reward, public spectacle and pageants as splendidly brilliant as the genius of man and the lavish expenditure of money could make them."

Creoles were less than ecstatic. *L'Abeille* published both French and English editions and, as not infrequently happened, took a different tack for each readership. As *L'Abeille*, the newspaper ignored Comus in its Mardi Gras coverage and mentioned the ball only a couple of weeks later when complaining that guests had not been served much of a supper. As *The Bee*, the paper gave Comus a favorable review on Ash Wednesday, reporting that the evening had gone off with great "eclat," but then turned equivocal the next day. While still conceding the "unsurpassed magnificence" of the tableaux at the Gaiety, *The Bee* professed iteilf unable to see the point of the whole exercise. "Such things will serve for a twelvemonth," its editors concluded.

The krewe, though it adopted the Creole trappings of the season—the grotesque masks, the private ball and banquet—

was obviously not driven by any desire to heal ancient rifts. Comus had suddenly co-opted the masked ball, which once entertained all classes of Creole, and made it an emblem for an emerging elite determined to keep the rest of the population at one remove. Comus was above the law from the beginning and was unaffected by an ordinance, adopted by the city council in 1857, that made it illegal "to abuse, provoke, or disturb any person; to make charivari, or to appear masked or disguised in the streets or in any public place." Mayor Charles Waterman was a member of Comus, and the police continued to clear the streets every year for the parading maskers.

Creoles were a small minority among the guests at the Gaiety for the inaugural Comus ball, where the atmosphere was far from Gallic. There were plenty of private, Creole balls elsewhere in town but, at the Gaiety, the conversation was in English. The entire evening was a radical departure from the old days, when street maskers were a motley of revellers more or less out of control. With the advent of Comus came the unfamiliar concepts of meticulous organization and a themed parade and ball. The theme—indeed, the name of the krewe itself—made no concessions to Creole sensibilities. The text for the first modern Mardi Gras was not some expression of Latin exuberance but two poems by the English Puritan John Milton, who spent his declining years in total blindness. Yet Milton, though nineteenth-century Creoles would hardly have agreed, is the perfect inspiration for a last fling before the self-denial and solemnity of Lent. Milton is always supposed to be with the holy faction, but cannot help giving sinners the most stirring and persuasive speeches. The necromancer Comus, son of Bacchus and Circe, is the villain of *A Maske Presented at Ludlow Castle*, which Milton wrote in 1634. Comus treats his guests to an "Orient liquor" that brings on a "foul disfigurement" not unlike a Mardi Gras mask. The krewe's insignia has from the beginning been a golden goblet, and Comus always has one in hand when leading the parade and when he opens the Mardi Gras ball. In the Milton poem Comus is eventually bested by the superior magic of a "Virgin pure," but not before he gets off some good, hedonistic lines:

> Mean while welcom Joy, and Feast,
> Midnight shout, and revelry,
> Tipsie dance and Jollity.
> Braid your locks with rosie Twine,
> Dropping odours, dropping Wine.
> Rigor now is gon to bed,
> And advice with scrupulous head.
> Strict Age, and sowre Severity,
> With their grave Saws in Slumber ly.
> We that are of purer fire
> Imitate the Starry Quire,
> Who in their nightly watchfull Sphears,
> Lead in swift round the Months and Years.

Comus delivers this speech to "a rout of Monsters headed like sundry sorts of wilde Beasts, but otherwise like Men and Women, their Apparel glistring, [who] come in making a riotous and unruly noise, with Torches in their hands." That sounded like just the ticket to John Pope when the club conceived in the Gem Saloon was looking for a name.

The krewemen in the parade of 1857 were got up as "The Demon Actors in Milton's 'Paradise Lost,'" which has Satan defying the Almighty in some of the most majestic poetry ever written. The imagery of the parade was perfect for the season, with nameless men enthroned as Comus on the first float and Satan on the second, personifying glorious, if futile, resistance to the imminent threat of virtue. The parade stopped once, the *Daily Crescent* reported, and "called on Mayor Waterman for the purpose, we suppose, of obtaining a license to raise the supernatural in the Gaiety Theater." At the Gaiety the krewe presented four elaborate diabolical tableaux, each exactly mirroring scenes described in *Paradise Lost*, to a highly appreciative audience. When it was over, the curtain opened again and "at the back sprang an arch of gas-jets, displaying in letters of fire, the words, 'Vive la danse.'" The maskers then danced with the ladies until it was time to repair to table. Altogether, an epic time.

The next morning the *Daily Crescent* published a rave review: "The different tableaux were arranged in accordance with descriptions in Milton's immortal poem, and they were acted out truly and successfully in a manner which reflected the highest credit upon the poetic taste and judgment of the gentlemen composing the Mistick Krewe of Comus."

The impact of the first Comus parade on New Orleans was all the greater because the public had no inkling what to expect. The nineteen men who took part in the inaugural meeting at the Gem Saloon, having elected hardware store owner Charles Churchill their president, swore oaths of secrecy, which they took very seriously. They rented second-floor rooms uptown on Tchoupitoulas Street for organizational meetings and decided to post a "sentinel" downstairs to ensure that nobody entered without uttering the password. The six instigators were given authority "to introduce such persons as they might deem worthy of being members of the association," so that, when a meeting was called for February 8, the sentinel admitted fifty-seven men. A week later, Pope suggested the group name itself after what Milton, in the list of "persons" at the front of his poem, called "Comus and his crew." Pope took a couple of orthographic liberties to produce the faux-archaic "mistick" and "krewe," and the name was adopted. The whimsical spelling caught on so well that "krewe" became the generic name for Carnival organizations, although Pope seldom gets the credit he is due in New Orleans. Most assume that Saxons of earlier generations spelled the word that way, while the few who know whence Comus derived its name are generally under the misapprehension that Milton himself wrote "krewe."

Churchill did not take his responsibilities as history's first Mardi Gras krewe captain lightly, drilling his men unmercifully and rehearsing for the tableaux with everyone's place marked in chalk on the den floor. The first krewe, not being equipped with the magic wand wielded by its Miltonic namesake, could scarcely have been expected to banish vice and crime from the streets of New Orleans on Mardi Gras; nobody has ever figured out how to do that and, indeed, a sense of wickedness lies at the heart of Mardi Gras. Even so, the epiphany of Comus had startling effects, both immediate and long-term. By luring the citizenry outdoors, Comus does appear to have loosened the stranglehold of the hooligans. If there was any pelting of the Comus maskers, no broken heads or other mishaps were reported. Even the mob, it seemed, had been distracted by the new formula.

Pope was by no means solely responsible for all the innovations that have informed Carnival in New Orleans since 1857. Three of the drugstore crowd—Todd and the two Ellisons—had lived in Mobile, Alabama, and taken part in a New Year's Eve parade that dated back to 1831, its unlikely progenitor being a Pennsylvania German who had come to town to work as a cotton broker. Accounts of the events that led up to Michael Krafft's brainwave vary, but they all involve strong drink and a larcenous visit to Griggs, Barney & Co.'s hardware store followed by an impromptu strut through the streets of Mobile amid the sound of horns and the tinkling of cowbells draped over rake tines. It was a hit, and became an annual event under the auspices of what Krafft and his friends christened the Cowbellion de Rakin Society. The torchlit parade rapidly became more sophisticated, featuring floats as early as 1840, and was known far and wide at the time. The New Orleans press, when it reported the advent of Comus and referred to "Cowbellions," had no need to explain. The *Picayune* used the word in its Mardi Gras report of 1837 and, twenty years later, *The Bee*, on the second day after the inaugural Comus parade, in an attempt to be cutting, observed that the krewe's "mobile movements rather indicate a Mobile parentage." No question about it. A large contingent from Mobile's Strikers Independent Society, an offshoot of the Cowbellions, was invited to the first Comus ball to see how its New Year's Eve parades had been adapted to Mardi Gras. The three refugees from Mobile who frequented the Pope pharmacy must have had a lot to contribute when conversation turned to the question of how to cure Carnival's degenerate condition.

Doubtless feeling pleased with themselves, the members of Comus met on June 8, 1857, to adopt a constitution with this preamble:

> Holding it to be a self-evident truth that man at his creation was so constituted that social and intellectual enjoyment should ever be the accompaniment of labor and that an agreeable relaxation from daily toil is always conducive to the proper exercise of his mental faculties and a sure solace to all the ills which flesh is heir to: we, duly impressed with the above and desiring properly to celebrate the Carnival as one of the occasions afforded for relaxation and in the true spirit of Charity, desiring to benefit our fellows and for the purpose of better carrying out our intentions do, hereby, associate ourselves together.

The krewe adopted the motto *Sic voleo, sic jubeo*. The constitution established an initiation fee of twenty-five dollars and annual dues of the same amount. Members were required to be at least twenty-five years old, although this provision was not infrequently violated. On signing the constitution each member swore an oath of secrecy. Nobody could ever reveal who was behind the masks at the parade and ball or who had received the honor of being crowned as Comus. At the same meeting, the members voted to give themselves a public persona by forming a gentlemen's club. Membership would be identical with the krewe's and provide a cover for its clandestine activities. All that was needed was a name for the new club, and English literature filled the bill once more. It was named the Pickwick Club in honor of the Charles Dickens novel published twenty years earlier. The Pickwick was not the first of New Orleans's gentlemen's clubs, for three were already in existence in 1857. The most venerable club still in operation is the Boston, founded in 1841 and named not for the city but for a card game popular at the time. The initiation ceremony in Comus/Pickwick was somewhat intimidating, one early member recalled: "The darkened room and black veil, the death's head and the owl, the solemn voice of the captain, the administering of the oath were all a part of the ritual."

If more Americans than Creoles were taking that oath, the krewemen were at least closer to an ethnic rapprochement than the politicians of the city. The Creoles were "very sensibly seeking alliances with the go-ahead blood of the Anglo-Saxon race," an English visitor observed at the time, but there was no suggestion of entente cordiale about the mayoral election of 1857. Major Pierre Beauregard, distinguished veteran of the Mexican War, was the Creole standard-bearer and faced Gerard Stith of the American Party. The campaign turned ugly when Beauregard seized the arsenal and courthouse and erected fortifications around Jackson Square, while Stith partisans occupied Lafayette Square with a cannon. No shots were fired; however, Beauregard met the Creole's inevitable fate on election day and Stith was installed as mayor of a city the great engine of trade had transformed into one of the world's most stylish and luxurious cities, where opportunity seemed limitless. Negro gangs sang their "wild, fantastic yet harmonious" worksongs all day as they loaded and unloaded cargoes at a port "crowded with vessels of all sizes and of every nation, together with hundreds of large and elegant steamers and a multiplicity of river craft." The port had become "the grandest quay in the world" nestled in a great curve of the Mississippi; "Tyre, nor Carthage, Alexandria nor Genoa, those afore time metropoles of merchant princes boasted no quay like the levee of New Orleans." The *Illustrated London News*, however, was still convinced that Bienville must have been crazy: "New Orleans has been built up on a site that only the madness of commercial lust could ever have tempted men to occupy." Still, antebellum New Orleans, according to J. B. Priestley writing in *Harper's Weekly* in May of 1938, was "one of the famous places of the world, glittering capital, a gaudy metropolis."

Slaves—the women in neat calico dresses, the men in blue cloth suits, vests, white shirts and high beaver hats—were auctioned at the city's two swankiest hotels, the St. Charles in the American section and the St. Louis in the French Quarter. The auctioneers, known for their repartee in both English and French, were much admired by visitors as they adroitly raised the bidding on all kinds of slaves from burly field hands to nubile "fancy girls" and all manner of other specialists. The St. Charles, "a palace for creature comforts, a college for the study of human nature and an exchange for money and appetite," accommodated a thousand guests and seated four hundred for dinner. It had a large rotunda, an enormous bar, confectionery and cigar stores, a telegraph station, steam baths, a barber shop, a bakery, a laundry and ordinaries for ladies and gentlemen. The St. Louis was slightly smaller, but its furnishings were even choicer. Not even the great hotels, however, could better the "luxurious furniture, beautiful carpets, elegant curtains and superb linens" to be found on such a steamboat as the *Peytona*, a veritable "river palace," according to the *Daily Picayune* in 1846. The boats, the driving force behind New Orleans's ascent as a trade center, were already racking up some impressive times, the *J. M. White* two years earlier having made the twelve-hundred-mile run to St. Louis in less than four days. Everything and everyone arrived and departed by boat; as late as 1852, there were only sixty-three miles of railroad track in the entire state of Louisiana. By 1860, fifteen-hundred-ton paddlewheelers were a common and stunning sight in the Mississippi, their holds crammed with cargo while gamblers, sightseers and businessmen strolled the decks, lounged in the saloons, listened to the orchestra and ate sumptuous meals.

The various delights of the city in the 1850s attracted hosts of visitors, many of whom were deceived by appearances into thinking it a bastion of racial tolerance. Free people of color could saunter into some of the city's restaurants and be waited on by Irishmen. On construction sites, Irish hod carriers could be seen rushing to keep colored masons supplied with bricks. The races lived in the same neighborhoods; many free people of color were prosperous, owned slaves, and indulged in some social, and considerable sexual, intercourse with white people. Intermarriage, though illegal, was by no means unknown. No southern city had a free colored population to compare with the one in New Orleans, either in size or sophistication, before the Civil War.

The free people of color were mostly of a light complexion that testified to the amorous propensities of generations of slave owners. Often educated and bilingual, free people of color owned real estate valued at $2,214,020 in New Orleans by 1850. They worked extensively in the skilled trades before the Civil War, and many sent their sons to school in the north or in France. Their numbers included doctors, engineers and architects. A free black named Norbert Rillieux invented a vacuum pan that became standard equipment in sugar refining, and another, Eugene Warbourg, earned some renown as a sculptor in Europe. But the free people of color were most famous for the "quadroon balls," where white men went, at a cost of two dollars, in hopes of finding a suitable mistress. If all went well the suitor could enter into an arrangement called a placage, whereby he would set a girl in a love nest and agree to provide for any children that might result. It was an axiom in New Orleans that *un bon placage est mieux qu'un mauvais marriage*. The "quadroon" girls, who frequently had much less black blood than the term suggests, captivated many a traveler from Europe. An English visitor wrote in 1841 that they resembled "the highest order of Hindoos, with lovely countenances, full, dark, liquid eyes, lips of coral and teeth of pearl, long raven locks of soft and glossy hair, sylph-like figures, and such beautifully rounded limbs and exquisite gait and manner, that they might furnish models for a Venus or a Hebe to the chisel of the sculptor." The New Orleans Carnival establishment's own chronicler, Perry Young, refused to believe that the local white quality would have had any truck with "off-shade harlots," and claimed that the patrons of quadroon balls were "visitors." But even he conceded in a 1939 book that some of the girls must have been remarkably good-looking. That, Young explained, "can happen when the tarbrush strikes."

The free people of color, though they could not vote and were required to show deference in the company of whites, had full property rights and standing to litigate. Even the slaves, in New Orleans if not on the plantations, enjoyed considerable freedom of movement. Many owners, of course, were pretty free with the lash and frequently asserted the *droit du seigneur*, but city slaves could earn money and spend their leisure like free men. They had, since colonial days, been given Sundays off to go drinking and gambling or to sing and dance in Congo Square, close to what is now the site of Louis Armstrong Park, across Rampart Street from the French Quarter. Many owners took to hiring out their slaves and letting them keep some of their wages, which in many cases were spent in saloons. Although antebellum laws forbade the sale of liquor to slaves, numerous New Orleans taverns openly catered to them. It was not unusual for white passers-by to be harassed or assaulted by drunken slaves. For slaves to pass themselves off as free people of color became a fairly simple matter, especially as plenty of them were similarly light-skinned, to judge from the presumably reliable descriptions of runaway slaves in antebellum newspaper advertisements. When Aimee deserted her owner in 1850, for instance, she was described as having "the appearance of a German girl," with "beautiful teeth, fine auburn hair, white eyelids." The same year another master sought help in retrieving the light-skinned Robert, who "blackens his face to disguise himself." Of the runaway slaves advertised for in 1850, more than 20 percent were described as "mulattoes." Almost half were "griffs"—one-quarter white. Many officially white Creoles, meanwhile, had swarthy countenances that were said to betray a Moorish taint from ancestral miscegenation in France and Spain and, perhaps, some illicit dalliances in colonial times.

Since strict discipline over the colored population was impossible, the city fathers moved early to enforce racial segregation. An 1816 ordinance required separate seating for whites and blacks at theaters and public exhibitions, and the council subsequently decreed strict segregation in hospitals, jails and cemeteries. For black people to enter a white hotel or restaurant was unthinkable. Familiarity between the races before the Civil War nevertheless reached the point where high-born ladies pranced around naked with Negroes performing voodoo rites on the shores of Lake Pontchartrain. Plenty of northerners remarked that racial prejudice seemed less marked in New Orleans than at home. One C. G. Parsons even went so far as to declare in 1855, "If the slaves could be set at liberty today, there would be nothing of this kind to exclude them from genteel society." This was a major misapprehension, for the free and easy ways of the colored population were making white society increasingly uneasy and repressive. Soon after Comus first appeared on the streets of New Orleans, the state legislature in 1857 banned the manumission of any slave, and two years later adopted a resolution urging free people of color to find a master. Many black people fled the city.

The frolics of '57 set Comus back ten thousand dollars, but the next year's parade and ball, when the membership cap had been raised from 100 to 150, cost twice as much. The theme in 1858 was "Deities of Heathen Mythology," and the spectacle was even more dazzling than the first year's had been. The banner at the front of the parade read: "Marry, but you travelers may journey far and look not on this like again. Here do you behold the Gods and Goddesses; presently you shall see them unfold themselves." That year saw the introduction of *tableaux roulants*, with the maskers aboard mule-drawn floats in front of all manner of mythological paraphernalia that were hauled onto the stage for the subsequent celebration at the theater, now renamed the Varieties. It was back to the Saxons in 1859 with the theme "The English Holidays," and tableaux illustrating the traditions of "Twelfth Night, or the courtly pageant of misrule," "Mayday," "Midsummer Eve" and "Christmas Eve." Plenty of Creoles were nevertheless delighted to join Comus and the Pickwick, as membership was further increased to two hundred. Notwithstanding the aggressively Anglo nomenclature, a mood of reconciliation reigned behind the portals. This was partly the result of an upper-class solidarity; the members of Comus, whatever their ancestry, had much in common as wealthy men of a social bent. That a chasm remained in New Orleans between Creoles and Americans was not to be doubted, but there were unmistakable signs that a much larger conflict would soon engulf their animosities and force them into an alliance.

Although the men behind the Comus masks were indisputably of superior educational, social and commercial accomplishment, New Orleans in general belied the myth that the slave-owning elite of the antebellum South developed a high-toned society. Contemporary observers found that New Orleans, far from putting them in mind of ancient Greece, was merely a "half-way house between Civilization and California." New Orleans—the South's second-largest city, barely smaller than Baltimore—did possess the only opera in the United States to warrant comparison with the European houses, and had, in composer Louis Moreau Gottschalk and chess prodigy Paul Morphy, two sons of international renown. The city remained, however, a cultural wasteland. Its theaters were mediocre and relentlessly lowbrow, while book publishers continued to find New Orleans a pitiful market. They sold four times more books in Cincinnati, although the cities were of roughly the same size. New Orleans, moreover, supplied the needs of a vast hinterland and rich plantations stretching many miles upriver.

No city seemed to possess a more promising future, however, than New Orleans in the 1850s. The magnificent French Opera House, designed by James Gallier, opened on Bourbon Street in 1859, when political differences with the northern states were the only blot on the horizon for a vibrant, polyglot city of 170,000 people, including 25,000 Irish and almost as many Germans. It was a sporting town with plenty of horse racing and boxing matches. Men played cricket and raquette, a game resembling lacrosse, or took their sailboats out into the lakes. The mood of the city was buoyant and secure, and few doubted its superiority to anything the North could offer or had any qualms about slavery. "We seriously question," the *Daily Picayune* editorialized in 1859, "whether the slavery of the South is not comfort in comparison with the slavery of poverty in the north."

In 1860 a statue of Henry Clay was erected in the middle of Canal Street, where the late Great Compromiser became the symbol of the new social and political order. Progress seemed unstoppable. The railroad was now spreading through the state, bringing the prospect of faster transportation between the port and the plantations and even greater accumulation of wealth. The streetcar was introduced in 1860, and New Orleans seemed safely established as a great metropolis of the modern world.

Then, however, the blue cockade, emblem of the secessionists, began to appear on lapels all over the city. Several Comus members, including Adley Gladden, president for the past two years of the Pickwick Club, were elected to a state convention that voted 113–17 to secede on January 26, 1861. Comus still managed to parade on Mardi Gras, February 12, with the theme "The Four Ages of Life," venturing for the first time into the realm of political comment with a group of krewemen in blackface carrying an effigy of Abraham Lincoln riding a split rail.

CHAPTER THREE

Comus Dons Confederate Gray

The first shots of the Civil War were fired on Fort Sumter by troops under the command of Pierre Beauregard, now a Confederate general, who, three months later, led the successful defense against the initial Union charge at the first Battle of Bull Run. Creoles and Americans alike celebrated the feats of the first Civil War hero from New Orleans. A new marching song was composed in Beauregard's honor, and his picture offered for sale. New Orleans's own Washington Artillery acquitted itself well at Bull Run, too, so that local pride and enthusiasm for the war ran high.

But not for long. Men were conspicuously absent from the streets, twenty thousand having enlisted as Confederate soldiers in New Orleans. A federal blockade kept sea vessels out of the port, and even steamboat traffic was reduced to a trickle. Bakeries ran out of flour, fish was scarcely to be found and soap was in such short supply that it was proposed that potash, retrieved from sugar refineries, be used in its stead. Shoes went up to nine dollars a pair, causing one local wag to observe that "these are the times that try men's soles," and a cup of coffee was so hard to find that a local druggist purveyed a substitute with a dandelion base. Unable to find oysters, the populace was reduced to eating sardines. Many citizens turned gray, though not because of the stresses of wartime: the city had run out of hair dye. The Union was roundly hated, and when citizens no-

ticed "the old escutcheon of the United States left over the upper window of the Orleans Artillery Arsenal," they climbed up
and tore it down.

By February of 1862, two thousand families depended on
government relief for food, and New Orleans had ground almost to standstill. Those members of the Pickwick Club who
were still in town had no stomach for Carnival and ran this notice in the *Daily Picayune*:

> WHEREAS, War has cast its gloom over our happy homes and
> care usurped the place where joy is wont to hold its sway. Now,
> therefore, do I deeply sympathizing with the general anxiety,
> deem it proper to withhold your Annual Festival in this goodly
> Crescent City and by this proclamation do command no assem-
> blage of the
> —Mistick Krewe—
> Given under my hand this, the 1st day of March, A.D. 1862
>
> Comus

Mardi Gras had such a hold on local affections, however, that
the Washington Artillery interrupted its campaign in Virginia
to hold a makeshift party on the appointed day, March 4. The
weather was bitterly cold, and the ladies at the dance were
young soldiers in disguise, but spirits were raised by memories
of Carnival fantasy. At home, reality was about to set in at its
most brutal.

When the Pickwick adopted a charter in 1859 the first two
signatories were its president, Adley Gladden, and William
McBeth, club secretary. At the battle of Shiloh on April 6,
1862, Captain McBeth was killed and General Gladden mortally wounded, while Louisiana regiments suffered enormous
casualties. The fleet of Union Admiral David Farragut, meanwhile, had established a base on Ship Island not far from the
mouth of the Mississippi in the Gulf of Mexico, and New
Orleans was under Confederate martial law. The railroads had

barely finished delivering the Shiloh dead and wounded when, on April 25, Farragut ran the downriver forts and dropped anchor with guns trained on New Orleans, awaiting support from troops under General Benjamin Butler. The Confederate army immediately began to withdraw and the citizenry set about burning bales of cotton and tobacco on the quay, torching boats, woodyards and coalyards, sinking the drydocks, smashing machinery and dumping sugar and molasses in the river. Foreign consuls stationed in the city formed a fifteen-hundred-strong "European Brigade" to maintain order until Mayor John Monroe, a former day laborer in the docks, surrendered on April 27.

Butler, though he was to become one of the principal figures in krewe demonology, was good-humored enough when he arrived May 1 to take command of New Orleans. A popular song of the era had been written in honor of "Picayune" Butler, a black West Indian who had come to New Orleans in the 1820s to make a living playing his banjo on the streets. When the conqueror was about to disembark in New Orleans, with thousands of onlookers gathered at the quay, the cry arose for "Picayune Butler" to come ashore. This no doubt appealed to the crowd's sense of humor; "Picayune," the name for a Spanish coin worth six and a half cents, which used to circulate in Louisiana, had now come to denote smallness or insignificance. The word was also familiar in the city from the *Daily Picayune*, so called because, when it first appeared in 1837, it was the cheapest newspaper in the city, retailing at six and a half cents.

Preparing to disembark, General Butler is said to have asked bandmasters if they had the appropriate music, but none did, and he was forced to enter the city to "Yankee Doodle" and "The Star-Spangled Banner." The crowd, yelling such pleasantries as "Yellow Jack [yellow fever] will have you before long," and "Go home, you damned Yankees," jeered at his unprepossessing appearance, his corpulent figure and his gauche

attempts to keep step with the music. Butler was born in Deer-
field, New Hampshire, in 1818, five months after his father
died in the West Indies of, as luck would have it, yellow fever.
As a captain of dragoons, Butler père fought under, and greatly
admired, Andrew Jackson when he beat the British at the
Battle of New Orleans in 1815.

Bald on top, Benjamin Butler was, as Mary Boykin Chesnut
confided to her diary, "a hideous cross-eyed beast." Union Colonel Theodore Lyman wrote that Butler "presents a combination
of Victor Emmanuel, Aesop and Richard III, which is very con-
fusing to the mind." Butler, famous for harboring fugitive slaves
in Virginia as "contraband of war," had nothing to commend
him to the propertied classes of Louisiana.

While the crowds were making sport of Butler, the editors
of the *Daily Delta* decided to take a lighthearted dig at the
sybaritic habits of the clubmen who made up the Confederate
Guards and who had vanished as soon as Farragut's fleet was
sighted in the river: "Lafayette Square has undergone a sudden
and violent change. The gay, gallant and luxurious Confederate
Guards, who a few days ago occupied the grounds with their
beautiful tents and sumptuous camp equipage, their gas-lighted
guard houses and elegantly dressed and most substantially con-
ditioned soldiers, have suddenly and mysteriously disappeared,
and whither no one hereabouts can inform us, and, even if we
knew, General Butler's proclamation would not permit us to
say." They had, in fact, retreated into Confederate territory and
were disporting themselves at the Manassas Club in Mobile.
There they bumped into some real soldiers from the Washington Artillery, one of whom, William H. Owen, himself later a
member of the Boston Club, wrote a book about his wartime
experiences. Owen reported that, when defending the home
front, the Guards had lived "luxuriously—tents floored, cots,
sideboards etc, plenty of servants—but had at times great pri-

vations for Joe Lovell told me that once it rained very hard and there wasn't an umbrella in the whole regiment."

Whatever mood of levity may have prevailed after the fall of New Orleans was quickly dispelled. A couple of days before Butler's arrival, some of Farragut's officers raised the United States flag over the New Orleans mint, whereupon four locals pulled it down, paraded it around the city to fife and drum, tore it up and distributed the pieces among the crowd. The *Daily Picayune* was full of admiration: "The names of the party that distinguished themselves by gallantly tearing down the flag that had been surreptitiously hoisted, we learn, are W. B. Mumford, who cut it loose from the flagstaff amid the shower of grape, Lieutenant N. Holmes, Sergeant Burns and James Read. They deserve great credit for their patriotic act." If it did not occur to the *Picayune* editors that Butler might take a different view, and that publicity might expose the patriots to reprisal, Mumford, a professional gambler, also miscalculated. He was a handsome man, forty-two years old, with thick brown hair and moustache and a cocky manner. He made no attempt to hide, but swaggered around town, turning up on one occasion outside the St. Charles Hotel, where Butler had established his headquarters, to relate his exploits to an admiring throng. Butler had him arrested, tried and hanged in the grounds of the mint.

By the time of Mumford's execution, Butler had already proved to the citizenry that the nickname by which he is still universally recognized in New Orleans today—"Beast"—was by no means solely attributable to his looks. He had, indeed, attracted international obloquy by this edict of May 28: "As the officers and soldiers of the United States have been subjected to repeated insults from the women (calling themselves ladies) of New Orleans, in return for the most scrupulous non-interference and courtesy on our part, it is ordered that hereafter, when any female shall, by word, gesture or movement insult or show contempt for any officer or soldier of the United States, she shall be held liable to be treated as a woman of the town plying her avocation." Most newspapers in Confederate country promptly published "An Appeal to Every Southern Soldier" from "The Daughters of New Orleans." It began: "We turn to you in mute agony! Behold our wrongs! Fathers! husbands! brothers! sons! we know those bitter, burning wrongs will be fully avenged—never did southern women appeal in vain for protection from insult! But, for the sake of your sisters throughout the south, with tears we implore you not to surrender your cities." Europeans were outraged by what they took to be an invitation to rape, and the English magazine *Punch* published a verse with this refrain:

> Yankee doodle, doodle doo,
> Yankee doodle dandy;
> Butler is a rare Yahoo
> As Brave as Sepoy Pandy.

British prime minister Lord Palmerston rose in the House of Commons to aver: "An Englishman must blush to think that such an act had been committed by a man belonging to the Anglo Saxon race." New Orleans Creoles were no doubt less shocked to find the race capable of such crassness, but Her Majesty's government adopted a resolution condemning Butler's order. As Butler himself noted in a letter to a friend, "some portions of the northern press" took a dim view of his order, too.

There is no doubt that Butler and his troops had been provoked. New Orleans women would flounce away, or affect nausea, when Union soldiers appeared, or even spit in their faces. In the French Quarter it was all the rage to empty chamber pots from the upper floors into the narrow streets when Yankees were passing. Butler himself had no second thoughts. In an article published in the *Boston Journal* on July 2, 1862, he pointed out that "[w]e were two thousand, five hundred men in a city seven miles long by two to four wide, of a hundred and fifty thousand inhabitants, all hostile, bitter, defiant, explosive." Had the "bejeweled, crinolined and laced creatures" of New Orleans not been stopped, they would have precipitated "disturbances and riot, from which we must clear the streets with artillery." Instead, "these she-adders of New Orleans themselves were at once tamed into propriety." Not quite all of them. Anna Larue, wife of a professional gambler, appeared in front of the St. Charles Hotel on July 10 displaying a Confederate flag, and almost started a riot by reviling Union soldiers and predicting their defeat. Butler took no action against Mrs. Larue.

Still credited today with being "the most hated man in Louisiana folklore," Butler was an efficient enforcer of the Confiscation Act, seizing $245,760 that belonged to the Confederate government and untold property from those who had held military or civil office under it. This meant ruin for many of the city's most prominent businessmen, and Garden District mansions were seized and auctioned wholesale together with furniture, jewelry, works of art, horses, silver and even clothes. Butler found four hundred church and plantation bells that had been sent to New Orleans from all over the Confederacy to be cast into cannon and shipped them north for auction. He relieved the citizenry of six thousand weapons, paying informants ten dollars to locate a musket or rifle, seven dollars for a revolver, five dollars for a pistol or saber and three dollars for a dagger or bowie knife. He forbade assemblies of more than three people on the street and required an oath of allegiance from anyone "asking or receiving any favor, protection, privilege, passport or to have money paid them, property or other valuable thing whatever delivered to them, or any benefit of the power of the United States extended to them, except protection from personal violence." Within two months the oath had been administered to more than 5,000 former members of the Confederate army, 11,723 other citizens and 2,499 foreign residents. Butler was not inclined to brook dissent even from clergymen. Those who refused to include a prayer for President Lincoln in their services were taken prisoner and sent to New York, replaced in the pulpit by army chaplains. When the newspaper *Le Propagateur Catholique* refused to abandon its pro-Confederate stance, Butler closed it down and put its editor, Fr. Napoleon Joseph Perche, in jail. Somehow, another priest, Fr. James Ignatius Mullon, pastor of St. Patrick's, escaped a similar fate although he was notably turbulent. Butler once complained that Mullon had refused to allow a Union soldier to be buried from his church. Not so, said Mullon—"I would gladly bury the entire Union army." Many white people felt the same, and the newspapers were full of praise for the steady stream of men leaving the safety and comfort of the city for the dangers and hardships of Confederate territory, now dubbed "Secessia." Butler made no attempt to stop the exodus, reasoning that his enemies could do less harm behind Confederate lines than they could in the city. Slaves, meanwhile, encouraged by Union soldiers, deserted their masters in the city and on the outlying plantations and descended on army camps looking for food and shelter. Butler's troops confined many of them a few miles upriver from the city at Camp Parapet, which had been under construction as a Confederate defense against an attack from the north when Farragut sailed in from the south. All that remains of Camp Parapet today is a Confederate powder magazine with a marker erected by local historians noting that the federals "occupied the area with many negro troops and contraband." It stands in the middle of an area known as Shrewsbury, one of the few black enclaves in Jefferson Parish.

The flight of the slaves gathered pace as word spread that Butler's army could provide menial tasks and even hire fugitives to work plantations seized from refractory Confederates.

Whites began to complain that they were losing jobs, and the city became a nervous place. Some people still remembered the great slave uprising of 1811, and, shortly after Butler's arrival, a New Orleans schoolgirl, Clarissa Solomon, wrote in her diary: "I fear more from the negroes than Yankees and insurrection is my continual horror."

Alone of the city's gentlemen's clubs, the Pickwick—possibly because its secretary, J. Q. A. Fellowes, was a Union man—remained open throughout the Civil War, although no board meetings were held and the place must have been pretty quiet. Altogether Louisiana had fifty-six thousand men in gray, more than half of whom were killed or wounded or died of disease. The federal army, meanwhile, included more black soldiers from Louisiana—twenty-four thousand—than from any other state, as well as some five thousand white New Orleans unionists, mostly disgruntled Irish and German immigrants.

Beast Butler did not last long in New Orleans, but he had time enough to earn a second sobriquet, "Spoons," bestowed because it was alleged that silverware would be found missing after he came calling at dinner time. That Butler presided over an administration riddled with corruption is not in dispute, but the "Spoons" evidence is slight. The Confederate Museum in New Orleans exhibits a receipt signed by J. D. Denegre, president of the Citizens' Bank, for a "box to contain silver" together with some spoons that are "said" to have been deposited there, and it is not inconceivable that he could have committed prandial misdemeanors, wealthy though he had become as a lawyer in Lowell, Massachusetts. But it is something of a cliché to suggest that people of dubious character will steal your spoons. Samuel Johnson used the line in 1763, and American as well as other English writers have adopted it since. In a city where Milton and Dickens had provided the first names in modern Carnival, Boswell's *The Life of Samuel Johnson* must have been familiar reading, and it may have been that Butler the spoon thief was merely the invention of literary types seeking any opportunity to defame him.

Not that it was necessary to make up stories about Butler to impugn the integrity of his administration. His agents habitually helped themselves to the proceeds when confiscated property was auctioned, and Butler was evidently guilty of conniving at the widespread profiteering and graft that made his elder brother, Andrew Jackson Butler, among others, a rich man. The federal War Department warned Butler that he "ought not to be involved in private trade and profit arising out of his official power and position," and U. S. Senator Reverdy Johnson of Maryland, who visited New Orleans in the summer of 1862, concluded that corruption in Butler's administration was "without parallel in the past history of the country."

For all that, the evidence does not support the traditional New Orleans view that Butler's regime was malignant from beginning to end. He put gangs of laborers to work cleaning up the feculent streets of New Orleans and produced what, by his own assessment, was "the healthiest city in America." The newspapers conceded that New Orleans had never been so clean. Butler had levees repaired, shanties demolished and canals flushed. He provided rations for the multitudes, black and white, left destitute by the war. On May 9, Butler announced the capture of provisions intended for "rebels in the field" and ordered it "distributed among the deserving poor of this city, from whom the rebels had plundered it." He noted, "The United States have sent land and naval forces here to fight and subdue rebellious armies in array against her authority. We find, substantially, only fugitive masses, runaway property-burners, a whisky-drinking mob, and starving citizens with their wives and children. It is our duty to call back the first, to punish the second, root out the third and protect the last." The threat of Confederate reprisal, however, was not quite so remote as Butler

suggested, and he spent the summer vainly requesting reinforcements from the North. When they were not forthcoming,
he started recruiting local blacks for the Union army, and soon
put together three regiments. He decided, meanwhile, that the
best way to pay the bills for feeding the poor and cleaning up
the city was to levy a tax on "those who have brought this calam-
ity on their fellow-citizens." Those responsible, the general decided, were all corporate and individual contributors to Confederate coffers and those brokers who had told plantation owners
not to ship cotton to New Orleans lest it fall into Union hands.

This was not the first time Butler had struck at the wealthy
elite of New Orleans, for he had already taken steps to preserve
the citizenry from the depredations of the bankers. After the
surrender of New Orleans, many merchants refused to accept
Confederate money, which the banks were therefore able to
scoop up at a discount, and which Butler decreed would not be
considered legal tender after May 27. When the banks instructed their customers to withdraw their deposits by that
date, obviously intending to fob them off with worthless paper,
Butler ordered them to pay in U. S. Treasury notes, gold or silver. The bankers, naturally, thought him a beast.

So did the staunchly pro-Confederate foreign consuls in New
Orleans. Butler cooked his own goose when he tried to extract
a cache of coin from the vaults of the Dutch and French con-
sulates. The money was intended for transfer into foreign accounts, partly in payment for Confederate munitions, and European governments squawked. The federal government blocked
the confiscation order and, on Christmas Eve, 1862, Butler was
recalled and replaced by Gen. Nathaniel Banks. Butler left behind a remembrance, inscribing "The Union Must and Shall be
Preserved" in the base of the city's Andrew Jackson statue that
stands in the middle of the square named after him. The legend
is a quotation from Jackson himself.

Butler, as "one whose name is to be hereafter indissolubly

connected with your city," delivered a farewell address calculated to ensure that, in the best local circles, that name would be anathema: "I saw that this rebellion was a war of the aristocrats against the middling men—of the rich against the poor; a war of the landowner against the laborer; that it was a struggle for the retention of power in the hands of the few against the many; and I found no conclusion to it, save in the subjugation of the few and the disinthrallment of the many." As for slavery, "I found the dungeon, the chain and the lash your only means of enforcing obedience in your servants. I leave them peaceful, laborious, controlled by the laws of kindness and justice."

The same day that Butler left town, Confederate president Jefferson Davis branded him "a felon, deserving of capital punishment," and "an outlaw and common enemy of mankind." In the event of his capture, he was to be immediately hanged. Butler escaped that fate but was still internationally notorious for his supposed atrocities in New Orleans, becoming the villain of an English melodrama, *The Confederate's Daughter or the Tyrant of New Orleans*, in 1865. In New Orleans a cartoonist depicted Butler as a hyena feeding on the corpses of Confederate martyrs. When Butler's grandson visited the city in 1938, elderly ladies were still debating "the propriety of receiving him socially." Perhaps they were worried about their spoons.

Or perhaps they recalled that Butler had upset the social order of the Old South when he put blacks from New Orleans into federal uniforms. Butler's recruits, though they included some fugitive slaves of undiluted African heritage, were mostly free people of color. Though black in the eyes of the law, they by no means all looked it. Union soldier Silas E. Fales complained in an 1863 letter to "Mary" that "[i]t is hard telling who is white here. The Creoles are blacker than some of the mulattos," and Butler himself could be baffled. When two young ladies of the city asked permission to present a set of colors to his regiment on the Fourth of July, 1862, for instance, he assented and rode forth in best uniform, "with chapeau and feathers," to review the guard and deliver a brief address. A few days later one of his officers came into Butler's office in an agitated state. "General," he said, "we have been deceived. They were negroes."

"What? Those lovely blondes, with blue eyes and light hair? Impossible."

"General, it's as true as there's a heaven above us. The whole town is laughing at us."

Two free people of color fought a duel in the city because of a difference of opinion over the war, and one was killed, although whether he favored the Union or the Confederacy is not recorded. The white citizenry expected the free blacks to protect their own interests by supporting the Confederacy, and some three thousand of them did enlist in the first year of the war, although whatever enthusiasm they felt for the cause soon evaporated. By the time Farragut appeared in Mississippi, the colored regiments had decided their interests lay with the Union, and they refused to join the Confederate retreat.

Butler, though at first reluctant to enlist colored soldiers, grew so desperate for reinforcements that he sent for "several of the most influential of this class" and asked them why they had "accepted service under the Confederate government which was set up for the distinctly avowed purpose of holding in eternal slavery their brethren and kindred." They answered that they "had not dared to refuse; that they had hoped by serving the Confederates to advance a little nearer to equality with whites; that they longed to throw the weight of their class into the scale of the Union, and only asked an opportunity to show their devotion to the cause with which their own dearest hopes were identified." After some hesitation, Butler decided to accept them in August of 1862, and three regiments of Native Guards were promptly formed. They went on to earn national recognition the next year for their spirited assault on the rebel fort at

Port Hudson, Louisiana, where Capt. Andre Callioux was killed after such heroics that thirty-seven black societies marched at his funeral. By that time, former slaves were flocking to the Union army, where they received a mixed reception. Many were taught to read and write and emerged at the end of the war with money in their pockets. But racism was rife in the Union ranks; black soldiers were sometimes refused supplies or forced to do all the fatigues, and many black officers resigned in the face of the contemptuous treatment they received from their white counterparts. General Banks in 1863 was "entirely satisfied that the appointment of colored officers is detrimental to the service," and dismissed them wholesale.

When New Orleans surrendered in 1862, its population of 170,000 included 14,000 slaves and 11,000 free people of color. This gave New Orleans a tripartite social structure without parallel in the United States and a colored middle class somewhat ambivalent toward the prospect of emancipation. For the free people of color the obvious danger was that they might face a loss of privileges; their initial enthusiasm for the Confederate cause no doubt owed something to the prospect that a Union victory would put all black citizens on the same legal footing. Certainly, the federals remained suspicious of the colored faction, notwithstanding its service to the Union army. Troops broke up a voodoo rite in July of 1863 and put four hundred people on trial, alleging that their incantations were on behalf of the Confederacy because free people of color dreaded the repercussions of a Union victory. All the accused were acquitted.

The departure of Butler was the occasion for some jubilation among the white citizens of New Orleans, but conditions hardly improved under Banks. A quarter of the population still depended on government relief for food, and the war had taken such a toll that the occupying forces ran ten orphanages. Banks was as happy as Butler had been to see disaffected citizens depart for Secessia, although he was much displeased on February 20—three days after Mardi Gras would have been celebrated in normal circumstances—when hundreds of women and children waving handkerchiefs appeared on the steamboat landing to bid farewell to the latest group of departing rebels. Union forces were ordered to present their bayonets, but the absurdity of the scene made many of them smile as they did so. The confrontation gave Marion Southward an easy opening to deride the federals in her verses "Beauty and Booty," which include this stanza:

> Five hundred kerchiefs we had snatched
> From Rebel Ladies' hands,
> Ten parasols, two shoes (not matched),
> Some ribbons, belts and bands,
> And other things that I forgot;
> But then you'll find them all
> As trophies in that hallowed spot—
> The cradle—Faneuil Hall.

All hope of a Confederate victory disappeared in the carnage of Gettysburg at the beginning of July 1863. Once again trainloads of corpses arrived in New Orleans, and more and more wounded and disfigured young men were to be seen hanging around its streets. Financial ruin and widespread want left a pall of depression over a city resigned to prolonged military occupation. The teeming waterfront of a few years earlier was practically idle. It was, the *Daily Picayune* observed, a good time for taking moonlight walks along the levee, for "trade offers no impediments in the way of heaped-up bales and barrels and the steamers are too few to prevent the balm-freighted winds from wandering where they list."

Much of Louisiana was still Confederate territory, under the governorship of Henry Allen, but the Union now controlled eighteen parishes, as counties are called in Louisiana, in addition to New Orleans. General Banks, on orders from President Lincoln, now moved to establish a new government that would be required to abolish slavery, to which end federal troops supervised the election of Bavarian-born Michael Hahn as governor and James Madison Wells as lieutenant governor. After their inauguration on March 4, 1864, where integrated bands provided the music, a convention was called, with federal judge Edmund Durell presiding, to adopt a new state constitution. Wells, a Unionist but, as a wealthy planter, no fan of manumission, attended to urge that slave owners be compensated for their losses. With a good field hand commanding more than a thousand dollars at auction before the Civil War, slaves constituted a sizeable investment for their owners. The convention, however, rebuffed Wells and abolished slavery unconditionally, also coming out in favor of free education for all children regardless of race. Delegates decided that the vote should remain limited to white males, although Lincoln himself had asked Hahn to consider "whether some of the colored people may be let in; as, for instance, the very intelligent and especially those who have fought gallantly in our ranks." The convention did, however, leave the way open for the legislature "to pass laws extending suffrage to such other persons, citizens of the United States, as by military service, by taxation to support the Government or by intellectual fitness may be deemed entitled thereto." Several delegates used the same term to express their opposition—"nigger resolution." Public officials in Louisiana had already developed a habit of entertaining themselves lavishly, and the constitutional convention set taxpayers back $125,000, including $9,421.55 for liquor and cigars, $4,304.25 for carriage hire and $150 to buy a pen for General Banks.

Outsiders continued to find that it was often impossible to keep up with the racial shibboleths of New Orleans society. One visitor, journalist Whitelaw Reid, who accompanied U. S.

Supreme Court Chief Justice Salmon Chase to the city in 1865, described their experiences of quadroon society: "Nowhere else in the world could that scene have been witnessed. There were elegantly dressed ladies, beautiful with a beauty beside which that of the North is wax work, with great swimming, lustrous eyes, half-veiled behind long pendent lashes, and arched with coal-black eyebrows, complexions no darker than those of the Spanish senoritas one admires in Havana, but transparent as that of the most beautiful northern blonde." The men present "whether in complexion, clothes or conversation, would never have been suspected in any mixed company at the North of being other than intelligent and polished ornaments of the Anglo-Saxon race." In New Orleans, however, white society was more fastidious: "The Chief Justice was eternally disgraced (according to the talk of the city next day) for having so forgotten dignity, and even decency, as to enter a parlor filled with niggers trying to play lady and gentleman." New Orleans, Reid noted, was "at once the most luxurious, the most unprincipled, the most extravagant and, to many, the most fascinating city in the Union—the only place that before the war could support the opera through an entire winter, the only place where the theaters are open on Sunday evening; where gambling is not concealed and keeping a mistress is not only in no sense disreputable but is even made legal."

The constitutional convention of 1864 had adjourned with a provision that it could be reconvened by Durell, and its recommendations were approved in a referendum. When the Confederacy finally gave up the ghost with Robert E. Lee's surrender at Appomattox on April 9, 1865, the soldiery came dragging home, and Hahn called elections. Returning soldiers voted en masse to produce a legislature dominated by former Confederates who were able to run for public office thanks to an amnesty from President Andrew Johnson, a Unionist from Tennessee with mixed feelings about the South. The new Louisiana legislature promptly adopted a resolution "that this is a Government of white people, made and to be perpetuated for the exclusive benefit of the white race," and quickly began passing laws to ensure that blacks were returned to a condition strongly reminscent of slavery. The legislature adopted a series of statutes that incorporated many provisions of the antebellum *code noir* restricting black people's freedom of movement. They were required to sign long-term labor contracts and were forbidden to leave their masters. Blacks who refused to work on these terms were arrested under the vagrancy laws and, if unable to pay their fines, hired out to the highest bidder. A convict-lease system was also instituted and lasted until the turn of the century. The brutality to which leased convicts were subjected appears to have been even worse than anything they had experienced at the hands of slave owners. A slave, at least, had an economic value, but there was no such incentive to keep a convict alive. As one lessee noted in his diary, "If one dies, get another." Records are sketchy, but it appears that the annual mortality rate among leased convicts was around 20 percent. The North's victory in the Civil War was said to have left Louisiana blacks somewhere "between peonage and serfdom."

While returned rebels were tightening their grip on the political institutions of New Orleans, many of them were also busy preparing for the first appearance of Comus since 1861. He emerged on Mardi Gras of 1866 with a spectacle that moved many onlookers to tears. Everyone knew that behind the masks were what the *Daily Picayune* called "recently grim visaged warriors, who had played conspicuous parts in the recent sad scenes of havoc and slaughter." Under the rubric "The Past, The Present and The Future," Comus presented tableaux depicting the horrors of the Civil War and the joys of reconciliation. The show culminated with a vision of American posterity living in harmony amid the "fruits of industry, science and all the peaceful arts." That glorious future, of course, was lily white.

CHAPTER FOUR

The Krewes and the Klan

*A*fter Comus's return to the streets in 1866, dashing Confederate general Harry Hays became president of the Pickwick Club. This was not the first election Hays had won since returning to New Orleans from the war, for he was now administrator of the city's court system as civil sheriff. He was also determined to put down blacks and radicals with any means at his disposal. Nobody in the city was more admired among the white population than Hays, whose Civil War brigade, among the most fearsome in the Confederate army, had performed celebrated feats of derring-do at various battles including Antietam, Fredericksburg and Gettysburg. Hays, who had been badly wounded at Spotsylvania in 1864, was also one of the leading ornaments of New Orleans society. A member before the Civil War of the Boston Club, he played a leading role in reorganizing it afterwards. He had become a member of Pickwick/Comus in 1858. The list of officers in Hays's Brigade reads like a page from the social register. Among the Pickwickians who fought under Hays were French-born Lt. Col. Charles de Choiseul, killed at Port Republic in 1862, Maj. Davidson Penn, who was also a member of the Boston Club, and two subsequent captains of Comus, Col. Walter Merriam and Capt. Samuel Gilman. Divisional commanders included Pickwickians George Clark, William Rickarby and Samuel Flower, also a Bostonian.

Around the time Hays became president of the Pickwick Club, state supreme court justice Rufus Howell called on delegates to the constitutional convention of 1864 to reassemble and consider Negro suffrage. Howell's authority to issue such a call was dubious, but he had the backing of James Madison Wells, who was now governor, and Judge Durell was out of town. A few hundred blacks, northern transplants and white liberals were milling around the hall during a recess on the first day of the convention, July 30, 1866, when gunfire was heard outside and bullets shattered the windows. The police, with a white mob in support, burst through the doors, shooting, stabbing and clubbing delegates and spectators. When it was all over, thirty-four blacks and three whites were dead or dying and more than a hundred and fifty others wounded. The coroner reported that he believed more blacks had been killed and wounded than he had been able to document. Among the casualties were some of the city's most prominent white champions of universal suffrage. Dr. Anthony Dostie, a dentist, former state auditor and long-time abolitionist, was shot, run through with a sword and thrown in jail. Bailed out by a federal army officer, he died six days later. Capt. C. Loup, a German immigrant who had fought for the Union, was shot and smashed in the head with a brick. "We have fought for four years these Goddamed Yankees and sons of bitches in the field and now we will fight them in the city," one of his assailants yelled. Loup died on the spot.

Dr. William Hire, a well-known physician in New Orleans for almost thirty years, was beaten and stabbed but survived. The killing and mayhem went on for a considerable time, witnesses reported, while the mob hunted down delegates and spectators in the streets and in the Mechanics' Institute, the temporary state capitol where the convention was being held. The New Orleans papers applauded what they portrayed as the defense of civil order and legitimate government, pooh-

poohing suggestions that the civil authorities were responsible for the massacre. This elicited an indignant reponse from attorney Henry Dibble, an ex-Union officer who had lived in New Orleans since 1863. "You have no respect for truth, and lack the ability to hide your falsehoods," he wrote in a letter to the editor of the *New Orleans Times*. A congressional committee investigated and concluded in a report published February 11, 1867, that the mayhem was the result of "a purposed attack by the police force of the city." The report noted that, though some members of the convention had been prosecuted for a breach of the peace, no action had been taken against the policemen and others responsible for the killings. It was impossible, various witnesses said, to impanel a jury that would convict a Confederate sympathizer of any crime against a Union man, for rebel sentiment in the city was even stronger than it had been before the war. In any case, Sheriff Hays controlled jury selection, and he had blood on his own hands.

The soldiers who had fought in Hays's Brigade during the Civil War stuck together afterwards, and the newspapers published periodic calls for reunions in the name of charitable and social purposes. But they had remained ready for action and, on the eve of the massacre, Hays had sworn in hundreds of them as deputy sheriffs to augment the police force. Inside the convention hall, delegates could hear the mob outside shouting, "God damn you. Now you're fighting Hays's Brigade." Witnesses told the congressional committee that they had been brutalized and arrested by Hays's old soldiers. Several members of the gentry either participated in or encouraged the slaughter. Hays's old company commander, fellow Pickwickian and, now, city councilman, George Clark, was one of the those spotted at the scene.

Governor Wells, testifying before the congressional committee, noted that 80 percent of state legislators were Confederate men and that "loyal" government was impossible in the circumstances. That "returned rebels" were ascendant was "eminently true" of New Orleans, the committee found. The "bold and bad man" John Monroe, who had risen from the ranks of the city's Know-Nothing thugs in the 1850s, was still mayor, and the constabulary consisted entirely of "men who have rendered efficient service toward the overthrow of the government of the United States." Wells, who had owned three plantations and hordes of slaves until emancipation, now declared himself in favor of suffrage for blacks and disfranchisement for rebels. But he was just trimming his sails according to the prevailing political winds, and Gen. Philip Sheridan, headquartered in New Orleans as commander of Texas, Louisiana and Florida at the time of the convention massacre, had Wells's number. Sheridan wrote Secretary of War Edwin Scranton, "Governor Wells is a political trickster and a dishonest man. I have seen him myself, when first I came to this command, turn out all the Union men who had supported the government, and put in their stead rebel soldiers, some of whom had not yet doffed their grey uniforms. I have seen him again during the July riot of 1866, skulk away where I could not find him to give him a guard, instead of coming out as a manly representative of the State and joining those who were preserving the peace. I have watched him since, and his conduct has been as sinuous as the mark left in the dust by the movement of a snake." Even by his own account, Wells's response to the massacre was less than heroic. He said that when he perceived that "the riot was increasing to a fearful extent," he took the streetcar to his home in Jefferson Parish and holed up. But Sheridan was a little slippery himself. He could not have seen Wells "skulk away" or do anything else during the riot. Sheridan left town July 23 for the "Rio Grande frontier," leaving Gen. Absalom Baird in command, and did not return until July 31. If Sheridan did not expect violence at the constitutional convention, he must have been the only man in town who failed to sense the racial tension of the preceding weeks. On July 6, a white girl cried, "Oh, there goes a nigger with a flag," precipitating a mass set-to between whites and blacks that left scores injured. Convention delegates and unionists were threatened, the newspapers worked themselves up into a lather at the prospect of Negro suffrage, and Anthony Dostie was all over town advocating disfranchisement for Confederates. Many people regarded Dostie as slightly crazy. A native of Saratoga, New York, he settled in New Orleans in 1852 but went back north at the outbreak of civil war after assuring the local citizenry that he "would rather see every human being wiped out from the southern states than to behold the triumph of treason." He returned to New Orleans during Butler's regime, was appointed to the school board and soon had the students singing patriotic songs. He was known as "the Robespierre of New Orleans," and gave one of his most incendiary speeches, a few days before the constitutional convention massacre, to a large crowd of blacks gathered outside the Mechanics' Institute. Henry Dibble also addressed that meeting, which was followed by a confrontation with the police. Two blacks were killed, several arrested and four policemen injured.

The federal troops that could have prevented the convention massacre did not appear at the Mechanics' Institute until too late, although Baird was asked in good time to send them in. On his return Sheridan wrote to Gen. Ulysses Grant, "It was no riot. It was an absolute massacre by the police. It was a murder which the mayor and the police of the city perpetrated without the shadow of a necessity." As for public reaction, Sheridan told the congressional committee, "There were a great many respectable people in New Orleans who condemned the riot. There were also a great many respectable people in New Orleans who made use of the worst description of language in respect to it—such language as regretting that any members of the convention escaped alive."

The committee recommended that the government of Louisiana be replaced by "a provisional government established and maintained by military power." Nobody in New Orleans appears to have taken much notice at the time, because Mardi Gras was less than a month away—March 5 was the great day that year—and Comus was preparing to make a splash with "The Feast of Epicurus." Comus led on his float, followed by krewemen on foot, each costumed to represent a dish or accessory from a sumptuous banquet. They lined up thus:

Absinthe   Sherry   Bitters   Epergne
Oysters   Johannisberger
Soupe a la Tortue   Soupe a la Julienne
Salt Cellar
Shrimp   Crawfish
Crab   Lobster
Celery   Pickles
Horseradish   Claret Club Sauce
Codfish a la Jonathan   Sheepshead a la Shoddy
Westphalia Ham   Irish Potatoes   Boarshead a L'Ecossais
Candelabra
Knife   Fork
Peas Corn Pumpkin Squash
Boeuf Gras
Beets Rice Carrots Cabbage
Bread   Tomatoes
Candelabra
Mutton Venison Epergne Pork Potatoes Turkey
Peacock Duck Macaroni Bird Pie Chicken Curry
Chicken Marengo Partridge Pie Snipe Sausage Epergne
Candelabra
Frog Lettuce Salad Fork and Spoon Coleslaw
Cauliflower Castors Artichoke Asparagus
Ice Cream Jelly Epergne Pudding Strawberries
Macaroni Champagne Sherry Meringue

The Krewes and the Klan

Banana Fruit Pineapple Melon Nuts Burgundy Candy
Candelabra
Omelette Brulee Cigars Coffee Whisky Brandy
Kirsch and Curaçao

The huge crowds along the route were mightily impressed with the show, the shimmering gold of the ambulatory candelabra providing a striking centerpiece. After that night's ball, it is said that the krewe consumed the parade.

Not everyone dined well that night in a city bearing all the scars of ruinous defeat. So much of the city's manhood had perished on the battlefield that solitary women driving their own buggies were a common sight, and plenty of the poorer class were ill nourished. Patrons of the St. Charles Hotel could still order a ten-course dinner from the fifty-four dishes listed on the menu, and regular folk could eat well too, provided the household included a man who knew how to hunt and fish. The abundant game included deer, squirrel, rabbit, duck, goose, pigeon, quail, snipe, woodcock, dove, turkey, grosbec or even robin (greatly relished at the time); the waters offered a dazzling profusion of speckled trout, redfish, drum, croaker and crabs, and it was all within an easy walk. New Orleans was still so much the frontier town that black bears roamed within its limits.

It was also a blot on the glorious landscape. The clean conditions of Beast Butler's era were a dim memory, and filth and pestilence were back with a vengeance. The city stank from the open sewers and the rotting refuse along the mostly unpaved streets. With so many in the grip of poverty, crime was worse than ever, drunks lurched along the streets, and the smoky saloons were crammed with ruffians, fighting, cursing and playing cards, dice or billiards. The head of the local Presbyterian church worried that young men were fleeing "from the gloom of the present by plunging into every form of earthly pleasure."

It was not all depression, however, for the socialites of New Orleans, aided by a steady resurgence of commerce after the war, were back in something like full swing, unfazed by the tightening grip of federal occupation.

When the Louisiana legislature declined to ratify the Fourteenth Amendment, in common with every Confederate state except Tennessee, Congress responded in 1867 by dividing the South into five districts under military rule, with Sheridan still in command of Texas and Louisiana, but with even greater powers. This did not sit well with the whites of New Orleans, who reviled Sheridan for his wartime depredations in the Shenandoah Valley. Sheridan promptly ousted several public officials, including Wells, Hays and Monroe and, as required by the Military Reconstruction Act, disfranchised anybody who would not swear an oath that he had never voluntarily aided the Confederacy. Society women dressed to the nines continued to parade along Canal Street in New Orleans on Saturdays, however, and every night there was a ball, a party or a dinner to entertain the wealthy classes until the early hours.

White society may have been remarkably resilient, but it began to feel the winds of change when the black citizenry set out to challenge segregation with tactics that foreshadowed the civil rights campaigns of almost a century later. In April of 1867 a black citizen named William Nichols attempted to board a streetcar reserved for whites and was thrown onto the street, whereupon the militant black newspaper, the *New Orleans Tribune*, took up the cause, and several other doughty souls followed Nichols's example. In Faubourg Marigny a mob attacked white streetcars and commandeered one of them. Further streetcar attacks occurred around Congo Square, and racial riots broke out in various parts of the city. Sheridan, at a meeting with Mayor Edward Heath and car company executives on May 6, refused a request that he deploy federal troops to subdue the protesters, and the authorities had no choice but to integrate the system and remove the stars that had marked streetcars reserved for blacks. The rest of 1867, however, brought no further advances for the black crusaders. When they demanded entry to white restaurants and taverns, Mayor Heath issued an executive order that private businesses were free to choose their customers, and the *New Orleans Tribune* got nowhere with its editorial campaign to integrate the schools. White society was also relieved when Sheridan was replaced at the end of 1867, and his departure was hardly less welcome than Beast Butler's had been.

Meanwhile, another secret organization that shared Comus's taste for elaborate hierarchy and odd spelling had taken to parading the streets, but not in New Orleans. It was on Christmas Eve, 1865, that six former Confederate officers, seeking some relief from postwar ennui in Pulaski, Tennessee, formed the Ku Klux Klan as a purely social organization. It did not remain so for long, and its terrorist tactics soon spawned imitators throughout the South. Alcibiade de Blanc, a Confederate infantry captain wounded at Gettysburg and now a judge in St. Mary Parish, Louisiana, formed his own version of the Klan in May 1867, christening it first the Caucasian Club and then the Knights of the White Camellia.

Comus dipped into the poetry of Irishman Thomas More for a procession of horsemen, complete with Oriental costumes and scimitars, reenacting "The Departure of Lally Rookh from Delhi" on Mardi Gras of 1868. That year police chief J. J. Williamson banned masking after 6 P.M. on Mardi Gras, save for members of Comus, but the krewemen were preoccupied with weightier political matters.

Resentment among the disfranchised former Confederates intensified when federal authorities called a constitutional convention, with half the delegates elected being Negroes. Alarmed Confederates in New Orleans established the Crescent City Democratic Club, which was much more sinister than its name suggests. The Klan, the Knights of the White Camellia and Democratic Clubs established in Louisiana were "organizations working for a common purpose," according to a Congressional report, Ku Klux Conspiracy, published February 19, 1872. The organizers of the Crescent City Democratic Club were mostly members of a New Orleans gentlemen's club, the Chalmette, which established the second of the city's Mardi Gras krewes, the Twelfth Night Revelers, in 1870. The Chalmette and Boston clubs merged in 1873.

The convention of 1868 produced a draft that included, for the first time in Louisiana's constitutional history, a bill of rights. It gave blacks the right to vote and hold office and denied the franchise to former Confederate soldiers and anyone who had voted for or signed Louisiana's ordinance of secession. Also prohibited from voting were those who had written newspaper articles or preached sermons in the rebel cause. The only way for a member of the proscribed class to regain the vote was to sign "a certificate setting forth that he acknowledges the late rebellion to have been morally and politically wrong and that he regrets any aid he may have given it." The constitution, which also desegregated the schools and prohibited discrimination "in public conveyances and places of public accommodation," was approved in a plebiscite in April 1868, and Louisiana was readmitted to the Union. The same day the constitution was ratified, Henry Clay Warmoth, a twenty-six-year-old Republican and former Union officer, was elected governor. The new lieutenant governor, Oscar Dunn, was an ex-slave. Members of the new legislature promptly accepted a total of fifteen thousand dollars in bribes to authorize a state lottery that was to become a national scandal over the next twenty-five years.

For now, however, it was the imminent danger of a race war that occupied center stage. The Knights of the White Camellia and other Democratic Party forces responded to the new regime ushered in by the elections of 1868 with a reign of terror that caused Warmoth to write to President Johnson on August 1, 1868, requesting he assign "two regiments of cavalry, a regiment of infantry, with a battery of artillery" to repress "disorder and violence." Johnson did not reply. Warmoth estimated that 150 men had been murdered in the preceding month and a half. Many prominent citizens in Louisiana were leaders in the Knights of the White Camellia, he wrote, which was determined to drive out Union men. People were being "shot down in the roads, in their houses, and elsewhere, without a question being asked or any steps taken to bring the offenders to justice." In New Orleans Knights of the White Camellia "drill openly in our streets at night, or in halls, easily to be seen." Warmoth predicted "bloody revolution."

The presidential election of November that year bore Warmoth out. Johnson had been denied the Democratic Party nomination, having been impeached and acquitted in the Senate, on May 26, by only one vote. The Democratic candidate, Horatio Seymour, should have stood no chance in Louisiana, which had voted overwhelmingly for Republicans in state elections seven months earlier. But, thanks to the Knights of the White Camellia, the Republican presidential candidate, Gen. Ulysses Grant, had to win without any help from Louisiana. The congressional committee that investigated the Klan found that in Louisiana "over 2,000 persons were killed, wounded, and otherwise injured within a few weeks prior to the presidential election" while "half the State was overrun by violence; midnight raids, secret murders and open riot." Grant received only 1,178 votes in New Orleans—almost 13,000 fewer than Warmoth in the gubernatorial election—but returns from rural Louisiana were even fishier. In Caddo Parish, which had 2,987 Republicans, Grant got one vote. That was better than he did in St. Landry Parish, where all 4,787 registered voters went for Seymour. The committee explained how this came about:

Here occurred one of the bloodiest riots on record, in which the Ku-Klux killed and wounded over two hundred republicans, hunting and chasing them for two days and nights through fields and swamps. Thirteen captives were taken from the jail and shot. A pile of twenty-five dead bodies was found half buried in the woods. Having conquered the republicans, killed and driven off the white leaders, the Ku-Klux captured the masses, marked them with badges of red flannel, enrolled them in clubs, led them to the polls, made them vote the democratic ticket and then gave them certificates of the fact.

Despite the provisions of the new constitution Warmoth made no effort to integrate public education. "The white people were opposed to mixed schools. The masses of the colored people loved their children and knew too well what would happen to them if any of them should attempt to force themselves into white schools," he explained. The press continued to report periodic lynchings in New Orleans with former rebels bristling under what they saw as a corrupt and usurping government. Several black parents did, in fact, try to enroll their children in the public schools of New Orleans after the 1868 constitution was adopted, but they were all rebuffed by the fiercely racist board of school directors.

The temerity of the black parents and the general turmoil of Reconstruction put white society in an escapist mood that led ineluctably to an expansion of the Carnival calendar and a deepening love affair with the past. The Twelfth Night Revelers emerged to mark the start of the Carnival season in 1870 with a torchlit parade and ball under the aegis of a character transported from medieval Europe and known as the Lord of Misrule. A mask, of course, concealed the features of the distinguished citizen of New Orleans elected the Lord of Misrule, which was the name given in olden times to the humorous fellow who organized the revels from Christmas to Twelfth Night in the great houses of Europe. Given the erudition of the Carnival class, some of its members may well have recalled that the sixteenth-century *Holinshed Chronicles* included a reference to the custom: "On mondaie the fourth of Januarie, the said lord of merie disports came by water to London, where he was received by Wause, lord of misrule to John Mainard, one of the shiriffes of London." The Twelfth Night Revelers debuted with *tableaux roulants* representing each of the continents and a ball at which the first queen in New Orleans carnival history was due to be anointed. The lucky lady would be chosen, again according to European custom, when slices of a gigantic cake were distributed. Whoever got the slice in which a bean was concealed would be enthroned. But the Revelers were somewhat out of control at the ball, attempting to distribute slices from the end of the spears some of them had carried in the parade. Cake was deposited on the floor and in several genteel laps. If any lady found the bean, she kept quiet about it. Comus that year demonstrated the potential for tourism offered by Carnival, and the *Daily Picayune* estimated that thirty thousand visitors watched this parade depicting the history of Louisiana.

A referendum that year restored the franchise to former Confederates, although the political consequences were not significant. Fewer than ten thousand men had ever been deprived of the right to vote under carpetbag government, and the ascendancy of the Republican Party owed more to the fact that former slaves, with the encouragement of carpetbaggers and scalawags, registered to vote in greater numbers than white Democrats. New Orleans, meanwhile, became the cynosure of all eyes when two of the most majestic sidewheelers on the Mississippi, the *Robert E. Lee* and the *Natchez*, met in the greatest steamboat race of them all. They raced from New Orleans to St. Louis, with crowds yelling their approval from the river banks all along the route, until the *Natchez* ran aground on the approach to St. Louis and the *Robert E. Lee* steamed across the finish line first in a time of three days, eighteen hours and twenty minutes. Thoughts quickly returned to the bloodiest era in the state history chronicled in the Comus parade, however, when the death of Robert E. Lee himself was announced. A fund was started to pay for the statue that went up fourteen years later at Tivoli, renamed Lee, Circle. If the Confederate cause was still dear to many hearts in 1870, however, another blow to the customs of the Old South was about to be administered. The Republicans in the legislature, angered by the exclusion of blacks from the public schools in New Orleans, established a series of new boards, packed with supporters of integration, to supersede the old directorate, which challenged the move in court. Unfortunately for the old regime, the case came before a new judge, none other than Dr. Dostie's Unionist and abolitionist friend Henry Dibble. Judge Dibble upheld the Republicans in November 1870 and the color bar was lifted with astonishing speed. When the schools reassembled after the Christmas holidays, more than a dozen previously white schools registered black children. While this was going on, the Lord of Misrule made his second appearance, and Miss Emma Butler, acknowledging receipt of the fateful slice of cake at the ball, became the first make-believe queen of a white Carnival kingdom. Comus, meanwhile, continued to dazzle the crowds every year and was still wedded to the literature of England. His inspiration for 1871 was Spenser's *Faerie Queene*.

White parents, aghast at the integration of the public schools, removed their children en masse. Accordingly by the end of 1871 about a hundred new private and church schools had been established for the education of white children in New Orleans. Many of the new schools were, however, tiny, and the white exodus was by no means universal. All the high schools, and some of the elementary, remained exclusively white, while others admitted blacks but operated their own internal systems of segregation. The beginnings of a miracle, however, were observed in a handful of public schools, where students were integrated without any disturbances. The discovery that children of different races could learn side by side persuaded many white parents to transfer their children back to the public system, and even the newspapers began to make approving noises. The *New Orleans Times* in 1872 found the fully integrated Bienville School to be "in fine condition morally, mentally and physically."

Judge Dibble, meanwhile, struck another blow for civil rights when ruling on a lawsuit brought by a black civil sheriff, C. S. Sauvinet, against a French Quarter saloon in 1871. When Sauvinet had ordered a drink, the proprietor, J. A. Walker, had told him no blacks were allowed and ordered him to leave. Although Dibble did not accede to Sauvinet's demand that Walker's liquor license be revoked, he did award a thousand dollars in damages to "sanctify the principle involved and deter others from inflicting the same injury." Few other black citizens, however, were willing to venture into white establishments. The press continued to report the occasional lynching in the city, and the *Daily Picayune* was beside itself with rage at the carpetbaggers, who "live by the bargain and corruption growing out of a venal and irresponsible administration of public affairs, who, having been thrown out of employment elsewhere by reason of their gross and exceeding vileness, have swarmed to these states where the ignorance and incompetency of the mass of the newly enfranchized make it easy for these vagrant politicians to obtain office." The notion of antebellum life as an idyllic time for all concerned had also crept into the New Orleans papers, the *Daily Crescent* inveighing against the "white newcomers" who had deprived the "sable race, so much falsely pitied, of their lost happy condition under the protection of their indulgent masters and mistresses."

White citizens chafed under what they saw as a usurping and corrupt government. They had a point, for the Republicans now established returning boards to tabulate and verify election returns as a counter to the White Camellia's terror tactics.

For the rest of the Reconstruction era, Republicans were unbeatable at the ballot box. Democrats knew that, however many voters they could keep away from the polls, the Republicans could conjure up more from beyond the grave or simply cook the books to swing the election their way. The Democrats were impotent because, as the Republican speaker of the state house of representatives, Col. George Carter, put it in a speech delivered in New Orleans in 1871, Warmoth held "power more despotic than any King in Europe, and patronage more abundant and potent than any five governors in the Union." Warmoth, according to Carter, not only rigged elections, but took bribes, used the police and militia to intimidate whomever he could not corrupt and was "the greatest living practical liar."

There was no reason for Warmoth not to take bribes, for it was not against the law in Louisiana at the time. Warmoth grew rich in office not just from payoffs but by awarding contracts for printing official notices to a newspaper of which he was the majority owner. He was also able to buy up state warrants, discounted because of the parlous condition of state finances, and redeem them at face value for cash from his own government. On May 9, 1864, Warmoth had written in his diary, "I am twenty two years of age today. I have determined to persist in my course and not drink liquor of any kind nor smoke cigars or use tobacco in any way." But by the time he became governor he was chomping on cigars and downing spirits with enthusiasm. On his election, Warmoth declared, "I don't pretend to be honest. I only pretend to be as honest as anybody in politics and more so than those fellows who are opposing me now." It is doubtful that he retained even as much integrity as that, however, and he soon built up a national reputation for crookedness. He was by no means the first, any more than he would be the last, Louisiana politician lacking in probity. The question of whether Warmoth corrupted Louisiana or Louisiana corrupted Warmoth may never be settled.

The Krewes and the Klan

To the white Democrats of New Orleans, carpetbag corruption and Negro suffrage were inseparable. The enlightened provisions of the 1868 state constitution therefore misfired and, far from bringing the races closer together, hardened animosities that were still apparent in the basement of New Orleans City Hall 123 years later. New Orleans in the Reconstruction era lived under race laws of a liberality unknown in its history until recent times. But they were enacted in a city that most white men regarded as under occupation by an alien despot. Racial prejudice became, and would remain, respectable in the upper echelons of society. As late as 1939, a booklet published by the Louisiana State Museum described the Ku Klux Klan as "a secret order that was destined to grow and spread throughout the South and exert a strange influence, not without good." The booklet, *Carpet-Bag Misrule in Louisiana*, was dedicated to "the patriotic Louisianians who in the aftermath of the War between the States so soundly, valiantly and heroically gave their all to maintain White Supremacy as a cardinal principle of a wise, stable and practical government."

The leading lights of those "patriotic Louisianians" were to be found in the gentlemen's clubs and the Carnival krewes of New Orleans. Carnival was all the rage, with both Rex and Momus, named for the Greek god of mirth and ridicule, making their first appearances in 1872. If Creoles were irritated at the way perfidious Albion had come to dominate the themes of Carnival, no relief was in sight, for the Twelfth Night Revelers that year honored English humorists, and neither Rex nor Momus, when they made their first appearance that year, sought inspiration from any Gallic source. Rex was born to honor a royal Russian on Mardi Gras; Momus, whose parades were held in the early days on New Year's Eve, chose to depict scenes from a Scottish novel.

Gen. George Custer and the grand duke Alexis, younger son of Czar Alexander II, were fresh from a hunting trip out west with Buffalo Bill when they arrived in New Orleans February 11, 1872, two days before Mardi Gras. General Sheridan had also been with the hunting party, but he did not move on to New Orleans, where memories of his stint as military commander in 1867 would doubtless have taken the luster off the royal visit. A few Indian chiefs had been on hand to assist the grand duke in shooting buffalo, although they may have had reservations about associating with Sheridan, who, in 1869, coined a phrase that ensured him a place in the quotation books. Sheridan it was who first observed, "The only good Indians I ever saw were dead."

Following the announcement that the grand duke Alexis would visit New Orleans, two members of Comus—its captain, Colonel Merriam, and Edward Hancock, an assistant editor at the *New Orleans Times*—decided that the occasion called for a parade, led by a newly created king of Carnival. They put together a committee of forty, mostly drawn from the Pickwick and Boston clubs, and called on Mayor Ben Flanders to request that Rex be given nominal control of the city and its police force on Mardi Gras. Their request being granted, they commenced to issue a series of edicts under the authority of Rex, who ordered gun salutes on Mardi Gras and the early closure of all government offices, businesses and schools so that his subjects could attend the parade, the first to be held in the city in the daytime. Rex ordered Warmoth to quit governing for the day to avoid "any unpleasant complications which might arise from the conflict of authority." The governor was also to "disperse that riotous body known as the Louisiana State Legislature." Rex grew increasingly whimsical as edict followed edict. Number 12 abolished "the office of Collector of Internal Revenue," and ordered: "The following laws enacted by a previous government having been found to weigh grievously upon His Majesty's subjects—The Registration Law, Constabulary Law, Printing Law, Taxes and Judge H. C. Dibble—all of the same are hereby abrogated and abolished." Anyone breaching the peace was "to attend meetings of the Academy of Natural Sciences for an entire year." In the interests of ensuring general prosperity, Rex also decreed that "low middle grade cotton" should sell at fifty cents a pound and sugar at twenty-five cents. All those resident on the parade route were commanded to provide "extra support for their galleries, to festoon and decorate the same with the royal colors (green, purple and gold) under penalty in default thereof of permanent exile to the Balize" at the mouth of the Mississippi.

Carnival historians say that the organizers calculated that they needed five thousand dollars to do the grand duke justice, although it is by no means clear why, since time was too short to get floats ready for the parade or to arrange a ball and reception afterwards. At any rate, a Jewish banker and cotton factor named Lewis Salomon, Boston Club member and Confederate veteran of Shiloh and other battles, was elected Rex and given the chore of raising the money, which he accomplished by selling dukedoms in the parade at a hundred dollars apiece. Rex then called on the actor Lawrence Barrett, who was performing at the Varieties Theater, and borrowed his *Richard III* costume for the parade. The dukes donned flowing robes to impersonate Bedouins, and extensive newspaper coverage ensured that plenty of maskers on foot would tag along behind the official parade.

The grand duke stayed on board the steamer *James Howard*, which had brought him to New Orleans from Memphis, until the morning of February 12, when Mayor Flanders and a reception committee arrived to greet him. One of the grand duke's party addressed the committee in French, which he assumed to be the native tongue of the city. Nobody understood him because, as *L'Abeille* waspishly pointed out, no Creoles had been invited.

Rex had now issued another edict, published in the papers

February 10. All bands taking part in the parade were to "play
passing in review the Royal Anthem, 'If Ever I Cease to Love.'"
The command implied that the grand duke might have had an
ulterior motive for accepting an invitation to sample Mardi Gras
in New Orleans. "If Ever I Cease to Love" was a song from the
burlesque *Bluebeard*, performed by the ravishing Lydia Thompson, with whom the grand duke had dined tête-à-tête after seeing the show at Wallack's Theatre in New York late in 1871.
Now Miss Thompson's company was on tour in New Orleans.
Rex's gesture had permanent effects, for "If Ever I Cease to
Love" has been the signature tune of his balls and parades ever
since. It is de rigueur when the king's float pauses so that Rex
can toast his queen on her reviewing stand. Immortal though
the song is in New Orleans, the lyrics may not be widely known.
The first verse goes:

> In a house, in a square, in a quadrant,
> In a street, in a lane, in a road,
> Turn to the left on the right hand,
> You see there my true love's abode.
> I go there a-courting and cooing
> To my love like a dove,
> And swearing on my bended knee,
> If ever I cease to love,
> May sheepsheads grow on apple trees.
> If ever I cease to love,
> If ever I cease to love,
> If ever I cease to love,
> May the moon be turned to green cheese,
> If ever I cease to love.

Lydia Thompson is supposed to have sung "If Ever I Cease to
Love" at her intimate supper with the grand duke in New
York, but he was hooked nevertheless.

The grand duke moved into the St. Charles Hotel, with Custer in the next suite. They dined well, the *Picayune* publishing

the extensive menu and adding that the finest wines and cigars were served. Custer, according to the *Picayune*, was "as amiable as he is gallant," while the twenty-two-year-old grand duke stood "over six feet high" and was "a finely proportioned young man, with an extremely light complexion, well shaped features, framed in neatly trimmed moustache and side whiskers and withal much handsomer than any of the numerous woodcuts of his appearance that have been published."

Rex, meanwhile, had adopted English titles for the members of his court. Rex proclamations were issued through such imaginary nobles as Lord High Chamberlain Bathurst or Earl Marshal Warwick, and duly certified by Seventh Secretary Espy. The conceit caught on so well that the newspapers continued to publish the communiques of mock aristocrats until after World War II. Even after Dorothy Mae Taylor set her sights on the old-line krewes, Rex maintained the courtly style for public announcements, although his tone became somewhat less peremptory.

Ever since the first parade, Rex has, with a few exceptions, been chosen from the ranks of the Boston Club, but one feature of 1872 has never been repeated. No Jew has ever been king of Carnival since. The Boston Club has for generations banned Jews, while Rex has admitted only a few. The other old-line krewes are rigidly anti-Semitic. Perry Young in 1939 praised Salomon thus: "Only Jew yet Carnival king, but noble citizen who shouldered an imperious duty that no one else would dare, and carried it to such an amazing success that the circumcised have never had another chance to earn that kind of glory." But prejudice against the Jews had evidently not taken hold of New Orleans clubmen in the mid-nineteenth century. In fact, the Boston Club had many Jewish members in its early years, the most distinguished being Judah Benjamin, who went on to become "the brains of the Confederacy." The club held a lavish banquet in Benjamin's honor when he was elected in 1853 to the U. S. Senate, where he remained until the outbreak of the Civil War. Jefferson Davis appointed Benjamin attorney general, secretary of war and then secretary of state. When the Confederacy collapsed Benjamin moved to England, becoming a highly respected barrister.

The weather for Mardi Gras of 1872 was perfect, sunny with a soft breeze, and the grand duke took his place outside Gallier Hall, then the seat of city government, as the sound of artillery indicated the parade was underway. In due course, Salomon rode by on a "spirited" horse, waving gaily to the grand duke, who bowed stiffly in return. Then came a mass of "lords of yeomanry" in their eastern garb, and "a live cow symbolic of the occasion." The *Picayune*, though somewhat skeptical, quoted estimates that put the pedestrian maskers following the principals at three or four thousand, and described the mood on the streets in terms that will strike a chord with anyone who has attended Carnival: "Mardi Gras is a festival with which our brethren of more Northern climes have little or no acquaintance. They know nothing of its laughter-provoking incidents, its ludicrous enactments, nor the gorgeous displays that are made, all taxing ingenuity to the utmost, that the day may be made 'the day of days.' In New Orleans, when Mardi Gras comes, Comus ascends his throne, and age, sex, color and previous condition are all ignored. Fun is the predominant passion and cynics are shoved aside that 'the man who laughs' may have his fill of it."

The parade was hardly the triumph of themed organization that the crowds had become used to with Comus. There were "Ku Kluxes, Chinamen, Japanese, brigands, clowns, monkeys and Knights of McGraw." Another section featured "kings and peasants, devils and saints, Indians and negroes, women of high and low degree, clowns and harlequins, birds, beasts and fishes." *The Bee* noted, "The kleptomania of carpetbaggism was typified by couples carrying the burdensome sack." Flags, flowers, colored lamps and "emblems dear to those who labored in the 'lost cause'" were all along the route. Nobody thought, in the early days, to turn up his or her nose at the commercialization of Mardi Gras, and the first Rex parade included advertising vans touting the Gem Saloon, Warner's Bitters, Singer Sewing Machines, Mme. Tigau's Elixir for Ladies, Carter's Mucilage, Leighton's Premium Shirts, the Old Reliable Furniture Company and Dr. Tichenor's Antiseptic, among others. Rex subsequently appeared in newspaper advertisements announcing that he dined at Mme. Begue's restaurant, drank at the St. Charles Hotel, and bought his comestibles at Chick Lalande's in the French Market and his hats from the Robert E. Lee store.

After the Rex parade, Alexis was on the reviewing stand again for Comus—"Dreams of Homer" was the theme that year— and then went on to the Varieties to view the tableaux, although he declined to dance. Whether the grand duke had an assignation with Lydia Thompson in New Orleans is unknown, although tradition has it that the Mardi Gras crowd sang a verse that she had made up. It concluded:

> If Ever I cease to love,
> May the grand duke ride a buffalo,
> If ever I cease to love,
> If ever I cease to love,
> If ever I cease to love,
> In a Texas rodeo,
> If ever I cease to love.

Alexis is supposed to have been so offended by this lèse-majesté that he ceased to love Lydia Thompson and transferred his affections elsewhere for the remaining four days he spent in New Orleans. But the grand duke was not so inconstant as folklore suggests. The *Daily Picayune*, on February 16, reported that Alexis, through General Custer, had requested that "'If Ever I Cease to Love' be introduced in the performance this evening at the Academy of Music, the farewell benefit of Miss Lydia Thompson." Then he steamed away, leaving the ersatz kings of Carnival to outlast the Romanov dynasty and memorialize his brief dalliance with a showgirl down the generations. The year came to an end with the first appearance of the Knights of Momus, who included several sons and nephews of Pickwickians and formed their own gentlemen's club, the Louisiana. They rode out on horseback and in carriages, taking as their text *The Talisman* by Sir Walter Scott.

If 1872 had been a great social year in New Orleans, it had not prevented the titans of the krewes and the gentlemen's clubs from taking a leading role in the inceasingly turbulent political scene. When Governor Warmoth, under threat of impeachment, decided not to seek reelection, he threw his support behind the Democratic ticket, which also happened to represent the Carnival elite. The gubernatorial candidate was John McEnery of the Pickwick Club, a Confederate infantry lieutenant colonel who had fought at various battles, including Vicksburg, Jackson and Missionary Ridge, during the Civil War; his running mate was the eminently clubbable Davidson Penn of Hays's Brigade. The election was chaotic; the state returning board split into two factions, one declaring McEnery the winner, the other plumping for the Republican, William Pitt Kellogg, a native of Vermont, whose commission as customs collector at the port of New Orleans in April 1865 bore the last official signature of Abraham Lincoln. The rival returning boards also certified the election of two different state legislatures. Amidst the confusion, Louisiana got its first and only black governor, albeit for only thirty-five days. The outgoing state legislature impeached Warmoth, and he was replaced by P. B. S. Pinchback, who had become lieutenant governor on the death of Oscar Dunn.

The federal government recognized Kellogg, a U. S. Senator since 1868, as the new governor, and Judge Durell, though in his cups as usual, signed a 2 A.M. order forbidding McEnery to take office. The Democrats still regarded McEnery as the rightful victor, however. When Pinchback stepped down, early in 1873, Kellogg and McEnery held simultaneous inauguration ceremonies. Kellogg moved into the governor's office in the Mechanics' Institute; Governor McEnery set up shop in the Odd Fellows' Hall. An air of foreboding descended on New Orleans and the entire state. The smell of blood was in the air.

But first came Carnival. For the first time Rex, who this year was E. B. Wheelock, chose a queen for the day, as succeeding kings of Carnival have done every year since. Rex had not yet adopted the habit of choosing a debutante as his royal consort, and Wheelock's choice was Mrs. Walker Fearn. That night, Comus outdid himself with "The Missing Links to Darwin's Origin of Species." The parade featured a host of beasts, each unmistakably representing some despised figure. The tobacco grub was President Grant, the snake was Warmoth, the bloodhound was Metropolitan Police Superintendent Algernon Badger, and nobody needed any help identifying Beast Butler in the shape of a hyena, complete with a silver spoon. Darwin himself appeared as "the Sapient Ass." Krewemen dressed as asses walked alongside, bearing transparencies on which the stanzas of a lengthy poem written specially for the occasion could be read in the glare of the flambeaux. The verses, a fine effort to satirize the theory of evolution in the style of yet another English literary giant, Alexander Pope, facetiously related how the spark of life led to amorous adventures in dozens of species. Here, for instance, is Comus on crustacea and fishes:

> There warmed the spark in its crustacean bed,
> Till shrimps, enraptured, on its sweetness fed;
> Impassioned Lobsters clasped seductive claws,
> And jealous Crabs succumbed to Hymen's laws.
> But kindling more—the piscine tribe prevails—
> Its incandescence gauds the Dolphin's scales,

Transforms Sea Dragons into sighing swains,
And distracts Sheepheads with bewitching pains.
The Flying-Fish then onward wafts the spark,
Till lovelorn passions thrill the cruel Shark,
And sweetest transports swell the mighty deep
To where the Whales uxorious vigil keep.

The lines were a worthy complement to the splendid designs for the costumes featured in the parade and at the ball afterwards. Swedish lithographer Charles Briton submitted seventy-one watercolors of creatures he envisaged for the Darwin satire, but a krewe committee reluctantly rejected them, fearing that such intricate papier-mâché figures would not survive the journey from Paris, where all Carnival figures were made, and the rigors of a parade. One George Soulie, however, approached Comus members and declared that he could not only reproduce Briton's animals in New Orleans but could do so in masks and costumes that would make it through the streets on Mardi Gras and arrive unscathed at the ball. He put together a sample and took it to the Pickwick Club, where members administered a severe pummeling before declaring Soulie's work admirably robust and ordered costumes made from every one of Briton's designs. Soulie remained New Orleans's preeminent papier-mâché artist for more than forty years after that, and the practice of importing Carnival art from Paris was abandoned.

It was the custom in those days for every guest at the ball to be presented with a lavishly illustrated book expounding on the day's theme. This year's effort reproduced the heroic couplets that had stretched from beginning to end of the parade and was illustrated with pictures of the outlandish Comus bestiary that visitors to the ball could spy strutting around the ballroom. The Comus verses, of course, are anonymous, but speculation on the authorship is bound to center on Edward Hancock, the *Times* assistant editor who helped found Rex and became its second captain in 1874. Hancock's jeux d'esprit included all of

Mistick Krewe of
Comus designs for
characters in the Missing
Links parade of 1873.
Photos by Tyrone Turner,
courtesy of Tulane
University.
Clockwise from top left:
The Tobacco Grub (President
Ulysses Grant); The Snake
(Governor Warmoth); The
Bloodhound (Police Chief
Algernon Badger); The Hyena
(Benjamin Butler); The Sapient
Ass (Charles Darwin)

Rex's edicts for many years, and he was remembered by a contemporary as a man of "wit, ingenious mind and fluent pen." The combination of Hancock's verses, Briton's designs and Soulie's costumes in the "Origin of Species" set a standard of artistry that has never been exceeded. The racism that informed the satire of Darwin's work has never been exceeded either. Supposed lord of all creation was a banjo-playing gorilla, who was seated on a throne in the tableau, "with Queen Chacma on his right and Orang, the Premier, on his left." Underneath, a staircase descended through the inferior species until Comus himself was discovered ruling humorously from the bottom of the evolutionary heap.

The political metaphor cannot have been lost on anyone. The *Daily Picayune* the next morning noted that Comus's gorilla was "a specimen, too, so amazingly like the broader-mouthed varieties of our own citizens, so Ethiopian in his exuberant glee, so at home in his pink shirt collar, so enraptured with himself and so fond of his banjo, that the Darwinian chain wanted no more links."

Someone—probably Walter Merriam—was so pleased with the krewe's wit that he sent a copy of the Comus book to Darwin, together with a *New Orleans Times* article reviewing the parade and blasting evolution theory. Darwin replied:

> Dear Sir,
>
> As I suppose that Comus and the newspapers were sent in good faith, I thank you for your kindness and for your letter. The abusive article in the newspaper amused me more than Comus; I can't tell from the wonderful mistakes in the article whether the writer is witty, ignorant, or blunders for the sake of fun.
>
> Yours faithfully,
> Ch. Darwin.

Before Lent was over, the sound of gunfire shattered the peace of Jackson Square. On March 5, a militia loyal to McEnery, and under the command of Gen. Fred Ogden, attempted to take over the police station, then located in the Cabildo on Jackson Square. Ogden, a cavalry commander in the Civil War and a member of the Pickwick Club, ordered his men to open fire on the Cabildo from an exposed position in the square but was soon forced to move to the shelter of the walls of St. Louis Cathedral. The Metropolitan Police, who were under Kellogg's control, then opened fire on the Democrats with a howitzer, driving them out of the square and into St. Peter Street. At this point, the federals turned up; the McEnery forces surrendered, and sixty-five of them were arrested. The next day, the Metropolitan Police raided the Odd Fellows' Hall and arrested such members of the McEnery legislature as were unwise enough to be around. Shortly afterwards federal troops had to be called out to put down a citizens' revolt, led by Alcibiade de Blanc, in rural Louisiana. White supremacists continued to terrorize the countryside, dragging prisoners from the Colfax jail for a mass lynching that left fifty-nine blacks and two whites dead. Of the ninety men indicted for murder and conspiracy, eight were put on trial, but the jury was unable to reach a verdict. At the second trial, five were acquitted and three sentenced to hang.

Discontent among the white people of New Orleans deepened. A national economic depression set in, adding to the woes of former Confederates already living in dramatically reduced circumstances. Kellogg added insult to injury by appointing blacks in unprecedented numbers to his administration; he was by now even more hated than Warmoth had been. Violence across the state was worse than ever. White gangs, calling themselves regulators, lynched Negroes supposedly guilty of theft or other crimes, churches were torched and various minor elected officials gunned down in the streets.

New Orleans society, however, was not to be denied its diversions, and Momus staged his second parade on New Year's Eve, 1873, styled "The Coming Races" and featuring various caricatures of human development in the future. For some reason the krewe lapsed into German, declaring, on the placard at the front of the parade, that the populace was to be treated to an *Entwicklungsgeschichte*. Charles Darwin's theories, having provided Comus with his theme that year, now informed the verse Momus displayed at the front of his parade:

> These oddities, from nature drawn,
> May surely raise the question:
> Will critics say by chance they're found
> Or natural selection?

Rex, E. B. Wheelock, rang out the New Year by rewarding his poet laureate, Xariffa, otherwise known as the fashionable Mrs. Mary Ashley Townsend, for her services that year. Shortly before midnight, the *Daily Picayune* reported, Earl Warwick, head of Rex's War Department, was dispatched to Xariffa's house, where he "ushered forth a huge Nubian slave of jet black hue and horrid features, who tottered under an immense butt of malmsey wine, which in accordance with the custom of all sovereigns, was due the honorable poet laureate of the realm."

But the political situation ensured that the mood of the city was far from festive at the beginning of 1874. Kellogg was anathema to the upper class, which, in hopes of galvanizing opposition, organized a Committee of 70, headed by attorney Robert Marr of the Boston Club. An immense crowd showed up for a New Year's Day meeting called by the committee and adopted a resolution repudiating "the government of Mr Kellogg and his fellow conspirators as an odious usurping tyranny, foisted into and continued in power by the bayonets of the United States government."

In the rural areas, meanwhile, the marauding bands, who were now forming themselves into chapters of a new organization, the White League, had become quite brazen. They would ride, unmasked and in broad daylight, with hangman's nooses dangling from their saddles, to the doors of parish courthouses. There they would suggest the resignation from public office of all blacks and scalawags, who were invariably quick to comply. Certainly six white Republicans in Coushatta were in no mood to argue when the League rode into town; they agreed not only to resign but to leave the state. The League was out for some sport that day, however, and all six were lynched. Conversation in the Boston and Pickwick clubs turned increasingly to the possibility of revolution, although there was still time to make Mardi Gras a glittering success, and Rex that year adopted a charter under the title "School of Design" to "advance art; entertain, amuse and instruct the people, and do other things which will redound to the good of society, the State and the Nation." Also that year Rex introduced the myth that he journeyed from distant parts aboard his royal yacht for Mardi Gras. Thus, William Pike disembarked from a steamer at the foot of Canal Street on Lundi Gras to be greeted by his adoring "subjects," as did subsequent Rexes every year until World War I.

The clubmen and krewemen of New Orleans had come to regard membership in a white-supremacist organization as a mark of manhood and resistance to a northern government that sustained Negro and carpetbag tyranny. They resented more than anything that the Reconstruction government was intent on disarming them. In several cases, the police seized guns from white citizens and refused to return them when ordered to do so by the courts. Held in contempt, the officers routinely received pardons from Governor Kellogg. Fred Ogden, Samuel Flower and other leaders of the Crescent City Democratic Club decided that the cause of the white race needed some new life. On July 2, 1874, therefore, the club was renamed the Crescent City White League with Ogden as president and several other prominent members of the Pickwick and Boston clubs among its officers. The League's platform, published that day, stated: "Where the white race rules, the negro is peaceful and happy; where the black rules, the negro is starved and oppressed." But it was no use explaining this to black people. "They have become maddened by the hatred and conceit of race, and it has become our duty to save them and to save ourselves from the fatal probabilities of their stupid extravagance and reckless vanity by arraying ourselves in the name of white civilization, resuming that just and legitimate superiority in the administration of our State affairs to which we are entitled by superior responsibility, superior numbers and superior intelligence."

While the League's purpose was "not to interfere in any way with the legal rights of the colored race, or of any other race," it was "determined to maintain our own legal rights by all the means that may become necessary for that purpose and to preserve them at all hazards." To achieve that end, the League was organized into two regiments of infantry and one of artillery.

CHAPTER FIVE

The Battle of Liberty Place

The steamer *Mississippi,* with a cargo of guns ordered by the White League, arrived from New York on Saturday, September 13, 1874, and docked at the foot of Canal Street. When Governor Kellogg stationed a contingent of the Metropolitan Police on the quay to prevent unloading of the ship, League members were fit to be tied, as readers of the next morning's *Daily Picayune* discovered. They were greeted with an appeal to the "Citizens of New Orleans," written by local physician J. Dickson Bruns and signed by fifty-four pillars of the community, including thirty-four who belonged either to the Pickwick, the Boston or both. It read:

> For nearly two years you have been the silent but indignant sufferers of outrage after outrage heaped upon you by an usurping government.
>
> One by one your dearest rights have been trampled upon until, at last, in the supreme height of its insolence, this mockery of a republican government has dared even to deny you that right so solemnly guaranteed by the very Constitution of the United States, which, in article two of the amendment, declares that "the right of the people to keep and bear arms shall not be infringed."
>
> In that same sacred instrument, to whose inviolate perpetuity our fathers pledged "their lives, their fortunes and their sacred honor," it was also declared that even Congress shall make

no law abridging "the right of the people peaceably to assemble and to petition the government for a redress of grievances." It now remains for us to ascertain whether this right any longer remains to us.

We, therefore, call on you on MONDAY MORNING, the 14th day of September, 1874, to close your places of business, without a single exception, and at 11 o'clock A.M. to assemble at the CLAY STATUE on Canal Street and, in tones loud enough to be heard throughout the length and breadth of this land, DECLARE THAT YOU ARE, OF RIGHT OUGHT TO BE AND MEAN TO BE FREE.

A sense of foreboding had been upon the city for months, with the daily newspapers railing against the "Africanization" of Louisiana and reporting the occasional lynching. A Black League had supposedly been formed and, General Ogden averred, was conducting armed drills. The *Daily Picayune* reported, on June 30, that the "colored population" was planning a "grand coup" on Independence Day to enforce their civil rights, "if need be, at the point of a bayonet; certainly insofar as drinking-saloon, soda-water and refreshment stands are concerned, and, as far as possible, otherwise." It was a false alarm, and the Black League may have been no more than a figment of the white imagination or propagandist invention. But by now Robert Marr and his Committee of 70 were meeting regularly at the Boston Club to plot the overthrow of the Kellogg government.

Davidson Penn, at a meeting of the Committee of 70 in the Boston Club, suggested that the governor and his top aides be kidnapped and taken out to sea while the White League seized the statehouse and installed the rightful McEnery government in power. McEnery vetoed that idea, and the committee concluded that armed insurrection was the proper course. McEnery would not be able to participate, because after the skirmish at the Cabildo the previous year he had been spared arrest only on his promise never to attempt the forcible removal of Kellogg. McEnery told the committee that he would leave town for the duration of any affray and put Penn in charge.

Thus, McEnery was in Vicksburg, Mississippi, when a crowd of some six thousand white men of all classes, Creoles and Americans, Germans, Italians and Irish, assembled in response to Bruns's appeal. Liberal sentiment was not entirely lacking in the city, and a group of well-known citizens, including Confederate generals Pierre Beauregard and James Longstreet, had organized a Unification Movement that advocated power-sharing between whites and blacks, with each race filling its quota of public offices. The proposal was a starry-eyed one, rejected by Republicans, in part because black voters were not inclined to put their faith in any deal made with their erstwhile masters, and by Democrats to whom the notion of equal rights for former slaves remained an absurdity. Kellogg's excesses also helped to still the voice of white moderation, and many former supporters of the Unification Movement joined the White League gathering at the Clay statue in the middle of Canal Street.

The statue was a natural rallying point; it was here that Dr. Samuel Choppin of the Boston Club, son of a foreign Frenchman, had delivered a famous recruiting speech for the Confederacy in 1861. His cry—*"Aux Armes, Citoyens!"*—was long remembered as the climax of the most stirring Civil War oratory delivered in New Orleans. Choppin was present this time too, but it was committee chairman Marr who harangued the crowd. Penn, meanwhile, had issued two proclamations. The first ordered "the militia of the state, embracing all persons between the ages of 18 and 45, without regard to color or previous condition, to arm and assemble under their respective officers for the purpose of driving the usurper from power." From early that morning groups of White Leaguers had been appearing in the streets uptown from Canal Street, leaning on their rifles and awaiting the call to action. Penn's second proclamation, addressed to black citizens, read: "We war against thieves, plunderers and spoliators of the State, who are involving your race and ours in common ruin. The rights of the colored, as well as of the white races, we are determined to uphold and defend."

The crowd around the Clay statue thunderously endorsed Marr's resolution that a five-man deputation call on Kellogg to demand his "abdication." Amid cries of "hang Kellogg," "we'll fight," and "call out the troops," the crowd dispersed after Dr. Cornelius Beard instructed everyone to return, armed, at 2:30 P.M. Marr, Dr. Choppin, their fellow Bostonian, J. M. Seixas, Jules Tuyes and J. B. Woods made up the committee that then strode into the French Quarter and into the statehouse. There they were received, somewhat to their disgust, by none other than Henry Dibble, now a colonel on Kellogg's staff. Dibble accepted a copy of the resolution from Marr and disappeared, promising to show it to the governor. When he returned, Dibble informed the committee that Kellogg refused to accept any communication from an armed force. Marr then led his men back along Royal Street to the Gem Saloon, where he announced from a gallery that Kellogg would not step down as governor or even grant an audience.

Shortly thereafter, uptown from Canal Street, the White League prepared to face attack from the mostly white Metropolitan Police, under Gen. Algernon Badger, and from the black state militia, led by Longstreet, who was in overall command. The White Leaguers commandeered streetcars to serve as barricades, constructed breastworks from barrels and logs, pulled up pavements to create ditches in front of their defenses and readied their weapons, which included plenty of old army rifles, muzzle-loaders and pistols. At the police station in the Cabildo in the French Quarter, Badger's force of 550 men wheeled out a

Gatling gun and three twelve-pound cannons before heading up to Canal Street, where Longstreet was riding around urging curious citizens to get out of the way. Longstreet was given much of the blame for the debacle at Gettysburg, where he was Robert E. Lee's second in command. This, however, appears to have been a canard started by former Confederates who felt that Longstreet had betrayed the cause after the war. Contemporary newspaper accounts of the Battle of Liberty Place suggest that Longstreet's strategic skills had not improved since his alleged blunders at Gettysburg, but the White League may have taken full advantage of the victor's opportunity to write history.

The accounts we have suggest that the White Leaguers were cock-a-hoop when they saw Badger's men stationing themselves on Canal Street in front of the customhouse, where Kellogg had now taken refuge. The customhouse stands a few hundred yards from the river, so that Badger's left flank was completely exposed, as he pointed out to Longstreet. But Longstreet curtly told Badger to follow orders and rode back into the French Quarter, where about four hundred of his militia were posted at the statehouse.

How many citizens were armed and on the streets that morning is impossible to say, but several thousand seem to have followed Dr. Beard's instructions. The organized and trained rebel force, according to a congressional committee that met the next year, numbered twenty-eight hundred. With Ogden in supreme command, the prominent Pickwickian, Col. William Behan, was put in charge of the White League, aided by the First Louisiana Regiment, consisting mostly of former Confederate soldiers, under Col. John Angell. One of Angell's soldiers that day was Edward Douglass White, who less than a month later became a member of the Boston Club and who went on to be appointed Chief Justice of the United States Supreme Court in 1910.

As it turned out, what was to become known, somewhat

grandly, as the Battle of Liberty Place, boiled down to a ten-minute confrontation between a few hundred White Leaguers and the Metropolitan Police. Badger's men were still awaiting orders in the middle of Canal Street when a freight train appeared, heading downtown, very slowly, along the tracks at the foot of the Mississippi River levee. According to Longstreet's report, some three hundred White Leaguers, led by General Ogden, crept along the levee under cover of the train until it reached Canal Street, where the engineer, presumably wishing them luck, sped away. The White League opened fire from behind the cotton bales that lined the track and from the corners of a couple of cross-streets. The Metropolitan Police responded with ordnance and rifle. Several bullets and one cannonball struck excursion boats en route to the Carrollton Regatta, as passengers crowded to the rails to watch the action. On shore, spectators were at every window and on the streets, while "newsboys" were reported darting around the scene of the fighting. The fight was as bloody as it was brief; almost as soon as it started, sixteen White Leaguers and eleven Metropolitans were dead, with scores injured on each side. Among the wounded was Badger himself, who had his horse shot from under him and was hit four times. As Badger himself put it, "When my men saw me fall, they left the field in quite a hurry." The press reported that Badger shot and killed one of his own men, Sgt. James McManus, in an attempt to stop the retreat.

The White League chased the Metropolitans into the French Quarter, where the state militiamen promptly turned tail despite Longstreet's efforts to rally them. The Kellogg forces threw down their guns, in many cases discarded their uniforms and ran for their lives. Longstreet made for the safety of the customhouse, knowing that the White League would not dare attack federal property. A few shots were fired from a window in the customhouse, for which dastardly act everyone blamed Henry Dibble. Longstreet, however, came in for the most obloquy. He

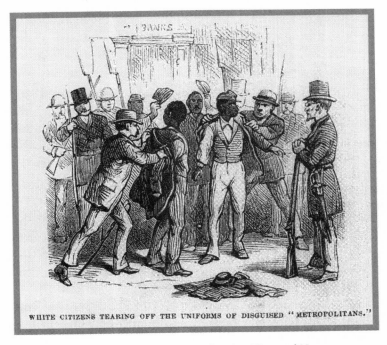

WHITE CITIZENS TEARING OFF THE UNIFORMS OF DISGUISED "METROPOLITANS."

Scene from the Battle of Liberty Place, Frank Leslie's Illustrated Newspaper.
Photo by Tyrone Turner, courtesy of Tulane University.

had, the *Bulletin* noted the next day, met defeat at the hands of "men who mostly fought under him in Virginia—men whose bravery and soldierly qualities made his reputation." The revered Confederate was now transformed into a craven scalawag, so far as the *Bulletin* was concerned: "General Longstreet was seen for a few moments, but judiciously made himself scarce in a most unaccountable and ungallant manner, when he heard the well known yell of his old troops. The men who fought under him in Virginia from Bull Run to Gettysburg would have been pleased to see more of him." Badger, on the other hand, was widely admired for the courage he displayed under fire. A native of Boston, Badger had come to New Orleans as a colonel with Beast Butler, and had remained after the war, marrying a local woman. He had begun his day on September 14 riding the same streetcar as Davidson Penn, who was on his way to a meeting of the putsch committee at the Boston Club. Shortly after 4 P.M. Badger was lying on Canal Street with wounds that appeared to be mortal. A few bystanders suggested finishing him off there and then, whereupon Capt. Douglas Kilpatrick of the White League appeared with a revolver in one hand and a sword in the other. Bestriding Badger's body, Kilpatrick announced he would kill the first man who tried anything. Badger survived, although he lost a leg, and acknowledged in his report: "The members of the White League took me up and treated me very kindly indeed; they took me to the hospital and did everything that was within their power to give me comfort and assistance." The roster of the White League includes many of the social elite whose descendants remain prominent in the clubs and krewes of today. Indeed, John Minor Wisdom of New Orleans, who has sat on the federal court of appeals since the Eisenhower administration, is the son of a Liberty Place veteran.

With the White League in full control of the city, Penn telegraphed President Grant that the people had had no choice but to take up arms against oppressors who "heaped upon them innumerable, faults, burdens and wrongs." Penn promised to defend federal property and officials and asked of Grant only that he "withhold any aid or protection from our enemies, and the enemies of republican rights, and of the peace and liberties of the people." The next day, the White League retrieved their guns from the steamer at the foot of Canal Street, and Penn, McEnery still being in Vicksburg, was inaugurated governor. The *Daily Picayune* that morning published an editorial exulting in the overthrow of the usurper and declaring: "Nothing can be more false than to claim it as a victory of a political party, least of all as a race victory." A few paragraphs later, the *Picayune* asserted that, had Kellogg remained in power, "the state would have been Africanized" and that "nothing could have been darker, bleaker and more hopeless than the prospect of Louisiana under such a government."

Kellogg, meanwhile, was still holed up in the customhouse, pleading with Grant to restore him to power. Grant declared that the overthrow of Kellogg was the work of "turbulent and disorderly persons" and ordered "said turbulent and disorderly persons to disperse and retire peaceably to their respective abodes within five days of this date." The president, the press concluded, was merely uninformed and would reverse himself when he discovered that the uprising was led by men of the utmost respectability. The city was calm, and no racial clashes were reported in the aftermath of the battle. "There is no class of our population which will derive more advantage from the success of the movement to expel from office the men who have kept this State and city in perpetual ferment and discord than the colored people," the *Picayune* opined. Penn, the newspaper said, was gratified that "no colored man was slain" at Liberty Place, although, in fact, four of the dead Metropolitans were black. McEnery returned on September 16 to be inaugurated as governor, but it was becoming clear that Grant was not going to change his mind. A federal warship was on its way and Grant ordered Gen. John Brooke to move his regiment to New Orleans from Brookhaven, Mississippi. Brooke assumed command of the city shortly after McEnery returned. The Mistick Krewe's reign over Louisiana was therefore a brief one. McEnery and Penn issued an address to the people of Louisiana declaring that they were "no longer citizens of a State, but inhabitants merely of what was once a free State." Their forebearance and valor would nevertheless command the respect and sympathy of the civilized world, McEnery and Penn assured the citizens before withdrawing in favor of Kellogg, who was restored to office September 19.

The White Leaguers, of course, were heroes in the city. A campaign to raise money for a monument had been instigated by the *Daily Picayune* two days after the battle, and two new tunes quickly became popular at the city's dance halls—"The White League Waltz" and "The People's Rights Quickstep." The Louisiana Supreme Court gave its sanction to the White League, ruling that it was "not a mob or riotous assembly," and dismissing a suit brought against the city by ten property owners seeking compensation for damage caused during the hostilities. The court found that the insurgents were "a well organized body of citizens and patriots, acting under the orders of, and in obedience to, a State government ordained by the people and wielding legitimate power, and that these citizens were exercising the sacred rights of resistance to oppression and usurpation, under which their dearest rights were being destroyed." There was plenty of sympathy in the North, too, for the White League cause. The *New York Tribune*, adopting a tack similar to that of many other newspapers, editorialized: "[Grant] has taken away from Louisiana the right of choosing its own officers, and sent his soldiers down there to put into power the persons whom he deemed most fit to rule. He has sustained them while they plundered the State and overturned even the semblance of popular government, and for all the wrongs and sore distress which have attracted for Louisiana the commiseration of mankind, his only remedy is more troops."

Kellogg may have been restored to the governorship, but Liberty Place had made it plain that he could be sustained only through the intervention of federal troops. He did, however, feel sufficiently cocky, a few weeks later, to make an obscene gesture from a cab to Maj. Edward Burke, who had been in charge of the White League commissary during the Battle of Liberty Place. Burke stopped the cab, reached inside and struck the gov-

ernor with his fist. As the cab started moving again, Kellogg
fired a shot at Burke, but missed. Burke returned fire but was
off the mark, too. Kellogg, meanwhile, had offered a reward for
the return of two cannons captured by the White League during the Battle of Liberty Place, but they remained hidden until
the end of Reconstruction, when they reappeared in the possession of the city's Washington Artillery. Nicknamed "Resurrec-
tion" and "Redemption" by the White League, the cannon are
now on display at the adjutant generals' office of the Louisiana
National Guard in New Orleans. Kellogg was apparently unaware that the White League had seized three other twelve-
pound howitzers during the battle. Those guns are now in the
possession of the Louisiana State Museum, one of them—
diplomatically unidentified—on display outside the front of
the Presbytere on Jackson Square a few yards from the *Pioneer*, a
Confederate submarine scuttled when New Orleans surrendered to Farragut.

A collateral casualty of Liberty Place was New Orleans's
highly promising experiment in integrated public education.
Regardless of the conciliatory announcements made by the
White League, the battle had deepened racial mistrust, and
when a few black parents tried to enroll their children in the
city's high schools, riots broke out. A delegation of White
Leaguers turned up at an integrated girls' school on Royal Street
in the French Quarter, in order, the principal was told, "to remove the colored pupils." Telling who was colored and who
was white proved, as usual in New Orleans, to be no easy matter, and a few girls of mixed ancestry managed to deceive the
White Leaguers and escape expulsion. One white-loooking girl
pretended to faint at their approach and was carried off to a
bedchamber, thus avoiding interrogation on the subject of her
mother, a quadroon who had married a German sea captain.

White high schoolers and their fathers toured the integrated
elementary schools and evicted all children whose complexions

they deemed too dark. While they were about this task one day, they encountered a group of angry black men who set upon them with fists, bottles and bricks, killing at least one. The White League and blacks armed with knives, pistols and razors patrolled the streets all night. The white mob continued to purge the schools of black students the next day, whereupon the schools all closed down for the Christmas holidays a week early. Some schools remained desegregated after the holidays, but the mood of the city had changed too much for any further narrowing of the racial divide.

With Kellogg back in precarious control, there was talk that New Orleans might have to relive the darkest days of Union occupation. The *New Orleans Bulletin*, on September 27, 1874, reported: "Some of the Northern Radical papers are threatening us with Butler and a Terre Haute paper puts this quotation (slightly amended) in our mouths: 'For all the sad words of tongue or Penn, / The saddest are these—we may have Ben.'" The editors, however, pooh-poohed the notion: "There is no danger of Butler's coming to New Orleans. Our spoons and money are gone, and there is no inducement to bring him down here." They were right. Butler did not come. But the city could hardly have been more outraged if he had, for Grant now sent General Sheridan down once again.

Sheridan arrived ready to punish the White Leaguers, and almost his first official act, on January 5, 1875, was to telegraph Washington: "It is possible that, if the President would issue a proclamation declaring them banditti, no further action need be taken except that which would devolve upon me." This plan, which would apparently have subjected civilians to court martial, was rejected. Sheet music for another new tune— "March of Those Louisiana Banditti"—later appeared in the stores. Sheridan also reported that "some of the banditti have made idle threats they might assassinate me," and generally portrayed the local citizenry as outside the law. He added that he was "not afraid," which amused everyone mightily. "I am not afraid" became a catch phrase around the city. The day after Sheridan's "banditti" dispatch was Twelfth Night, but the Revelers had lost their enthusiasm for partying and published this proclamation in the morning *Picayune*:

> Whereas joy having fled for a season from our happy city; armed hosts becoming interpreters of public opinion, driving gaiety from our homes, hope from our labors, and commerce from our port, and even slander has clothed itself in "official orders" to malign our citizens; and,

Bayonets surround the Lord of Misrule on the invitation to the Twelfth Night Revelers' Ball of 1875, which was to have kicked off the first Carnival season after the Battle of Liberty Place. The ball was canceled because of civic unrest. Photo by Tyrone Turner, courtesy of New Orleans Auction Galleries.

Whereas the present offers us no time for revelrie;
Be it ordained, That the Twelfth Night Revelers postpone
their annual festival to a more fitting season.

Lord of Misrule

The other krewes followed suit, and there was no Mardi Gras that year, which the *Daily Picayune* thought appropriate, since the city had the White League "martyrs to commemorate." The *Picayune*, in its Shrove Tuesday editorial, wrote: "Blood has been poured where Rex's columns would have marched today; tears which no mortal touch could check, or human consolation sweeten, have fallen in the interval since Comus last saluted us."

New Orleans looked elsewhere for amusement and was gripped with a mania for spelling bees. Comus, naturally, supplied the champion, in the person of Edgar Farrar, of what the newspapers termed "orthographomachy" in 1875. Finally, there was enough to eat in New Orleans, and prices were reasonable. Robins were fifty cents a dozen. Life was cheap throughout Louisiana, too, and the editor of the *Shreveport Times*, Henry James Hearsey, was churning out reams of fulminating, racist prose. "White men may have burned and killed in Louisiana," he wrote on Christmas Eve of 1875, "but the responsibility belongs to the radical government of the state." What was happening in Louisiana was "the natural and irresistible organization of conservatism and intelligence against Communism in its worst and most dangerous phase."

The Lord of Misrule and the Twelfth Night Revelers made their last appearance on the streets of New Orleans in 1876. The annual ball and tableaux have continued ever since, but the Revelers became the first Carnival organization in New Orleans to dispense with a public parade.

CHAPTER SIX

Confederate Krewemen Rise Again

Although the Revelers had retreated from the public domain in 1876, there was more than enough misrule left to go around. When Louisiana voters went to the polls that year, they wound up once again with two governors and two legislatures, but this time they had two presidents as well, rival boards certifying that both Republican Rutherford Hayes and Democrat Samuel Tilden had carried the state. Confusion reigned elsewhere, too, and Congress took its time settling the presidential dispute in favor of Hayes. The White League was more decisive so far as the state elections were concerned.

The Louisiana Democratic ticket was headed by Francis Tillou Nicholls, a Confederate brigadier general, who had lost his left arm at Winchester and his left foot at Chancellorsville. "I nominate what is left of Francis Tillou Nicholls," some waggish delegate announced at the Democratic convention. A Pickwickian who had fought alongside Alcibiade de Blanc in the war, Nicholls was inaugurated, along with his lieutenant governor, former New Orleans mayor Louis Wiltz, on January 7, 1877, at St. Patrick's Hall. The same day, the Republican Stephen Packard and his black lieutenant governor, Caesar Antoine, took their oaths of office in the statehouse at the St. Louis Hotel.

On January 9, the White League, six thousand strong and led by General Ogden, marched across Canal Street and into the French Quarter, where troops loyal to Packard surrendered. President Grant, on the verge of leaving office, was not inclined to intervene this time and the League patrolled the streets for the remaining few months of Reconstruction. With Nicholls in full control, the age of Bourbonism dawned in Louisiana. The Bourbons were so called because they, like the French royals restored to power after the fall of Napoleon, were said to have "learned nothing and forgotten nothing." They believed in the values of the antebellum oligarchy, which meant that government's role should be limited to the protection of life and property, taxes kept to a minimum and white supremacy maintained at all costs. Nicholls was not, unlike several members of his administration, a rabid bigot, but was more inclined to view blacks with the condescension of those belonging to a paternalistic upper class. He would not have been out of place in the white section of the city hall basement in 1992. On taking office, Nicholls promised to "obliterate the color line in politics and to consolidate the people on the basis of equal rights and common interests." The new legislature resolved to promote "kindly relations between the white and the colored citizens of the state upon a basis of justice and mutual confidence." These promises quickly proved just as false as the liberal pronouncements of the White League in 1874.

A few weeks later, a black barber and school director named Joe Craig tried to take a seat in the rotunda of the St. Charles Hotel. He was dragged out and thrown into the street. At the same time, the new government quickly squelched the bold experiment in the integration of public education in New Orleans, and all Negro students were reassigned to their own schools. Whatever opportunities Reconstruction may have offered for racial progress in New Orleans had largely been lost already. Nicholls himself was not without a sense of noblesse oblige, and frequently deplored racial violence, but there were plenty of men in powerful positions who were made of sterner stuff.

Those men now had a newspaper that gave voice to their views with great panache. Four social lions—former governor John McEnery, Fred Ogden's brother Henry, Dr. Samuel Choppin and B. F. Jonas, a future U. S. Senator—established the *New Orleans Democrat* in 1876 and did not agonize long over who should be editor. Henry James Hearsey, who had achieved considerable renown in the Red River Valley for his vigorous advocacy of white supremacy in the *Shreveport Times*, was an obvious choice, and he quickly made a mark in New Orleans. Born at Thompson's Creek, West Feliciana Parish—even today a remote and depopulated area—Hearsey had as a youth started a small newspaper, the *Feliciana Constitutionalist*, and built enough of a reputation to be hired, at the age of nineteen in 1860, as editor of the *Woodville Republican* in Mississippi. After writing a series of editorials clamoring for secession, he quit at the start of the Civil War to enlist as a Confederate private, eventually rising to the rank of major. In Shreveport after the war he had heartily approved the Colfax and Coushatta massacres and arrived in New Orleans as master of the incendiary editorial. He was in perfect tune with the temper of the times.

For now, however, the most devastating and impudent political comment appeared not in the public prints but on the public streets. Momus had moved his parade from New Year's Eve to the Thursday night before Mardi Gras. When he appeared for the parade on February 8, Momus was preceded by a United States army band, which made the satirical theme all the more biting: Momus was out to hold every prominent figure in national government up to ridicule. Entitled "Hades—A Dream of Momus," the parade presented Republican officials as denizens of Hell. Beelzebub, of course, was President Grant.

Baal was unmistakably General William Tecumseh Sherman. A most obscure devil called Eurynome—not to be confused with the mother of the Graces—was there "impersonating that murderer of Piegan invalids, the devastator of the peaceful homes of Virginia, the man who was never afraid, and the hero of the Banditti proclamation—Phil Sheridan." Eurynome appears to have been mentioned only once in English literature and that en passant by Milton in *Paradise Lost*. Momus had consigned scores of high officials to damnation, along with such Louisiana bêtes noires as William Pitt Kellogg and Henry Warmoth. There was also a float entitled "Knights of the Black League," bearing "a monstrous serpent of the sea whose mottled body, full thirty feet in length, supported a head of huge dimensions, black as Erebus, and with human features." Those features were recognizable as belonging to one Eliza Pinkstone. Perry Young explained thus: "Eliza was a black prostitute of Ouachita, whose family were murdered. There were many accounts and conjectures regarding the murder, including her own several versions, one of which was a trump card of the Republicans in their claims of terrorism and intimidation during the 1876 election. The float was an odd variation of the term, 'riding the nigger into office.'" Stephen Packard was among the characters lampooned with the Knights of the Black League. The last, and nineteenth, float showed the ship of state foundering in a sea of fire with several well-known figures on deck. They included Beast Butler, without whom no Hell-bound party would have been complete, so far as the krewemen were concerned. The Momus reception committee that day included a future chief justice of the United States Supreme Court, Edward Douglass White, who was elected president of the Louisiana Club soon after the parade, Frank Adair Monroe, later chief justice of the Louisiana Supreme Court, Joseph Ellison, one of the founders of Comus, and various other names

Confederate Krewemen Rise Again

The final float in the 1877 Momus parade, "Hades—A Dream of Momus," shows the ship of state foundering in a sea of fire. Harper's Weekly; *photo by Tyrone Turner, courtesy of Tulane University.*

familiar to New Orleans society for generations. So far as Carnival is concerned, for instance, the Denegres have always been with us and one of them, Henry, was on the Momus committee of 1877. Jules Aldige, who was to become Rex in 1883, was there, too.

Governor Nicholls had dispatched Maj. Edward Burke to lobby in Washington for recognition of his administration. The Momus parade was clearly not calculated to help that cause, and Nicholls telegraphed Burke: "The sentiment of the whole community is opposed to what occurred at the celebration Thursday. It was the act of a few private individuals, entirely unauthorized and unknown and universally condemned and regretted." That, from a prominent member of the Carnival establishment, was thoroughly disingenuous. The *Picayune*, reporting on that Thursday evening, said: "The large area of the Opera House could scarcely accommodate the multitude of ladies and gentlemen who desired to gain admittance to the charmed precincts. The beauty and fashion of the city were represented in the brilliant gathering." Nicholls, in any case, need not have worried that Momus would bring federal wrath on Louisiana. When Rex appeared five days later, he had the 16th U. S. Infantry Band to play in his parade and the navy to provide salutes. Rex that year was Charles Howard, head of the Louisiana lottery, which was showing a profit of between $20 million and $30 million a year by retaining approximately half the revenues while using the rest for prizes, advertisements and political payoffs. The lottery company contrived to put on a veneer of respectability in 1877 by hiring the revered Confederate generals Pierre Beauregard and Jubal Early to draw the numbers. Beauregard and Early, who were paid ten thousand dollars a year each to begin with but probably got significant raises thereafter, conducted the drawings with scrupulous fairness. The lottery company also did its best to allay public suspicion through contributions to New Orleans's Charity Hospital, the French Opera House and other eleemosynary causes.

Rex's theme in 1877 was "The Military Progress of the World." Comus followed with a parade and ball dedicated to "The Aryan Race" and its responsibility for all the achievements of civilization, beginning, on dubious anthropological grounds, with the ancient Egyptians, and ending with the conceit of a 1976 presidential election contested by women candidates. That people were desperate to get into the Comus ball, and krewemen were anxious to keep undesirables out, was evident from a Comus proclamation published on the morning of Mardi Gras:

Confederate Krewemen Rise Again

Whereas two invitations to our festivities each numbered 22
have been stolen by some disloyal subject, now, therefore,

Be it known that a reward of $1,000 each will be paid by the
keeper of my private purse for the return of the same to the
Custodian of our Royal Archives.

This done in the 20th year of our reign, A.D. 1877.

Packard relinquished his claim to the governorship and, on
April 20, President Hayes withdrew federal troops from Louisiana, the last state to have the yoke of Reconstruction lifted.
Nobody was more pleased than Hearsey, who inveighed against
the iniquities of Reconstruction so effectively that when he died
in 1900 even the rival *Daily Picayune* acknowledged, with perhaps a dash of hyperbole, that "to his brilliant and courageous
labors was largely due the uprising of the people which resulted
in the regaining of the white citizens of the state of control of
their public affairs."

Hearsey, according to one of his friends, "never became rec-
onciled to General Lee's defeat," and, indeed, cut a faintly ri-
diculous figure, a florid-faced caricature of the pre–Civil War
southern gentleman, downing mint juleps, challenging rival
editors to pistol duels, striding around town with his cane and
goatee beard and urging the younger generation to revere the
"war whoops and cries of the Confederacy." He was drunk on
whiskey every night, returning home by the streetcar, mule
drawn until electrification in 1893. Sometimes, at the end of
the evening, he could still negotiate his way from the streetcar
to his house unaided. On other occasions, the driver would enlist the help of a few passengers and deposit his unconscious
form on the doorstep. Hearsey had a pugnacious temperament,
but was of no great physique. Certainly Mark Bigney, with
whom Hearsey began to feud in 1878, towered over him.
Bigney, editor of the rival daily, the *New Orleans Item*, started
things by suggesting that the *Democrat* was printing stories

reminiscent of a "schoolboy essay." Hearsey responded by terming the *Item* "a sickly little evening sheet, which subsists mainly by puffing the lottery" and said it did not deserve even the dignity of a kick from the *Democrat*. Bigney produced this riposte: "Whenever a person, whether in a newspaper or out of it, boasts of his achievements in the way of kicking, he proves himself an insignificant creature and a coward, who has learned all he knows upon the subject by an unwilling familiarity with other people's boots." This was too much for Hearsey, who sent an employee round to the *Item* offices demanding either a retraction or a duel. He got neither, Bigney explaining that duels never solved anything and that he, in any case, was "too old to indulge in such foolishness."

Shortly afterwards Bigney was walking on the street when Hearsey charged up and started raining blows with his ever-present cane. Bigney wrestled the cane away, knocked Hearsey to the ground and administered one kick. Hearsey was led away, and Bigney related the episode to his readers: "He was completely at my mercy. I could have jumped on him and disfigured him and the law would have justified me. He was down and I was not, but I could not find it in my heart to be so cruel to him as he had attempted to be to me."

The *Item* at the time had just hired one of the finest writers ever to work in New Orleans, certainly the most effective promoter of its exotic and romantic image. Lafcadio Hearn joined the *Item* in June of 1878, eight months after he "first viewed New Orleans from the deck of the great steamboat that had carried me from gray northeastern mists into the tepid orange-scented air of the South," and found it "drowsing under the violet and gold of a November morning." The lithographer Briton, whose parade designs included the Dream of Hades as well as the Origin of Species, fell ill around this time, calling on his fellow Swede Bror Anders Wikstrom to help him out. By the early 1880s Wikstrom had become the doyen of Carnival artists during an age of rare beauty in floats, royal jewels, invitations and proclamations. Hearn was among the artists and intellectuals who gathered frequently at Wikstrom's ornately furnished atelier, hung with armor and covered with Oriental carpets. Until World War I Carnival continued to inspire works of the highest order, notably from the hands of Carlotta Bonnecaze, Jenny Wilde and Ceneilla Bower Alexander, whose designs were all captured in papier-mâché by Soulie.

Hearn, who lived in New Orleans from 1877 till 1888, left vivid accounts of Mardi Gras in halcyon days. In the *Item* on February 2, 1880, he wrote:

> The Night cometh in which we take no note of time, and forget that we are living in a practical age which mostly relegates romance to printed pages and merriment to the stage. Yet what is more romantic than the Night of the Masked Ball—the too brief hours of light, music amd fantastic merriment which seem to belong to no century and yet to all? Somehow or other, in spite of all the noisy frolic of such nights, the spectacle of a Mardi Gras ball impresses one at moments as a ghastly and unreal scene. The apparitions of figures which belong to other ages; the Venetian mysteries of the domino; the witchery of beauty half-veiled; the tantalizing salutes from enigmatic figures you cannot recognize; the pretty mockeries whispered into your ear by some ruddy lips whose syllabling seems so strangely familiar and yet defies recognition; the King himself seated above the shifting rout impenetrable as a Sphinx; and the kaleidoscopic changing and flashing of colors as the merry crowd whirls and sways under the musical breath of the orchestra— seem hardly real, hardly possible to belong in any manner to the prosaic life of the century. Even the few unimpassioned spectators who remain maskless and motionless form so strange a contrast that they seem like watchers in a haunted palace silently gazing upon a shadowy festival which occurs only once a year in the great hall exactly between the hours of twelve and three. While the most beautiful class of costumes seem ghostly

only in that they really do belong to past ages, the more grotesque and outlandish sort seem strangely suggestive of a gob-
lin festival. And above all the charms of the domino! Does it
not seem magical that a woman can, by a little bright velvet
and shimmering silk, thus make herself a fairy? And the glorious Night is approaching—this quaint, old-time night, star-
jeweled, fantastically robed; and the blue river is bearing us
fleets of white boats thronged with strangers who doubtless are
dreaming of lights and music, the tepid, perfumed air of Rex's
palace, and the motley rout of merry ghosts, droll goblins, and
sweet fairies, who will dance the dance of Carnival until blue
day puts out at once the trembling tapers of the stars and the
lights of the great ball.

In *Harper's Weekly*, on February 24, 1883, Hearn advised that
Carnival, with its "artificial picturesqueness," was not the best
time to sample the charms of New Orleans: "To see the Queen
of the South in her most natural and pleasing mood, one should
visit here during that dreamy season called St. Martin's summer, when the orange blossoms exhale their fragrance, and the
winds are still lukewarm, and the autumn glow bronzes those
faint tints which the old-fashioned edifices wear." For those
who did choose to visit New Orleans at Carnival time, Hearn
had a few tips:

That Canal Street offers, in a large sense, the best view of the
procession is beyond dispute; but the strictly local picturesqueness of the exhibition may be studied to advantage in the anti-
quated French by-ways. The Canal Street spectacle is impos-
ing, but not unique. Under similar conditions a street of equal
breadth in any other great modern city would offer a spectacle
of magnificence scarcely inferior. The grotesque silhouettes of
the moving panorama are partially lost in such a street—the
shadows cannot reach the sides of the buildings. But through
the queer old streets of the French Quarter the Carnival procession must almost squeeze its way, casting eccentric shapes of

darkness upon the walls, and lighting its path with torch-light that flings upwards the shadows of projecting galleries, and lends much Rembrandtesqueness to the faces peering down from balconies or dormer-windows.

Already in Hearn's day Carnival hardly represented a respite for an otherwise hard-working and ambitious populace. Indeed, the elaborate and complex rituals of the season could hardly have developed in a city without a healthy respect for leisure and amusement. As Orson Welles observed in more recent times, "Wherever the money-changers have taken over, Carnival is no more. Wherever work is so hard that a holiday means rest instead of a good time, Carnival is only a word for a tent show."

With Lent in New Orleans came the prospect of even greater idleness, as Hearn, not disapprovingly, observed:

> Already the Carnival societies are secretly preparing for the display of next year. Ere long the moist and odorous spring will blow in the streets, and the city will gradually settle down into its long and dreamy summer languor; the pulses of its commercial life will beat more slowly with the lengthening of the days, the forest of masts along its eighteen miles of wharves will dwindle as the sultriness thickens, the wilderness of smoking chimneys at its sugar and cotton landings will diminish, and the somnolent and burning season will come, with warm winds and lightnings from the Gulf, with clouds splendid and ponderous as those of geologic eras, when the heavens were heavy with vaporized iron and gold.

The same year that Hearn's piece appeared in *Harper's*, yet another English memorialist set down his impression of Mardi Gras, albeit somewhat more prosaically than Hearn:

> The first essential in the successful conduct of the Southern Carnival is an entire and unswerving belief in the supremacy of Rex. Crowds have been gathering, evening after evening, be-

fore the window of a jewelry store in Canal Street, in which Rex's Crown Jewels—his diadem, his sceptre, his orb and his right—have been displayed. "Bathurst, Lord High Chamberlain" and "Warwick, Earl Marshal of the Empire" have continued to countersign royal edicts which are not only implicitly believed in, but as implicitly obeyed. These relate to the decoration of the city and the ships and steamers in harbor, and to general measures of police.

Hearn's New Orleans caught the fancy of the nation when magazines and northern newspapers began to publish his pieces, while his enchantment with its ambiance brought him into close contact with the novelist George Washington Cable, whose novels were almost invariably set in the French Quarter, but whose accounts of life there were regarded by the real Creoles of the era as an insult. Not only did Cable espouse the rights of black people, but he openly questioned the racial purity of the white Creoles and portrayed them as behind the times. He lived in the Garden District and eventually moved to Massachusetts.

The gentry displayed its altruistic side during the yellow fever epidemic of 1878, ministering heroically to the sick and the dying. The relief effort, directed by Gen. Fred Ogden, president of the Red Cross and vice president of the Howard Society, left no time for Carnival preparations, and neither Comus nor Momus appeared in 1879. Rex, however, did manage to put on a parade, followed by the Phunny Phorty Phellows, an irreverent Carnival club formed the previous year and specializing in poking fun at elected officials and the socially pretentious. Carnival that year was still a memorable experience, but things were not the same without Comus, as a European traveler recorded. "True, people surged in the streets and enjoyed themselves and welcomed the parade. But this year passion failed. One organization, the star of Carnivals past, did not take part at all. Though hundreds of masques and masqueraders usually participate, this one lifts the celebration to the heights it reaches in Rome and Venice. The Mystik Krewe of Comus puts its peculiar name on the locus of foolishness."

The Howard Society, formed more than forty years earlier to help yellow fever victims, earned the gratitude of the city in the 1878 epidemic and demonstrated a genuine sense of civic duty on the part of the Carnival fraternity. The society, named after the English philanthropist John Howard, certainly had no connection with Rex of 1878. Indeed, Charles Howard, though a member of the Boston Club, was always persona non grata in some polite circles because of his lottery connections and Republican affiliation. Rex, in the person of Howard, got the cold shoulder from Comus, represented by Governor Nicholls, in 1879, when the legislature, now controlled by the Democrats, passed a bill cancelling the lottery contract awarded by their Republican predecessors. Nicholls signed the bill, explaining his refusal to veto it thus: "At no time and under no circumstances will I permit one of my hands to aid in degrading what the other was lost in seeking to uphold—the honor of my native State."

Hearsey's *Democrat* was also a staunch opponent of the lottery, editorializing in 1878: "This overgrown and arrogant monopoly assumed that laws were only made to enable courts and public officials to make money by accepting bribes." But the lottery forces were too powerful both for Nicholls and the *Democrat*. The lottery company filed suit to overturn the law repealing its contract, the case being assigned to federal judge Edward Billings. Hearsey had no doubt how the case would come out, noting in an editorial: "The Lottery Company owns Billings body and boots, by right of purchase, and he will certainly obey implicitly the instructions of the company and its attorneys in all matters which come before him, and which interest that institution." Billings duly overturned the statute, but Hearsey did not have long to savor the accuracy of his prediction. He and George Dupre, who had become the *Democrat*'s principal stockholder, were forced to relinquish their interest when the lottery company contrived to have their lines of credit cancelled by the banks. Lottery supporters took over the paper and Hearsey was out of a job. His replacement as editor was Maj. Edward Burke, one of Charles Howard's most trusted lieutenants.

The Howard faction went to work wooing legislators, and succeeded in having a constitutional convention called in 1879. Burke, who had now been elected state treasurer, lobbied assiduously for the Howard interests, and helped persuade delegates to call elections immediately, cutting a year off Nicholls's term in office. Nicholls declined to seek reelection and returned to private life early in 1880. The 1879 constitution eliminated the requirement that public accommodations be desegregated and removed several other equal-rights guarantees, but the traces of fraternization were not to be wiped out overnight and some blacks and whites continued what appears to have been a free and easy association. Racially mixed families were not an uncommon sight on the streets of the city, while picnic grounds, bathhouses and barrooms on the shores of Lake Pontchartrain remained integrated until several years after the liberal provisions of the 1868 state constitution were rescinded in 1879. The streetcars remained open to all, blacks and whites attended the same Roman Catholic services, and some, though by no means all, of the city's brothels welcomed customers regardless of race. The races competed against each other on the baseball diamond and in the boxing ring. Black jockeys rode against whites at the fairgrounds.

Hearsey, meanwhile, was back in business, having established a new paper, the *Daily States*, so named, he said, because of his devotion to the cause of states' rights. Hearsey, New Orleans's dominant newspaperman for the rest of the century, started on a shoestring, as a *States* writer later recalled: "The first number was a small, six-column, four-page sheet, printed on an old-fashioned flat-bed press, the motive power of which was furnished by an old and blind, but willing and muscular, darkey." For the rest of his life Hearsey scarcely missed an opportunity to incite racial discord. But his first task was to write editorials insulting his successor at the *Democrat*, Major Burke, who responded in kind. Hearsey issued a challenge to a duel and, this time, it was accepted. The *Daily States* was less than a month old.

The two majors met just out of town in a Metairie field. They were both remarkably cool, Burke turning up with a glove on his left hand and a pink carnation in his buttonhole, Hearsey dapper in a dark suit with, of course, a cane in his hand. They faced each other and fired, both missing. After ambling around for a while and chatting with their seconds, they tried again. Still, neither was hit, and honor was declared satisfied.

Hearsey's mind was rooted in the antebellum South, but he was by no means alone in remaining true to the Confederacy long after it had fallen. Comus himself seemed unregenerate, as he demonstrated when, for the first time, he chose a queen and a court for the Mardi Gras festivities of 1884. The first queen of Comus was Mildred Lee, daughter of Robert E. The maids were her sister, Mary Lee, Jefferson Davis's daughter, Varina, Stonewall Jackson's daughter, Julia, and Confederate general D. H. Hill's daughter, Nannie. Two years earlier Rex, in the person of Joseph Shakspeare, mayor of New Orleans and a member of both the Boston and Pickwick clubs, had appeared at the Comus ball to honor his royal brother. Every year since then Rex and Comus have met at the ball just before midnight. In 1884, with the appearance of the Confederate daughters, the occasion became, and has remained, the "meeting of the courts" with glittering scepters and tiaras all over the place.

Just a few blocks away in the Odd Fellows' Hall a new Mardi Gras ball featured not a meeting of the courts but a meeting of the courtesans. This was the "Ball of the Two Well-Known Gentleman," which was staged by the city's pimps, procurers and hookers and offered sights never seen at Comus or Proteus. In the golden age of New Orleans prostitution, from Reconstruction to World War I, its bordellos ran the gamut from squalid cribs to sprawling buildings appointed with great taste and opulence. In the 1870s and early 1880s Kate Townsend operated a Basin Street brothel that is reputed to have been the grandest and most luxurious ever seen in New Orleans. She put her girls in ball gowns, required clients to wear formal dress and charged a hundred dollars for a night of pleasure and up to forty dollars for a bottle of champagne. Kate was stabbed to death by her Creole lover, Troisville Sykes, in 1883. In the splendid surroundings of the top-of-the-market houses, a masquerade ball must have seemed a logical way to celebrate Carnival, which brought an influx of visitors that made the season especially lucrative. The first Ball of the Two Well-Known Gentlemen was held in 1882, coinciding with the debut of Proteus, whose tableaux at the French Opera House featured the gods of the ancient Egyptians. At the rival ball, held at the Odd Fellows' Hall, the show was much fleshier. Part of the fun for the demimonde, of course, was in spoofing the pretentious upper class, and an advertisement that appeared in the weekly newspaper, the *Mascot*, in 1883, announced that the forthcoming ball would be "given under the management of the two well-known gentlemen who gave previously the Mardi Gras ball at the French Opera House." Admission was two dollars, ladies free, and the Ball of the Two Well-Known Gentlemen was quickly established as the highlight of the season for assorted johns, politicians and policemen who grew rich on bribes for turning a blind eye to the whorehouses.

Among the policemen whose faces were well known in the brothels of New Orleans were brothers Michael and David

Hennessy, who, in 1881, gave Major Hearsey several opportunities to vent his editorial spleen. The Hennessys, detectives in the New Orleans Police Department, first hit the headlines when they helped federal marshals from New York arrest Giuseppe Esposito, a mafioso who had fled Sicily and settled in New Orleans to avoid arrest for the kidnapping and mutilation of an English tourist. Esposito was taken to New York and deported home, whereupon Hearsey wrote: "The kidnapping of the Italian fruit dealer Esposito and his removal by violence to New York, where after an unsatisfactory investigation, a subordinate official in the State Department at Washington, without the slightest authority, signed the extradition papers which consigned the captive to the tender mercies of the Italian authorities, is a most remarkable affair and ought to arouse the indignation of the country." Later that year the city's chief of detectives, Thomas Devereaux, charged Michael Hennessy with unbecoming conduct for turning up drunk at Kate Townsend's place and assaulting a customer. Devereaux wound up dead on the floor of a brokerage house, shot point-blank in the head, allegedly by David Hennessy, who was put on trial and acquitted. "We are astounded that a jury in a Christian and enlightened country could return such a verdict as not guilty in this case," Hearsey wrote. "Not even the savage tribes of the western plains would recognize such a mode of seeking protection or revenge as the Hennessys resorted to when they murdered Thomas Devereaux, for even savages will not tolerate assassination, and all the facts proved beyond question that this was a deliberate and bloody assassination."

After Mildred Lee's reign as the first queen of Comus in 1884, the krewe and the Pickwick Club went their separate ways, although remaining informally linked. Comus disappeared from the streets for five years, apparently because of money problems, leaving his slot on the evening of Mardi Gras to be taken over by Proteus, named for the Greek sea god who could assume any shape at will. The downscale Phunny Phorty Phellows gave up the ghost the next year, which also marked the emergence of a Carnival spectacle with roots deep in colonial times; this was to become a permanent feature of the season in New Orleans.

Black citizens continued to celebrate Mardi Gras dressed up as Indian braves, as they had for at least a hundred years, but it was not until 1885 that the first organized tribe appeared, apparently inspired by Buffalo Bill, who had come to town the year before hoping to make a buck from the crowds visiting the World's Industrial and Cotton Exposition, of which Maj. Edward Burke, now state treasurer, was director general. Buffalo Bill's Wild West Show, featuring Annie Oakley for the first time, was still going strong in New Orleans when Becate Batiste took to the streets the next Mardi Gras with warriors sporting turkey-feather headdresses and outfits adorned with shards of glass, eggshells, bottle caps and whatever else came to hand. Buffalo Bill's show employed plenty of black cowboys and about sixty Plains Indians, who had become a familiar sight around New Orleans when Batiste's tribe, which he called the Creole Wild West, made its debut. Soon thereafter another Wild West Show organized by the 101 Ranch of Oklahoma came to New Orleans, and the "101 Wild West" tribe duly appeared on the streets at Mardi Gras. That tribe has disappeared, but the Creole Wild West is still around.

Many of Buffalo Bill's black riders were veterans of the 9th U. S. Cavalry and felt close kinship with the Indians they had helped put down, while black spectators at the wild west shows by no means liked the way the mock battles came out. Audiences in black neighborhoods today still cheer for the Indians in western movies. Batiste himself was of black, French and Choctaw ancestry, and many members of the Wild Magnolias, the Golden Eagles, the Wild Tchoupitoulas, the Yellow Pocahontas, the Black Eagles and other tribes in existence today boast of Indian blood. The tribes' songs and chants are such a jumble of African, Indian, Creole French and English words that not even insiders are always sure what they mean. The most famous of the Mardi Gras Indian songs, included on records made by both the Wild Tchoupitoulas tribe with the Neville Brothers and the Wild Magnolias with Willie Turbinton, is nowadays known as "Hey, Pocky Way." It is more properly called "Too Way Pa-Ka-Way," and in a standard version with a habanera beat, begins thus:

> The Indians are coming,
> Too Way Pa-Ka-Way.
> The Indians are coming,
> Too Way Pa-Ka-way.
> The Big Chief is coming,
> Too Way Pa-Ka-Way.
> The Wild Magnolias are coming,
> Too Way Pa-Ka-Way.

Although the meaning of "Too Way Pa-Ka-Way" is obscure, some linguists point out that it sounds a lot like *toi pas kwe*, Creole French for "you can't believe that," which would make sense as a chant refrain. Others speculate that "too way" is a corruption of the French *tuer*, and that the phrase means "kill the guy over there." If the title does indeed imply an admonition to do in the competition, it was sometimes taken literally during early feuds between uptown and downtown tribes.

Downtown blacks were largely descended from the slaves imported in colonial times from the Senegal River Basin, progenitors of the accomplished and socially adept *gens de couleur libres*, whereas uptowners were more likely to trace their ancestry to "Virgina Negroes" or early nineteenth-century immigrants from Saint Domingue. Downtown tended to be supercilious toward the unruly and generally darker-skinned denizens of uptown, who naturally relished the prospect of bringing their detractors down a peg or two. The great New Orleans jazzman Jelly Roll Morton, Creole son of downtown who recorded a version of "Too Way Pa-Ka-Way" for the Library of Congress in the 1930s, recalled that, when he was a flag boy in the early years of the century, "many a time, in these Indian things, there would be a killing." Not for nothing are the tribes in New Orleans commonly referred to as "gangs."

Louisiana's Democratic Party, dominated by the Carnival elite, made no attempt to restrict the black franchise, but was not above a little fraud and intimidation on election day. In 1888, Louisiana had 127,923 black voters and 126,884 white, but the Democratic Party had a firm grip on power, and the governor, with the disproportionate power conferred by the 1879 constitution, was always white. John McEnery's brother Samuel became governor in 1881, remaining in office until 1888, although he was a most ineffectual character, and nobody doubted that the state was really under the control of Major Burke. Under Burke's influence, McEnery befriended the most corrupt elements in Louisiana public life and soon earned the nickname "McLottery." The Democrats, fearing that McEnery would hurt the party's chances of retaining power, nominated Francis Nicholls to replace him, and he was duly elected to a second term. No sooner had Nicholls taken the oath of office than Major Burke emigrated to Honduras. With an audit revealing that negotiable securities worth $1,267,905 were missing from the state treasury, Burke was indicted in absentia but never came back from Honduras, where he died in 1928.

Thanks in part to the laissez-faire attitude of the Bourbons, Louisiana remained pitifully backward for the rest of the nineteenth century. New Orleans was probably the filthiest and least salubrious city in the Union, while government starved the public schools of money, ensuring that the populace would remain largely ignorant and illiterate. Recovery from the economic depression of 1873–77, which had ruined many a rich man and sent Garden District values into precipitous decline, was slow. The vigorous entrepreneurial spirit of the pre–Civil War era seemed to have been dissipated, and the Anglo-Americans now joined the Creoles in posing as the refined products of a vanished civilization that put them above vulgar commercialism. New Orleans's strategic location as a transportation center nevertheless ensured the survival of a prosperous class. The city became not just a port for riverboats and ocean-going ships but also a major railroad center; in 1882 the connection was completed between New Orleans and San Francisco.

In race relations, the city continued to move steadily backward. Gangs of underfed black convicts, leased to construction and levee companies, labored under such brutal conditions that they died in appalling numbers. The *Daily Picayune*, in an access of humanitarianism, suggested in 1884 that anyone convicted of crimes carrying more than a six-year sentence be executed, since chances of living out a term that long were remote. The few remaining pockets of interracial association disappeared from New Orleans in the 1880s. White baseball teams quit playing against blacks, and the Fairgrounds kicked out all the black jockeys.

All this delighted the redoubtable Major Hearsey who, though his duelling pistol never hurt anyone, wielded a deadly pen. He was a friend of Jefferson Davis, who was said to have frequently complimented him for his "staunch adherence to the principles for which the Confederacy was founded," and who, as it happened, died on a visit to Judge Charles E. Fenner's Garden District residence in 1889. An estimated 140,000 people filed by the bier to view Davis's corpse before it was buried, clad in Confederate gray, in the Army of Northern Virginia tumulus in Metairie Cemetery. Two years later Davis's body was reinterred in Richmond, Virginia.

CHAPTER SEVEN

"Who Killa da Chief?"

hen David Hennessy was appointed police chief following Joseph Shakspeare's election as mayor in 1888, he did not feel constrained to sever his connections with the bawdy houses. In fact, it was an open secret that he controlled the Red Light Social Club, which, impressed by the success of the Ball of the Two Well-Known Gentlemen, started to organize its own Carnival balls. A few days before Mardi Gras of 1889, the *Mascot* editorialized that the ball should not be allowed:

> With reference to the Red Light Club, the Mascot has made an investigation and finds that the majority of its members, while holding good positions—many of them being persons of wealth—are nevertheless generally recognized, to use an expression of the day, as the lovers of women notoriously lewd and abandoned.
>
> The name of the Chief of Police is more than frequently mentioned in connection with the club, which, from all accounts, he appears to be a member of. Now with all due respect for Mr. Hennessy and for Mayor Shakspeare, we have no hesitancy in saying that it ill becomes the head of the police force to be so mixed up with an organization framed for God only knows what purpose and the members of which expect and do profit by their connection with the public women of the town.

It was not just the lubricious aspect of Hennessy's extra-curricular activities that earned the *Mascot*'s disapproval. Political cronyism and patronage apparently flourished there too, to judge from the breezy comments of columnist Bridget Magee the next year:

> So I see that old Jew Myers, the clothier, has been awarded the contract for putting some decent togs on Chief Hennessy's greasy police. Do any of you know how he came to get the job in spite of Godcheaux bidding lower than Myers? I tell you, Myers belongs to the Red Light Social Club, do you see? And so does the chief of the alleged police force. The chief told Shakspeare that as Mardi Gras was coming in, the men ought to have a fine fit and Godcheaux would not give it, so the old fraud, Shakspeare, said, "Well, then, let's give it to Myers." Now do you know what the Red Light Social Club is? Of course, you don't. It's a band of fellows that have immorality and indecency for their objects and unless you have the affection of or borrow a tip from the landlady of some bagnios you can't join it.

In 1890 Comus announced that he would resume his parade on Mardi Gras night, but Proteus refused to yield the slot he now regarded as his own. Proteus at the time was regarded as the most Creole of the krewes, and some lingering effects of ancient rivalries may have added to the intransigence of both sides. Although Comus started first, he encountered a delay and arrived on Canal Street at precisely the same moment as Proteus, heading in the opposite direction. Their combined flambeaux illuminating two rows of majestic floats produced as brilliant an effect as spectators could recall in the city, but a violent confrontation seemed imminent when Proteus blocked Comus's path and the two krewe captains, on horseback, commenced to exchange threats. It came to nothing, however, when someone emerged from the crowd and led the Proteus captain away. The krewe of Comus was back in charge of the Carnival season's last parade. Proteus, reverting to Monday evening, did come up with an idea a couple of years later that was promptly adopted by all the other krewes and remains a convention of Carnival balls. Proteus dreamed up the system of "call outs," whereby ladies who have been selected for the honor of dancing with krewe members sit in a special enclosure waiting to be invited onto the floor. Other guests at the ball get to watch the tableaux and the dancing. From the earliest days of Carnival krewe members have presented their dancing partners with "favors," which have sometimes been jewelry of considerable value.

Hearsey was never admitted to the rarefied world of the Carnival krewes, but his success in the newspaper business made it obvious that he struck a chord with white society. He was a dangerous man not just because of the extremity of his views but because of the great flair with which he expressed them. Writing shortly before Hearsey's death in 1900, a local historian noted that he was "the most conspicuous editor in the state," possessed of a "singular genius of bitterness, sarcasm and ridicule in controversy." By then, Hearsey had made the *States* "one of the most substantial newspaper properties in the south." His editorials were frequently "the talk, the sensation of the city." In his private life, it was said that there were "times when his too confiding nature and his loyalty to his friends led him into mistaken generosity." The *Item* obituarist said of Hearsey, "Brave as Caesar, he was as tender and sensitive as a woman."

But there was no softer side to the editorials he wrote after New Orleans Police Chief David Hennessy was murdered on the street near his home October 15, 1890. According to contemporary newspaper accounts, Hennessy and Capt. William O'Connor left Virget's Oyster Bar around 11 P.M. and started to walk home. They had just parted company when O'Connor heard gunshots and hurried back, to find Hennessy mortally wounded, sitting on a stoop. Hennessy had managed to get off three shots, but missed. J. C. Roe, a police officer assigned to guard the Hennessy house, had tried to return the assailants' fire, but his revolver jammed and he was shot in the ear. As O'Connor rushed up, Hennessy said, "Oh, Billy, Billy. They have given it to me and I gave them back the best I could."

"Who gave it to you, Dave?"

"Put your ear down here."

O'Connor did so and Hennessy whispered, "Dagoes."

A man with a decent sense of the dramatic would have expired there and then, but Hennessy remained conscious and talkative until he died in Charity Hospital the next morning. Joseph Shakspeare, who had won back the mayor's job in 1888 after being out of office for six years, ordered a mass roundup of Sicilians, who had been immigrating to New Orleans en masse over the previous decade. Many of them settled in the French Quarter, which became so lawless and violent that one stretch of Decatur Street became known as "Vendetta Alley." Shakspeare abhorred the Italian population, which numbered around thirty thousand at the time, although he was hardly alone in that or in the belief that New Orleans had become the Mafia's first stronghold in the United States. "No community can exist with murder associations in their midst. These associations must perish or the community itself must perish," he remarked at Hennessy's death. The *Item* also had no doubt that the Mafia had killed Hennessy, observing in an editorial: "How bold impunity has made the oath-bound brotherhood of Sicilians, the tragical event of last night shows." With the city in turmoil, the entire press forgot about Hennessy's frailties and sanctified him in death. Shakspeare turned for help to his peers in the Carnival establishment, appointing a committee of fifty business and professional men, headed by Edgar Farrar, to supervise an investigation. The committee, which included the aged Badger, evidently decided that its powers were unbridled. Discovering that Dominic O'Malley's detective agency had been hired to work for the defense, the committee sent him this note on October 22, 1890:

> The Committee of Fifty demand that you drop all connection instanter with the Italian vendetta cases, either personally or through your employees. They demand further that you keep away from the Parish Prison, the Criminal District Court and the recorder's courts while these cases are on trial or under investigation. That you cease all communication with members of the Italian colony. That you cease in person or through your employees to follow or communicate with witnesses in the matter of the assassination of D. C. Hennessy. The committee does not deny those accused a right to employ proper agency, but they do not intend to allow a man of your known criminal record and unscrupulous methods to be an instrument for harm to the public at their hands.

O'Malley was indeed something of a shady character and did have a police record, but he was not a man to be intimidated by a mayoral committee. He wrote back to Farrar: "Your extraordinary communication of this date has been received. In response I can but say that I propose to conduct the business of my office without instructions from you or the committee which you pretend to represent. Being unable to discover whence you derive any authority to 'demand' that I should obey your behest with respect to the character of my employment, I shall continue to reserve to myself the right to think and act without regard to your wishes."

Eventually, nineteen Sicilians were indicted and, on February 16, 1891, the first nine went on trial. Hearsey promptly assured his readers that Italians were liars who intimidated witnesses "lest they be assassinated with immunity by their murderers." He was already looking forward to a lynching and warned American citizens who helped administer a Sicilian Protection Fund that they had better make themselves scarce in the event of an acquittal or a hung jury. Otherwise, Hearsey said, "when the vengeance comes they may be partakers of its results." He further stoked the fires by reporting that unnamed jurors said that attempts had been made to suborn them. Hearsey declared the state's case watertight, but the evidence presented in court was in fact extremely feeble, to judge from newspaper accounts, which are all we have to go on. The official records of the trial are nowhere to be found. However, neither police officer Roe nor Captain O'Connor was called to testify, and the defendants' alibis could not be cracked. The jury acquitted six Sicilians and deadlocked on three. All nine faced other charges and were taken back to join their compatriots in jail. Several prominent men that evening were seen entering the law offices of W. S. Parkerson, Mayor Shakspeare's close friend and election campaign manager.

The next morning's papers carried a notice, bearing the names of sixty-one of New Orleans's club and krewe elite, headed "Mass Meeting." It read: "All good citizens are invited to attend a mass meeting on Saturday March 14 at 10 o'clock A.M. at Clay Statue to take steps to remedy the failure of justice in the Hennessy case." On the same page as that notice, the *Picayune* editorialized: "We trust, and believe, that the object of the meeting is wholly in the interest of peace as in the interest of justice. The names of the gentlemen who have signed the call would seem a ready guarantee of peaceful intentions, and so we accept them."

That was a mistake, for when a large crowd assembled at the statue in the middle of Canal Street, newsboys were hawking a *Daily States* extra full of Hearsey's fulminating prose. If the mob needed to be whipped into a homicidal mood, Hearsey was the man for the job: "Rise in your might, people of New Orleans!" he adjured. "Your laws in the very temple of justice have been bought off, and suborners have caused to be turned loose upon your streets the midnight murderers of David C.

"Who Killa da Chief?"

Hennessy, in whose premature grave the very majesty of our American law lies buried with his mangled corpse—the corpse of him who in life was the representative, the conservator of your peace and dignity."

Other newspapers were slightly less bloodthirsty. The *Times-Democrat*, created by a merger of two New Orleans dailies, hoped that the meeting at the Clay statue would not turn into a mob. President of the *Times-Democrat* was Ashton Phelps, a Boston Club man and veteran of the White League. The Phelps family is one of the oldest and most established, both in high society and in the newspaper business, in New Orleans. Ashton Phelps's grandson and namesake, Rex of 1970, was publisher of the *Times-Picayune*, the city's only daily newspaper since 1980. His great-grandson, another Ashton Phelps, is publisher today and a leading light of Carnival. Although Phelps's *Times-Democrat* of 1891 was somewhat more restrained than Hearsey's *States*, its editorials left no doubt that something had to be done: "This failure of justice creates a grave and threatening situation, and it is entirely meet and proper that good citizens should assemble to discuss the gravity of the situation and the steps necessary to remedy the wrong complained of." Hearsey's attitude towards both Italians and Hennessy had changed considerably over the preceding ten years. Now, he had no trouble transforming Hennessy into a "martyr" and encouraging riot: "Rise, outraged people of New Orleans! Let those who have attempted to sap the very foundation of your Temples of Justice be in one vengeful hour swept from your midst. Peaceably if you can, forcibly if you must!" Whatever chance of a peaceful resolution may have existed Hearsey was clearly out to destroy. "Who bribed the jury?" he asked in another piece appearing in the extra distributed at the Clay statue. As a favor to anyone who might be curious on the subject, he published the names and home and business addresses of each of its members. The meeting began at 10 A.M. with speeches from Parkerson,

Walter Denegre, who was to become Rex of 1899, and John
Wickliffe, an editor at the *Daily Delta*. Denegre wanted O'Malley, as well as the Sicilians, lynched. He told the mob that the
jury had been bribed. "And bribed by whom? By that scoundrel, D. C. O'Malley, than whom a more infamous scoundrel
never lived. The committee of Fifty have already notified him
to leave town without avail. More forcible action is now called
for. Let everyone here now follow us with the intention of doing his full duty." Whatever may have been the defects of the
O'Malley character, they did not include cowardice, for he was
standing in the middle of the crowd, looking perfectly cool.
He was recognized, but nobody touched him.

The mob, said to have numbered in the thousands, marched
to the parish prison, broke down a door and went hunting
for the Sicilians, who had been let out of their cells to find what
haven they could. Antonio Scaffidi, Joseph Macheca and Antonio Marchesi, discovered hiding behind a brick pillar, were
immediately shot to death. Frank Romero, Loretto Comitez,
Charles Traina, James Caruso, Pietro Monasterio and Rocco
Gerachi ran into the prison yard and huddled against a wall,
where they "begged for their lives, and got bullets in return."
The crowd outside the prison now demanding some share of
the sport, Manuel Polizzi and Antonio Bagnetto were dragged
onto the street. Polizzi was strung up on a lamppost but grasped
the rope with his hands. He was let down to the ground, and
his arms pinioned. No sooner had he been hoisted aloft again
than a hail of bullets dispatched him. Souvenir hunters tore his
shirt to pieces. Bagnetto, kicked and beaten almost to death by
the mob, was hanged from a tree, receiving one last kick in the
face from the man who adjusted the rope. Mayor Shakspeare
observed, "The Italians had taken the law into their own hands
and we had no choice but to do the same." Hearsey was full of
admiration: "Citizens of New Orleans! You have in one right-
eous upheaval, in one fateful gust of mighty wrath, vindicated

your laws, heretofore trampled underfoot by oath-bound aliens who had thought to substitute Murder for Justice and the suborner's gold for the Freeman's honest verdict." Other papers took a similar line, though in less coruscating style.

Major Hearsey was still working on his apotheosis of Hennessy in the columns of the *States*, when the Red Light Social Club went out of existence, its last meeting breaking up amid shouts of "Who killa da chief?," which had become a catchphrase in the city. There are still people alive in New Orleans today who recall that in their childhood "Who killa da chief?" was the customary taunt for anybody of Italian extraction. The consensus among the Carnival class today is that New Orleans was unlucky with its Italian immigrants, receiving the dregs of Sicilian society, while, as one prominent kreweman put it, "we got a good class of Jew, educated people from France and Germany." Jews and Italians remained equally unwelcome in the krewes and the clubs, however. Well into the 1980s, New Orleans restaurants continued to list "wop salad" on their menus and a glass of Chianti could be had by calling for a "dago red." Italians nevertheless have for decades been major players in the political life of New Orleans.

The jailhouse lynching of 1891 resulted in the recall of the Italian ambassador from Washington, and for a while the streets of New Orleans were abuzz with rumors that the Italian navy was planning to sail up the Mississippi and bombard. The crisis passed when the federal government paid $24,330 in reparation to the families of the three victims who had remained Italian citizens. Charges against the surviving Sicilians were dropped. O'Malley was charged with attempting to bribe a juror, but the district attorney declined to prosecute for want of evidence. No charges were brought against those who participated in the lynching, a grand jury concluding that it was "a spontaneous uprising of the people." Hennessy was entombed in Metairie Cemetery and a design competition held to find a monument worthy of the martyr. Even amid the ornate stone-masonry of that most exclusive of cemeteries, Hennessy's memorial sticks out. Designed by a German immigrant named Albert Weiblein, it is in the form of a broken shaft topped by a pall with a police belt and night stick dangling. Resembling nothing so much as an outsized, erect penis, it is one of the more noted local landmarks.

CHAPTER EIGHT

Honoring the White
League Martyrs

Having satisfied their thirst for justice in the David Hennessy case, the white people of New Orleans prepared to commemorate their finest hour, the triumph of Liberty Place. Thanks to the efforts of a committee of ladies, six thousand dollars had been raised by public subscription to erect a thirty-five-foot obelisk, made of granite from Maine, in the middle of Canal Street, where the fighting had been at its most intense. The eminent Bostonian Robert Marr, now a state judge, presided at dedication ceremonies when the cornerstone was laid on the seventeenth anniversary of the battle, September 14, 1891. Crowds packed the surrounding streets under a hot sun, as veterans of the battle marched past the site of the monument, one company displaying a United States flag captured along with the cannons from the Metropolitan Police. Former U. S. Senator B. F. Jonas delivered a stirring speech, recalling how the White League had "charged upon the hireling myrmidons of the usurping government and swept them from the field as the chaff is driven before the wind." He wound up by reading extracts from a statement issued by the Committee of 70 when federal troops restored Kellogg to the governorship in 1874. After complaining that the White League had been "grossly misrepresented abroad," the statement rehearsed the various injustices to which the citizenry had been subjected during Reconstruction. First among them was the disarming of the whites and the formation of the black militia:

> The white people of the state, thus stripped of every means of defense, were threatened, moreover, by a formidable oath-bound league of blacks, which, under the command of the cunning and unscrupulous negro, might at any moment plunge them into what they were anxious to avoid—a war of races. The incessant demand for offices from the city, state and federal government, for which they were utterly unfit and for which they proferred no other title than that of color; the development in their conventions of a spirit of proscription against white radicals, and even against honorable Republicans who had fought for their liberation, their increasing arrogance which knew no bounds, their increasing dishonesty, which they had regarded as a statesmanlike virtue, their contemptuous scorn of all rights of the white man. All these signs as set forth in the platform of the Crescent City White League, warned us that the calamity which we had long apprehended was imminent, and that we must either prepare for it or perish under it.

White attitudes had not changed by the time Jonas delivered his speech. Major Hearsey, on July 19, 1890, had urged blacks to "become non-voting friends to the whites instead of voting enemies," but they had not, apparently, been listening. Talk of a possible race war became commonplace in the 1890s while Jim Crow took hold. The white power structure decided that the disfranchisement of blacks was an urgent necessity, and in 1896 Gov. Murphy Foster asked the legislature to call a constitutional convention. That was the year the United States Supreme Court, in the case of *Plessy* v. *Ferguson*, upheld a Louisiana law requiring separate railway coaches for whites and blacks. Plessy, who was seven-eighths Caucasian, had been arrested for riding in a white coach and had sued, claiming the law violated the Fourteenth Amendment. The case was evidently a put-up job, since "the mixture of colored blood was not discernible" in Plessy, according to his own testimony, and he precipitated his arrest by identifying himself as a Negro to the conductor. A Negro, under the law at the time, meant anyone with a "traceable amount" of black blood. Indeed, the difficulty of telling who belonged to which race was one reason the New Orleans streetcars remained integrated at the time. Testifying against a law that sought to require separate accommodations for whites and blacks, the president of one of the streetcar companies pointed out in 1900: "Our conductors are men of intelligence, but the greatest ethnologist the world ever saw would be at a loss to classify street car passengers in this city."

The white elite, however, knew which families belonged to polite society and which didn't. A group of men who obviously didn't, and who lived in an area then known as Jefferson City, formed themselves into the first of the city's Mardi Gras marching clubs in 1890. Organized Mardi Gras was inexorably reaching into every social stratum of the city, the Jefferson City Buzzards inaugurating a decidedly working-class practice of marching to the beat of accompanying bands from barroom to barroom and ending the day well in the bag. Upper-class Carnival proliferated more discreetly in the 1890s with the establishment of several white male nonparading Carnival societies that maintained the tradition of choosing names from mythology. Poseidon ruled over the first Atlanteans ball in 1891, the Elves of Oberon materialized in 1895, the Krewe of Nereus a year later and the High Priests of Mithras in 1897. The members of Mithras formed the Stratford Club the same year. The black citizenry also decided to take a leaf out of white society's book with the formation of the Illinois Club in 1895. The driving force behind the Illinois Club was Wiley Knight, a black butler who came to town with his employers from Chicago and gave dancing lessons on the side. The Illinois quickly became a

MG becomes lower

black Creole version of the Pickwick and the Boston clubs, organizing Carnival cotillions, complete with mock royal courts, at which their daughters were introduced to society.

White society ladies, meanwhile, were donning masks on Mardi Gras night to slip into the Ball of the Two Well-Known Gentleman for thrills not available from their own class. The Gentlemen still had one rival for the bawdy trade, however, in the C. C. C. Club. The Gentlemen continued to hold their annual ball on Mardi Gras night, while the C. C. C. Club rented the Odd Fellows' Hall the previous Saturday. The madams of the city, meanwhile, formed a social club, which they named the Society of Venus and Bacchus. Whether they realized that Bacchus was the father of Comus is not known, although some of the members, like the daughters of old-line krewemen, evidently relished royal titles. The *Mascot* covered meetings of the Society of Venus and Bacchus and reported on October 27, 1894, that a brothel keeper known as "Nanon, the Western Beauty" was elected secretary and had this to say: "Last year Miss Gertie Livingston assumed the title of Queen of the Demi-Monde. This year Nellie Dorsey comes here from New York and tells that she has enjoyed the title of Queen in Gotham and does not intend to renounce that title in favor of any woman who used to be a chambermaid. Gertie's perusal of novels has made her very chic, but the only one who ever announced his allegiance to her was Baby Lou, and he renounced his allegiance when her majesty had him arrested for stealing her ring." Nanon declared her devotion to egalitarian principles: "In a democracy like ours we should have no queen. We are all queens and earn our money by being such. It is our duty to uphold the democracy, and I propose that any man who frequents nigger dives be boycotted by us." This observation, the *Mascot* reported, brought hearty applause, whereupon "Miss Julia Dean stated that she had been informed that a Japanese house had been opened on Customhouse Street at Annie Merrit's old stand, and that it should be discountenanced as much as possible. Miss Wilcox said that she was sure the Japs were niggers dressed up."

Although prostitution had flourished throughout the history of New Orleans, it had never been so widespread or pernicious as in the waning years of the nineteenth century, when countless children were sold into the bawdy houses that sprang up all over town, even in respectable neighborhoods. Much has been written about the glamorous surroundings in which the trade was conducted, and the astonishing number of fine early jazz musicians who played the bordellos, but the other side of the coin was filth and disease and a population habitually befuddled with cocaine, opium and alcohol. Violence and theft were commonplace, and government was so hopelessly corrupted that policemen would pay their superiors as much as $375 a week for the privilege of a Basin Street assignment and regular bribes from the houses. Any attempt to stamp out prostitution would have been futile, but pressure was mounting on the city council at least to control it as the trade became so blatant and brisk that honest burghers were horrified to see bawdy houses being set up in respectable neighborhoods. Alderman Sidney Story, a businessman of unimpeachable respectability, introduced an ordinance establishing legal prostitution in an area outside the French Quarter, which the city council adopted in 1897, to take effect on January 1 the next year. Much to Story's chagrin, and over his repeated protests, the press took to calling the red-light district "Storyville," although its denizens apparently never used that name. To the whores, pimps, musicians and hangers-on who made a living there, it was known simply as "the District." It was also nicknamed "Anderson County" after the dominant entrepreneur of the city's vice trade. Tom Anderson already owned, or had a stake in, several saloons, clubs and brothels in the area when prostitution was legalized, and was a partner, in business and bed, with Josie Arlington, one of the most celebrated brothel keepers of the era. Anderson was known as the "Mayor of Storyville" and wrote letters to the mayors of New Orleans as an equal, soliciting, and receiving, various political favors.

When the constitutional convention called by Governor Foster opened in 1898, Ernest Kruttschnitt, White League veteran, lawyer and son-in-law of Judah Benjamin, was in the chair and Hearsey had been appointed official printer. Kruttschnitt announced that the point of the convention was "to eliminate from the electorate the mass of corrupt and illiterate voters who have during the last quarter century degraded our politics." Other delegates similarly made no bones about their intentions. J. A. Sider wanted to "disfranchise as many Negroes and as few whites as possible," while Judge Thomas Semmes, chairman of the judiciary committee, acknowledged he was out to "establish the supremacy of the white race." Semmes, host of famous soirees in Richmond when he was a Confederate senator, had been president of the American Bar Association in the 1880s. His daughter, Myra, was married to Sylvester Walmsley, a member of Mayor Shakspeare's Committee of Fifty and a signatory of the advertisement that led to the jailhouse lynching. Walmsley chose Shakspeare's daughter, Nita, as his queen when he was Rex in 1890; he was Comus four years later and remained a pillar of the Carnival establishment for decades. The constitutional convention contrived to put black people in their place by inventing the infamous "grandfather clause," whereby voters who had been registered before January 1, 1867, or their sons and grandsons, were automatically granted the franchise. Everyone else, save Italians, had to demonstrate an ability to fill out a tricky form, which required the applicant, for instance, to give his age in years, months and days, and to own property assessed at three thousand dollars. The exemption for Italians was secured by delegate Martin Behrman, but not out of any passion for ethnic fair play. The Italians were known in New Orleans as loyal machine voters, and, indeed, helped elect Behrman mayor six years later.

The constitution was declared adopted without a referendum, and blacks virtually disappeared from the electoral rolls. On January 1, 1897, Louisiana had 130,344 black voters and 164,088 white. Three years later, 5,320 blacks were registered, and 125,437 whites.

That doubtless cheered Hearsey up as he began what was to be his last year on earth, which he departed in style. In private life Hearsey remained a man of great charm and unfailing courtesy, and was well known for his financial probity, not so common a virtue in New Orleans at the time as it might have been. But his animus against what he regarded as inferior races was unabated. When five Italians were lynched in Tallulah, Louisiana, in 1899, for instance, he launched into an editorial that showed he had not modified his views since the Hennessy assassination, scoffing at "efforts to arouse a spirit of indignation" and concluding that "Judge Lynch has administered more substantial justice than all of the criminal courts of the land combined."

The next year, a black laborer named Robert Charles provided him with one more chance to expound his racial theories. On July 23, 1900, Charles shot and wounded one of two police officers who apparently had tried to rough him up on the street; he then fled to the rooming house where he lived. When four policemen turned up to arrest him, two were dispatched by blasts from a rifle, whereupon the other two took refuge in a neighboring room, creeping out at dawn to find that Charles had disappeared. Readers of the *States* were promptly regaled with an editorial headlined "Negro Murderers." Hearsey pointed out that the "average negro is, after all, little else than a tamed savage." When aroused, the Negro became "an unreasoning brute and the most dangerous of murderers." Hearsey had been waiting for this. Only a month before, when two black men were lynched in Mississippi City, he wrote that, while he felt no sympathy for the victims, he regretted that, if guilty of the offenses alleged against them, they had been granted "a comparatively painless death." If they were innocent, "the severity so far inflicted will be calculated to temper the ferocity of the mob when the right fiend shall be come up with." Charles was that fiend.

A few hours after "Negro Murderers" hit the streets, a mob of two thousand gathered by New Orleans's statue of Robert E. Lee and went hunting for blacks, assailing them on the street and dragging them off streetcars to be shot or beaten. By the next morning, three blacks were dead, six seriously injured and at least fifty more in need of medical treatment. This was not a gentlemen's lynching, however—the upper class always assembled at the Clay, not the Lee, statue—which may help explain why Hearsey this time turned disapproving. His next editorial called on the authorities to "institute a rigid and far-reaching investigation into the genesis of this villainous riot and trace up its instigators and drag before the courts every scoundrel who was engaged in it."

When Charles's hiding place was discovered, a huge crowd of armed citizens turned up to help the police arrest him. Charles, having already killed two policemen and injured one more, clearly did not have much of a future, and he apparently decided to shoot as many white men as he could. Somehow he managed to survive the constant hail of bullets, and, appearing from time to time at a window with his antique Winchester, he proved a formidable marksman. By the time the police set the building on fire and flushed him out, he had killed another five people, including two policemen, seriously injured eight, of whom three were policemen, and wounded twelve more. Once Charles emerged from the house, he was shot to death. Long after he was dead, the mob continued to pump bullets into his body. Others kicked the corpse, and an effort was made to burn it, but the police intervened. Hearsey conceded that he could not help feeling "a sort of admiration prompted by his wild and ferocious courage," but observed that Charles was brave in the manner "of the brute, the lion or the tiger." A few days later, some white men assaulted a black woman on the street after she was heard expressing sympathy for Charles. Hearsey observed, "She was not hurt enough." Despite Hearsey's purported disapproval of the attacks on blacks while Charles was on the run, none of the rioters, though nine were indicted, was ever convicted of a crime.

Robert Charles's desperate defiance came at a time when race relations in New Orleans were at a historic nadir. The previous month, the *Times-Democrat* had published a series of articles by one Dr. Gustave Keitz, who wrote: "The fact that we are on the threshold of a race war cannot be denied." That was a widely held view at the time, and Keitz was in favor of forced deportation as a way of keeping the peace. Even as Keitz was propounding his views, Robert Charles was himself promoting the cause of black emigration as a member of the "Back to Africa" movement. A few days before Charles hit the headlines, Keitz reported that his fellow doctors "are agreed that the number of negroes should be reduced and have discussed asexualization, a measure which should be practiced at the earliest possible period of life."

Such half-measures were not for Hearsey, who stole the Nazis' thunder with the headline on his editorial of August 7, 1900: "The Negro Problem and the Final Solution." Some whites, he noted, had intervened to protect blacks from the mob while Robert Charles was in hiding. "But let the negroes remember that a race war is a very different thing from a hoodlum riot and that if they listen to the screeds of agitators in the North and if they harbor such characters as Charles among them here the result will be a race war and a race war means extermination. In such a war the race and every member of the race is held to be guilty. In such a war there will be no distinction between good negroes and bad negroes."

Hearsey at the time had a bee in his bonnet because the Clay statue was about to be moved from Canal Street, where it impeded improvements planned for the streetcar line, to Lafayette Square, where it still stands today. The statue, of course, was sacrosanct to white New Orleans. On June 4 the previous year, the *Times-Democrat* had reminded readers that "[d]uring the Reconstruction Days, the Boston Club was the gathering place of the leaders of the white element and should justly share much of the tradition that clusters around the sombre lines of the Clay statue. The Boston Club party grew into public utterance as an expression standing for the supremacy of the white man and the perpetuation of the white man's institutions." Removal of the statue, to Hearsey's mind, would "please the railroads and iconoclasts but it will be the shame of New Orleans." What was the world coming to? "Now let the work be thoroughly done. Aye, let some gentleman of the council move that the statue at Liberty Place be tumbled from its base and chucked into the river."

Two months later Hearsey was dead of Bright's disease at the age of fifty-nine. Everyone of consequence turned out in his honor. Gov. W. W. Heard and New Orleans mayor Paul Capdevielle headed the political contingent. Society was represented by eminent members of the krewes and clubs, and Charles Janvier, Rex of 1896, was an honorary pall bearer. Rival editors published fulsome obituaries and attended the funeral, at which the Reverend Benjamin Palmer delivered a eulogy to Hearsey as "the special advocate and exponent of those principles which the most of us believe lie at the foundation of all just and true government upon this sinful earth," and noted that "a beautiful consistency pervaded his whole career." Palmer, a Presbyterian from North Carolina who settled in New Orleans shortly before the Civil War, was one of those southern preachers who found justification for slavery in the Bible, and a fire-eating sermon he delivered in 1860 was said to have been instrumental in fanning the flames of secessionism. He never moderated his views and was still decrying the folly of manumission when he died a couple of years after Hearsey's body, wrapped in the Confederate flag, was placed in the tomb of the Army of Tennessee in Metairie Cemetery.

At the time of Hearsey's death, Carnival was an established tourist attraction, bringing more than a hundred thousand visitors to the city, including some distinguished guests at the old-line balls. In 1900, perhaps out of respect for the delicate feelings of outsiders, Rex decided that the Boeuf Gras would no longer have a place in his parade. Chinese Ambassador Wu Ting Fang was on the balcony of the Boston Club, seated behind Queen of Carnival Rosa Febiger, when Rex, Thomas Woodward, paused on the street for the traditional toast. That night the ambassador was at the Comus Ball. The same year the first women's Carnival organization, Les Mysterieuses, held its inaugural ball at the French Opera House, treating male guests exactly as Comus and Momus treated their females. The curtain rose to reveal two rows of masked ladies flanking their nameless queen, whose king, William Stauffer, sat alongside his dukes in a proscenium box. A couple of hundred male guests sat in the call-out section waiting for an invitation to dance. Les Mysterieuses did not hold a parade, and lasted only a few years, but women's krewes soon became a feature of the season.

President Teddy Roosevelt's daughter Alice was a guest at the Comus ball of 1903 and again six years later. President-elect William Howard Taft and his wife dropped in on Oberon and his queen, Laura Merrick. At the other end of the social scale, Carnival marching clubs along the lines of the Jefferson City Buzzards were all the rage, and the Broadway Swells, the Jassy Kids, the St. Roch, the Jan Jans and the Chrysanthemum came and went. Maskers took to outfitting themselves as the

Happy Hooligan, the Katzenjammer Kids, Mutt and Jeff and other popular cartoon characters of the day, while dancing in the street remained perfectly normal behavior on Mardi Gras. Although the pre–World War I vogue of such dances as the bunny hug, the bear and the turkey trot made no impression on the old-line balls, they did not lack enthusiastic exponents along the public thoroughfares.

Political satire comes naturally in New Orleans, and a recurring Carnival sideshow has been the maverick organization with a point to make about corruption. One of the drollest examples appeared in 1911 when members of the New Orleans Chess Club were joking about the number of dead men who were still on the electoral rolls. They formed themselves into the St. Louis Cemetery Marchers' Club, borrowed a hearse and resolved to proceed from the cemetery and trail along behind the Rex parade, although by Mardi Gras only thirteen men had the nerve to turn up. The horse-drawn hearse, complete with a skull-and-crossbones placard, was driven by the figure of Death, in black suit and mask, with Beelzebub riding alongside. Inside, a club member sat in a coffin with a ballot box next to him and displayed a sign that read "Dead but still a voter." One of the marchers, Edouard Henriques, was got up in a skeleton suit, while the rest wore death masks, white winding sheets and hoods and carried various signs suggesting a posthumous franchise. Among the legends were "Gabriel's Band," "Count me in for several votes" and "Vote for Adam, the people's choice." The marchers passed in mock review before sexton Moise Rodriguez and proceeded through the cemetery gates onto the streets, earning much applause before the police came along and forced them to disband.

If admission to old-line Carnival was the summit of social ambition in New Orleans, by no means everyone took it so seriously. In the early years of the new century, the upper classes had good reason to know that their pretensions were being riotously satirized in Storyville, for many of them saw it with their own eyes. It was now so fashionable to go slumming in the District at Mardi Gras that tickets to the Carnival balls there were among the hottest items in town. The balls were never-theless advertised every year in Tom Anderson's *Blue Book*, which, appearing for the first time around the turn of the century, listed the brothels, madams and whores of Storyville and gave rapturous accounts of the delights they offered. A 1905 advertisement, featuring a trim young woman in mask and evening gown, announced: "Fun! Fun! Fun! Don't miss the French Balls given by the C. C. C. Club and Two Well-Known Gentlemen." It went on to explain: "The Balls have been famous for years, so if you are out for a good time don't miss them."

Anderson was so widely recognized as an unsavory character that it was only natural that he would run for public office in Louisiana, and in 1904 he was elected to the state house of representatives. He had no challenger as boss of Storyville, where the most celebrated of the colored madams, Lulu White, in her red wig and dripping with diamonds, ran the magnificent Mahogany Hall, while Josie Arlington continued to dominate the white trade. The District was segregated by law, but the *Blue Book* reveals that a few black prostitutes operated on the same premises as whites, while some of the leading colored, mostly Creole, musicians—notably Mr. Jelly Lord himself—played the white bordellos. Storyville's Carnival queen—always white—reigned over the Ball of the Two Well-Known Gentlemen, where the hookers were becoming increasingly resentful of the society ladies who turned up to gawk at them every year at the Odd Fellows' Hall. The hookers' "warm French balls" offered a "grand time of high revelry," the *Sunday Sun* announced just before Mardi Gras of 1906, the year that Josie Arlington decided to teach the snooty intruders a lesson. Arlington contacted her friends in the police department and arranged for them to raid the Ball of the Two-Well Known Gentlemen and arrest every woman present who could not produce a prostitute's registration card. Several respectable ladies were taken to the police station and unmasked before being allowed to go home. Thereafter, the hookers had the balls to themselves.

Creoles of color may have been flattering the white establishment by imitating its clublife and debutante seasons, but members of the black Knights of Pythius shared Storyville's taste for mocking the elite. The Knights' inspiration came one night at their Pythian Temple Theater where the musical comedy *Smarter Set* was performed early in 1909. It featured an African skit entitled "There Never Was and There Never Will Be a King Like Me," which naturally put the audience in mind of Rex. That Mardi Gras, William Story, sporting ragged pants, a lard-can crown and a banana stalk scepter, appeared as the first king of Zulu, while Paul Johnson invented a character called "Big Shot from Africa," who was to become a staple of the parade. In keeping with the general desire to send up the ornate parades of the old-line krewes, the Big Shot carried what was supposed to be a huge diamond but was easily identifiable as a glass doorknob. Riders, lampooning the white man's racial stereotypes, wore grass skirts and daubed their skin with black dye, creating an effect so aggressively low-class that the parade, held under the aegis of what was called the Tramps' Club, became a continuing source of offense to many of the city's blacks, who thought it too close to Uncle Tom for comfort. The Zulu parade weaved through the uptown streets as the whim of the king dictated. Zulu took to issuing "letters of patent" and did a good job of imitating the florid Rex style, though naturally espousing a more liberal worldview than Rex. The Zulu king styled himself the "Prime Defender of the Gods of Fun and Toleration" and decreed: "All cares, quarrels and prejudices are hereby cancelled."

Still the rigid lines of demarcation that have always characterized New Orleans were barely shaded. Among the black musicians of Storyville, it was the same old story; Creoles were regarded as more presentable and better educated than uptown blacks and therefore commanded the best-paid gigs. Piano players were the aristocrats of the bordello musicians—indeed, they were called "professors"—and Morton has related what a good living he made in Storyville: "Tom Anderson was king of the District and ran the Louisiana legislature and Hilma Burt was supposed to be his old lady. Hers was no doubt one of the best paying places in the city and I thought I had a very bad night when I made under a hundred dollars. Very often a man would come into the house and hand you a twenty or forty or fifty-dollar bill, just like a match." Nobody doubts that Morton was a genius of jazz, but it may be doubted that the quality of his playing was always appreciated in the District. Plenty of the black musicians who played there were no slouches either—the roster of those who worked the Storyville joints amounts to a who's who of classic New Orleans jazz—and financial considerations eventually forced many Creoles to put aside their contempt for the untutored, but often richly talented, black musicians, as violinist Paul Dominguez has explained: "See, us downtown people, we didn't think so much of this rough uptown jazz until we couldn't make a living otherwise. If I wanted to make a living, I had to be rowdy like the other group. I had to jazz it or rag it or any other damn thing." Dominguez blamed legendary cornettist Buddy Bolden for this indignity. "He caused these younger Creoles, men like [Sidney] Bechet and [Freddy] Keppard to have a different style altogether. I don't know how they [uptown blacks] do it, but, goddamn, they'll do it. Can't tell you what's there on the paper, but just play the hell out of it."

Although under the law anyone with a "traceable amount" of black blood was deemed colored, racial classification in Louisiana remained exquisitely complex, as the state supreme court explained in a 1910 decision:

> We do not think there could be any serious denial of the fact that in Louisiana the words "mulatto," "quadroon" and "octoroon" are of as definite meaning as the word "man" or "child." There is also the less widely known word "griff," which, in this state, has a definite meaning, indicating the issue of a negro and a mulatto. The person too black to be a mulatto and too pale in color to be a negro is a griff. The person too dark to be a white, and too bright to be a griff, is a mulatto. Between these different shades, we do not believe there is much, if any, difficulty in distinguishing. Nor can there be, we think, any serious denial of the fact that in Louisiana, and, indeed, throughout the United States (except on the Pacific slope), the word "colored," when applied to race, has the definite and well-known meaning of a person having negro blood in his veins. We think also that any candid mind must admit that the word "negro" of itself, unqualified, does not necessarily include within its meaning persons possessed of only an admixture of negro blood; notably those whose admixture is so slight that in their case even an expert cannot be positive.

Storyville was not only legally segregated but was supposed to become all white when the city fathers got around to legalizing prostitution in an uptown area where black prostitutes operated openly. Those uptown whores became the first females to parade at Mardi Gras sometime around 1912, when they banded together as the Baby Dolls, hanging around the Zulu parade, cavorting on the streets—"walking raddy," they call it in New Orleans—and turning dollar tricks with maskers they met on the streets. A whore named Beatrice Hill, who claimed to have been the first Baby Doll, described the scene: "Women danced on bars with green money in their stockings, and sometimes they danced naked. They used to lie down on the floor and shake their bellies while the men fed them candies. You didn't need no system to work uptown. It wasn't like the downtown red light district, where they made more money but paid more graft. You had to put on the ritz downtown, which some of the girls didn't like that. You did what you wanted uptown." Groups calling themselves the Gold Diggers and the Zigaboos soon appeared to follow in the Baby Dolls' footsteps.

Morton was right about Hilma Burt; she had replaced Josie Arlington as Anderson's "old lady." Anderson remained on friendly terms with Arlington, however, until she died in 1914 to be buried in a plot she had bought in, of all places, Metairie Cemetery. She is reputed to have paid two thousand dollars for the plot and another eight thousand for her tomb and a memorial which she commissioned Albert Weiblein to design. Its centerpiece is a statue of a young girl with one hand clasping a wreath and the other reaching out to a bronze door as if she hopes to enter. What it signifies is unknown, although one story has it that Arlington meant it to show a virgin being turned away from her brothel where, she somewhat unconvincingly maintained, no innocent had ever been deflowered. Arlington's tomb became such a magnet for gawking tourists that her business manager, John T. Brady, having married her convent-educated niece, had the pieces removed to an anonymous receiving vault elsewhere in the cemetery. The tomb she commissioned was sold and now bears the name A. Morales.

Comus continued to affirm his Anglophile and literary bent. Having done "Scenes from Shakespeare" in 1898, his Miltonic eponym in 1906 and Tennyson in 1907, in 1914, when the European powers were on the brink of World War I, he staged a parade and ball with the themes "Tales from Chaucer." The upper class also staged a series of "Germans," as they had during the social season since the 1880s. A German, in the Carnival sense, was a formal ball, without masks, where that year's debutantes would parade, with a bouquet going to the one who most took the fancy of the menfolk and extravagant favors being handed out to all the ladies. The name came from the German Cotillion, a popular dance in the nineteenth century. Zulu, meanwhile, was becoming bolder in his lèse-majesté, and that year King Henry Harris, riding in a buggy and sporting a suit of flags saved from cigarette packs, trailed behind Rex with his parade. Zulu's role did not remain limited to the staging of Carnival parades and balls. In 1916, members incorporated the Zulu Social Aid and Pleasure Club, which operated as a self-insurance pool to meet the medical and burial expenses of its members in the tradition of black benevolent and mutual aid societies that have existed in New Orleans since 1783. Zulu's zest for tweaking Rex's nose was unabated, and, in 1917, in a parody of Rex's Lundi Gras ceremonial arrival by yacht, King James Robertson was rowed across the New Basin Canal in a skiff. That year was the end of Mardi Gras for a while, as the United States entered the war on April 6 and a newspaper notice appeared that might have rung a bell among older residents:

> WHEREAS, War has cast its gloom over our happy homes and care usurped the place where joy is wont to hold its sway. Now, therefore, do I deeply sympathizing with the general anxiety, deem it proper to withhold your Annual Festival in this goodly Crescent City and by this proclamation do command no assem-blage of the
> —Mistick Krewe—
> Given under my hand this, the 30th day of June, A.D. 1917
> Comus.

The outbreak of war also caused a delay in planning a consti-tutional convention to find new ways to disfranchise black citi-zens, which became necessary after the U. S. Supreme Court in 1915 threw out an Oklahoma "grandfather" clause similar to

Louisiana's. The Supreme Court opinion was written by Chief Justice White, veteran of Liberty Place and old-line Carnivals but now, to his former colleagues in the Louisiana Democratic Party, an apostate.

War was also the death knell for Storyville. In August 1917, by order of Secretary of War Newton Baker and Secretary of the Navy Josephus Daniels, prostitution was banned within five miles of a military installation. Mayor Behrman, who said of prostitution that "you can make it illegal, but you can't make it unpopular," travelled to Washington to appeal the order that Storyville be closed down, but failed to get an appointment with either President Woodrow Wilson or with Daniels. After Daniels informed Behrman that, if he did not close Storyville, the armed forces would do it for him, the city council, under protest, adopted an ordinance to do so. The denizens of the District were initially unconcerned, assuming that Tom Anderson would take care of everything. Indeed, Anderson's paramour and future wife, a madam named Gertrude Dix, sought a court injunction against what she argued was an unconstitutional confiscation of property, but she lost her case, and, by midnight of November 12, legal prostitution in New Orleans had come to an end. The result was not, of course, an end to the trade, which now went on all over town without the benefit of any regulation. Anderson remained in the state legislature until 1920, when he retired to spend the rest of his life in great prosperity.

Of the lavish Storyville buildings, barely a trace survives, and a public housing development now stands where the whores of yesteryear plied their trade. The Carnival Germans were now a thing of the past, thanks in part to widespread hostility toward the Kaiser, who was hanged in effigy on the streets of New Orleans during Carnival of 1917. Berlin Street, which commemorated a Napoleonic victory, was renamed General Pershing, while young women wrapped in the American flag rode around the streets to the strains of "The Star-Spangled Banner." Germans were abandoned not just on ethnic grounds but also because the younger generation, on the verge of the Jazz Age, found them intolerably formal and stuffy.

CHAPTER NINE

Comus and the Kingfish

The spirit of Liberty Place lived on in Comus and his ilk, for whom Huey Long was a bigger scoundrel than any carpetbagger and a worse tyrant than Sheridan. "It would be unfair to say that Long was Hitler, but he was certainly Mussolini," is how one veteran kreweman puts it. Revolution was in the air in various parts of Louisiana, but nowhere was the mood more defiant than along the shady avenues of uptown New Orleans, where many of the residents had cases of carbines stored in their closets. They grabbed their guns on January 26, 1935, and travelled to Baton Rouge, there to fight for the Square Deal Association, which had been formed with the intention of breaking Long's stranglehold, by assassination if necessary, on state and local government.

The events that brought the state to such a desperate pass began in 1918, when Long, son of dirt-poor Winn Parish, a hotbed of Populism, won his first public office, a seat on the state railroad commission. As he later did when running for governor and U. S. Senator, Long railed against the wealth and privilege that found its most conspicuous embodiment in the world of the krewes and the gentlemen's clubs. That world was slow to resume its diversions after the end of World War I, partly because the city's magnificent French Opera House, where Comus, Momus and Proteus had held their balls, burned down in 1919. Proteus reappeared in 1922, Momus in 1923 and Comus in 1924. Rex, however, was back in business in 1920, when Gen. John Pershing, commander of the American army in Europe, was named a peer of the realm by Rex John Clark and entertained on the balcony of the Boston Club as Queen Elinor Bright received the traditional royal salute when the parade halted on Canal Street. There was, however, one important difference that year: the queen could not be toasted, at least in public, with any alcoholic drink. Prohibition, wet weather and the absence of the other krewes combined to produce sparse crowds and perhaps the least jolly Mardi Gras in history.

The Rex parade of 1920 was followed by the United Ancient Order of Druids, a fraternal order, which, though far from top-drawer, presented floats that did not suffer much by comparison with the main event. The Druids retained their spot behind Rex for several years before, as countless Carnival organizations have done, fading from the scene. Rex did not resume his Lundi Gras tradition of arriving by boat after World War I, although Zulu King of 1920, Freddie Brown, crossed the New Basin Canal as usual, this time aboard a motor-driven skiff, and led his parade the next day.

Meanwhile, a group of young black Creoles in the Seventh Ward, who had banded together as the Autocrat Club in 1918, began to hold Carnival balls, which soon became highly fashionable in black society. The Autocrat, it is said in New Orleans, is where the "brown bag test" originated to provide a yardstick for the exclusion of people with too dark a complexion. To get in, a candidate had to demonstrate that his skin was lighter than a paper bag held up to his face. Plenty of people in Louisiana remember such a test being administered in a variety of contexts, but who first thought of the idea has not been determined. The Autocrat Club, in any event, was far removed from the earthy Carnival antics of Zulu, and, indeed, has never staged a parade. Neither has it cared to arrange formal debuts, leaving such affectations to the Illinois Clubs.

With the reemergence of Carnival after World War I, an innovation began to catch on as riders, hitherto largely static figures in a passing show, took to tossing trinkets to the crowds. It was not, as befitted a gentlemanly event, overdone, and was nothing like the wholesale dumping of "throws" that characterizes some parades today. Still, the opportunity to catch a gewgaw flicked from a languid wrist added a little extra spice to the occasion as life returned to normal.

Normal meant that the city's political and economic life was firmly controlled by its upper class—krewemen, directors of the Whitney Bank and members of the Tulane University Board of Administrators, who sometimes ran members of their own circle for public office but more often financed campaigns for candidates they could trust to do their bidding. One piece of business interrupted by the war was the rewriting of the state constitution following the Supreme Court's rejection of the "grandfather clause" whereby blacks had been virtually denied the franchise. Gov. John Parker, a prominent member of the New Orleans aristocracy who reigned as Comus in 1917, called a constitutional convention in 1921 in order, among other things, "to shut out the Negro," as the *Picayune* put it. That year Comus, in the person of Charles Claiborne, is said to have refused to greet the Rex queen, Beecye Casanas, at the meeting of the courts, because she was one-fourth Jewish. Whether or not the story is true, there is no doubt that anti-Semitism, largely absent in the early days of Carnival, was now rampant. Carnival types themselves suggest that the Jews who came from France and Germany in the nineteenth century fit in well with the refined elements of New Orleans society, but that the World War I-era immigrants from Russia and elsewhere were of coarser stock. The later arrivals, moreover, are supposed to have been Orthodox and disapproving of the way their pre-decessors had assimilated. In any event, the old-line krewes be-came keenly anti-Semitic, in order, according to their apolo-gists, to avoid unseemly disputes within their ranks. It did not strike any of the krewemen as odd that the intelligentsia of an American city could still be fussing over who got to go to a masked ball, in part because New Orleans was largely un-touched by the rapid industrialization that elsewhere wiped out the social customs of the eighteenth century.

Parker had been a member of the Committee of Fifty ap-pointed by Mayor Shakspeare to investigate the assassination of Police Chief Hennessy in 1890; he had also been, at twenty-eight, the youngest signatory of the advertisement convening the mass meeting that led to the lynching of the Sicilians the next year. He was a parishioner of the First Presbyterian Church and said that he had learned "true Christianity" from its pastor, Rev. Benjamin Palmer, who gave the eulogy at Major Hearsey's funeral and had a reputation for saintliness despite his unswerv-ing faith in slavery.

Theodore Roosevelt described Parker as "a mighty good friend of mine," but could still show some impatience with the racial attitudes of the landed southern class. In a letter from the White House dated October 3, 1906, Roosevelt remonstrated with Parker: "If I catch your meaning, it is that the increase of rape, with its lawless avenging and the great unrest in the rela-tions of the races, are due to my having had Booker Washing-ton to dinner five years ago. Is not that statement of the case sufficient to show its absurdity? If not, then the absurdity would be sufficiently shown by the fact that highest number of rapes punished with lynching (and the great majority of rapes are so punished) occurred in the last years of Cleveland's adminis-tration and have steadily decreased up to the present year." In a postscript Roosevelt added that "practically every graduate of Tuskegee and Hampton and similar institutes is a worthy, law-abiding citizen who does all he can to make the rest of his people law-abiding and industrious." Parker ran unsuccessfully for governor of Louisiana in 1916 as a member of the Progressive Party established by Roosevelt four years earlier, but returned to the Democratic fold to win the election of 1920.

Among the delegates to the constitutional convention of 1921 was former governor Ruffin Pleasant, who proposed that the exclusion of the Negro could be accomplished by limiting the vote to the descendants of those "who inhabited the earth North of the twentieth degree of North latitude prior to October 12, 1492, when Columbus discovered America." That suggestion was rejected, the convention voting instead to require potential black voters to answer recherché questions on constitutional exegesis. Although this device was to prove useful for segregationists in the 1950s, it was rarely, if ever, used before then; Louisiana was effectively a one-party state and the Central Democratic Committee banned blacks from its primary elections.

Parker was, at least by the standards of his Bourbon predecessors, an active governor, introducing the state's first severance tax on oil and the beginnings of a highway system, for instance. Almost from the beginning of his administration, however, Parker was mauled by Long as a tool of the Standard Oil Company and mocked for his alleged need to be "daily and weekly told of his wonderful greatness and beautiful characteristics." In 1921 Long, on a complaint from Parker, was found guilty on two counts of criminal libel, given a suspended thirty-day jail sentence and fined a dollar. The judge in the case sought election a few months later for the state supreme court, but was defeated by a candidate put up by Long, whose work on the railroad commission, now renamed the public service commission, was making him a hero of the rural poor. Long by this time harbored gubernatorial aspirations of his own and ran for the job in 1924, Parker being constitutionally barred from seeking reelection. But Parker was active behind the scenes, according to Long, who called his two opponents in the election the "Parker Gold Dust Twins." Another of Long's favorite butts was the hostile New Orleans press. Among the directors of the *Times-Picayune*, he pointed out, was the wealthy and aristocratic lawyer, Esmond Phelps, who also represented such exploiters of the common man as Western Union and the Texas and Pacific Railroad. Phelps, son of Ashton Phelps, veteran of Liberty Place and former managing director of the *Picayune*, was also one of the leading lights of old-line Carnival, at a time when the krewes' control of city politics was at its zenith. Later, Long, who loved to ridicule his enemies by bestowing nicknames on them, observed: "Esmond Phelps never spent a dime for a shoe shine in his life. He uses Shinola and if he has none rubs his shoes on his pants' legs." For the rest of his life Phelps was known as "Shinola."

Long lost the election of 1924, but ran a strong third and was beginning to make uptown New Orleans nervous. Certainly he had an enemy for life in Parker, the only Comus ever elected governor of Louisiana. In Parker's last year as governor the state legislature adopted a statute allowing larger cities to mandate segregation in housing, which the New Orleans City Council did one week later when City Attorney T. Semmes Walmsley appointed a special prosecutor to enforce segregation. It was not a task that Walmsley was likely to find distasteful; he was the son of Sylvester Walmsley, now veteran captain of the Mistick Krewe, and grandson of Confederate senator and archsupremacist Thomas Semmes. A number of black households in New Orleans were bombed before the U. S. Supreme Court overturned the housing-segregation law in 1927.

Parker was the main speaker in 1924 at ceremonies marking the fiftieth anniversary of the Battle of Liberty Place, for which his namesake father, also a member of the Mistick Krewe, had signed the impassioned call to arms written by Dr. Bruns. The same year Parker refused a reprieve for six Sicilians sentenced to death for the murder of a store owner outside New Orleans. As one of the condemned men was led to the gallows, he remarked: "Governor Parker has now made it seventeen Italians—eleven lynched and six hanged." Parker returned to private life, operating his cotton factorage—one of the biggest in the country— and playing the country squire at a plantation he owned close to Henry Hearsey's birthplace.

Gubernatorial election returns in 1928 showed that Long trailed the other two candidates in New Orleans, but he enjoyed such overwhelming support in the rest of the state that he won easily. The city's elite despised Long for the blatant corruption of his administration and the deliberate coarseness of his manner, but feared, correctly, that he would use his formidable political skills and power to punish them. New Orleans was not, in any case, much to the taste of Long's impoverished constituency, particularly in the dour and Baptist northern regions of Louisiana, which seem scarcely part of the same planet as the easygoing Catholic south. In many parts of the state, New Orleans was synonymous with sin and dissolution. Long quickly set about fulfilling his campaign promises, paving country roads, providing schoolchildren with free textbooks, establishing old-age pensions and providing the poor with various other boons that they had never known under the laissez-faire policies of the old Bourbon oligarchy. That New Orleans was out of step with the new era became all the more apparent in its choice of a new mayor—T. Semmes Walmsley.

Around that time, too, Esmond Phelps was working as a volunteer attorney for a group of legislators preparing to have Long impeached in the state house of representatives. Both sides in the impeachment struggle tried to put improper pressure on representatives, as one of them, Lester Lautenschlaeger, told

Long's biographer, T. Harry Williams. Lautenschlaeger was awakened by a knock on his hotel room at four o'clock in the morning and found Long outside. Long asked him to vote against impeachment and offered "anything you want the rest of your life in politics" in return, but Lautenschlaeger replied that he would have to hear the evidence before making up his mind. That was enough for Long to sever his political ties with Lautenschlaeger, who, later that same morning, encountered Phelps in the lobby. Lautenschlaeger was backfield coach for the football team at Tulane, where Phelps was on the board of administrators. When Lautenschlaeger gave Phelps essentially the same answer he had given Long, he was told, "Unless we can count on you now, your position at Tulane is at stake." Lautenschlaeger was fired by telegram an hour later, and reinstated only when the other coaches threatened to resign.

The house of representatives did vote to impeach Long on eight counts, mostly involving bribery attempts or the misappropriation of public money, but he escaped trial in the senate when fifteen of its members, enough to force acquittal, were persuaded to sign a round-robin declaring that they would not vote to convict under any circumstances. In June of 1924, a month after Long had beaten the rap in the legislature, some 250 rich New Orleans conservatives gathered to plan a strategy to rid Louisiana of Long's baleful influence. They decided to call themselves the Constitutional League, elected former governor Parker as president and put a staff to work finding evidence of waste and nepotism in the Long administration. This was not exactly a daunting task, and the League soon filed a lawsuit to remove legislators appointed by Long to executive posts. The supreme court duly ruled that the appointments violated the separation-of-powers principle and ordered the legislators to give up their second jobs, but the Constitutional League otherwise barely caused a ripple. To an electorate inured to political corruption, dual office holding seemed a venial offense and, besides, Long, though abhorred by the Carnival crowd, was growing increasingly popular among the masses, as he was soon to prove at the ballot box.

T. Semmes Walmsley, who had been appointed mayor on the death of his predecessor, was elected to the post in 1930 when Long stayed out of the campaign. If a truce existed between the governor and the city aristocracy, however, it was to be short-lived. Long was planning a series of costly state bond issues, which many of the clubland conservatives in New Orleans opposed, in part because they did not trust him to handle the proceeds honestly. Prominent in the opposition was wealthy attorney Arthur Hammond, who was married to Esmond Phelps's sister Hilda and whose clients included both the local levee board and the port authority. Long, having himself been pilloried for the double-dipping he allowed in his administration, seized the opportunity to feign moral indignation that Hammond was breaking a state law forbidding anyone to draw two state salaries. Whether legal fees constituted salaries was not a point Long was inclined to dwell on, and he ordered Hammond fired by both the levee board and the dock board. Hilda Phelps Hammond promptly organized her upper-class friends to form the Louisiana Women's Association, dedicated to Long's removal from public life.

Long believed that Walmsley had promised to support the bond issues, but he now refused to do so, and received for his pains a lesson in the superior powers of the state. Long ordered New Orleans banks to call in loans they had made to the city against anticipated tax revenues, which he said had been overestimated. The state then refused to return the city's tax records after a routine review. The city was thus unable to send out tax bills until it secured a court order compelling return of the records, and, for a while, teetered on the verge of bankruptcy.

Walmsley described Long as a "cur" and a "madman." Long nicknamed the long-necked, balding and red-faced Walmsley "Turkey Head."

Long was the first governor since the Reconstruction Republicans not to receive an invitation to a New Orleans Carnival ball, a slight he evidently deeply resented. He responded in public speeches by suggesting that the city leadership's obsession with the frivolities of Mardi Gras were responsible for a decline in the fortunes of its maritime trade and had handed a golden opportunity to the go-getters of Houston. Long's celebrated slogan, "Every Man a King," which he had adopted from William Jennings Bryan's "Cross of Gold" speech, hardly applied to New Orleans during Carnival season, and he bristled at old-line snobbery. Local historians in New Orleans assert that Long wanted to abolish Mardi Gras, but there is no evidence of his trying to do so. In 1930, however, he apparently decided to make himself a rival attraction, booking into New Orleans's Roosevelt Hotel for the Carnival season. He dined with ex-president Calvin Coolidge and his wife, posing for press photographers and suggesting the caption "The ex-president of the United States and the future one." He told reporters that, Coolidge having revealed that the White House was in a state of disrepair, he would, once elected president, "tear it down and build another one." On Sunday morning, March 2— two days before Mardi Gras—two distinguished Germans had an appointment to pay their respects to the governor at the Roosevelt. One of them, Lothar von Arnauld de la Periere, was commander of the German cruiser, *Emden*, which was on a goodwill tour of the United States. The other was the consul in New Orleans, Rolf Jaegar. The commander, in dress uniform, and the consul, in formal attire, were shown into Long's suite, where they were startled to find him emerging from the bedroom wearing green pajamas, a red-and-blue robe and blue slippers. After the interview, Jaegar demanded an apology for the insult to his country, and Long was ferried out on Shrove Tuesday, properly dressed, to make amends aboard the *Emden*, de la Periere concluding that he was "a very interesting, intelligent and unusual person." The Polish Countess de Topar Lakopolanki, also in town for Mardi Gras, issued a statement in Long's defense, noting that other great men, including Mussolini, received visitors in "intimate garments." The analogy between Long and Mussolini, though it was to become a truism of uptown New Orleans, left Long unfazed. His only concern was how the folks back home in Winn Parish would react when they read in the papers that he had become sufficiently pretentious to sleep in pajamas. Many street maskers in New Orleans took to impersonating "Kingfish," as Long was nicknamed after a character in the radio show *Amos 'n' Andy*. Others donned crowns and royal robes and waved placards emblazoned "Every Man a King."

A few months after what the Carnival fraternity considered his typically loutish behavior during the 1930 season, Long was elected to the U. S. Senate, and even came close to carrying New Orleans, but delayed taking his seat until he could ensure that his control of Louisiana remained absolute. Parker's Constitutional League disbanded, and Mayor Walmsley, recognizing who was boss, made peace with Long again and praised him extravagantly, while the city's high society did its best to continue as though their dominance remained intact. Comus remained in Eng. lit. mode, doing "Jewels of Byron" in 1931, and preparing for its seventy-fifth anniversary the next year. Sylvester Walmsley, now krewe captain, planned to mark the occasion by giving participants in the 1932 ball copies of a history of Comus written, with his assistance, by Perry Young. Young, as editor of a magazine called *World Port* and PR man for the New Orleans Dock Board, came into contact with prominent citizens who belonged to the old-line krewes, and he was himself a member of Alexis, one of the more exclusive

Carnival organizations of the time. He also wrote the Comus programs. He completed *The Mistick Krewe: Chronicles of Comus and his Kin* in 1931, whereupon Sylvester Walmsley hauled off and died, leaving his replacement as captain, Charles Claiborne, to reject the book. Young established Carnival Press in 1933 to market *The Mistick Krewe*, but managed to sell only a thousand copies, although it is now regarded as the classic work on Carnival.

Senator-elect Huey Long worked hard in 1931 to ensure that his puppet, O. K. Allen, would win the upcoming gubernatorial election. He achieved for Allen a triumph that was nowhere more astonishing than in the New Orleans suburb of St. Bernard Parish, where returns showed that his total exceeded the number of registered voters. Not only that, but his rivals did not receive a single vote, although the local sheriff told Long beforehand that they would get "about two." The next time Long saw the sheriff, he asked, "What the hell happened to those two fellows?"

"They changed their minds at the last minute."

Long took his Senate seat in January of 1932, but he made no attempt to conceal his continued domination of state government through Allen and other surrogates. New Orleans remained a primary target of his venom, losing control of various city departments to the state and seeing many of its tax revenues removed by the legislature. Twice, at Long's behest, Allen declared martial law in New Orleans, although confrontations between national guardsmen and local police never produced any bloodshed. Walmsley did manage to win reelection as mayor in 1934 over a Long candidate, but that was the last gasp of the city's ruling caste for a long time.

Long was by now becoming a major player on the national stage, and planned to challenge Franklin Delano Roosevelt for the Democratic presidential nomination in 1936. His radical share-the-wealth notions had extended his popularity with the dispossessed far beyond Louisiana, while the president and others recognized a danger that the United States could fall under the sway of a fascist dictator. Plenty of people throughout Louisiana thought that any means would be justified to remove Long from public life, and chapters of the Square Deal Association sprang up in Baton Rouge, New Orleans and elsewhere. Although this time the planned insurgency was not the brainchild of New Orleans's Carnival elite, many of its members signed cards pledging their support and answered the call to assemble in Baton Rouge. Mayor Walmsley and ex-governor Parker belonged to the Square Deal Association, although neither seems to have taken up arms, while Hilda Phelps Hammond was prominent in its women's division.

The Square Deal Association proved a good deal less efficient than had Hays's Brigade in 1866, the White League in 1874 or the Comus lynch mob of 1891. In the evening of January 25, 1935, about three hundred Square Dealers took possession of the courthouse in East Baton Rouge Parish, where the Long machine had just fired all local government employees. Allen called out the National Guard, and by daybreak the Square Dealers had dispersed from the courthouse. But Long had a spy inside the Association, who swore it was bent on assassination and who apparently furnished a list of its members. Square Dealers promptly received brief telephone calls from anonymous voices instructing them to reassemble, armed, at the Baton Rouge airport. About a hundred of them fell into the trap, and the so-called "Battle of the Airport" was over as soon as five hundred state militiamen appeared on the scene and subdued the Square Dealers with tear gas. Some surrendered, and some escaped into the nearby woods; the only casualty occurred when one of the insurgents was wounded by an accidental shot fired by a comrade hastening to flee. Long subsequently called off hearings into the uprising, and nobody was indicted.

Perhaps the New Orleans contingent at the Battle of the Airport would have been larger had the Square Dealers not chosen to make their move in the middle of the Carnival season. The weeks leading up to Mardi Gras, which in 1935 fell on March 5, were growing more and more hectic with the emergence of new organizations, elite and otherwise. The old-line krewes were still the dominant street spectacle, although Momus did not parade from 1933 through 1937, limiting his activities to the annual tableau balls. Rex picked up a new supporting act in 1935, when he was followed for the first time by a parade of decorated trucks put on by the Krewe of Orleanians, an offshoot of the Elks organization. Krewes appeared in parts of town where organized Carnival parades had never been seen before—in Mid City and on the west bank of the Mississippi, for example. They all, regardless of place and social class, faithfully followed the formula laid down by the old line.

Huey Long was not finished with New Orleans, and soon contrived to strip Walmsley of all the powers of his office. He had his tame legislature pass bills transferring the powers of various local officials to the state and prohibiting the collection of taxes that accounted for two-thirds of the city's revenues. With the city almost on its knees, a majority of the commission council defected to Long, who now controlled political patronage in New Orleans. Walmsley at first resisted demands that he resign, but did so in 1936 after kicking his heels in an office that had become meaningless. Walmsley did have the satisfaction of remaining at least a figurehead mayor after Long was mortally wounded by an assassin on the evening of September 8, 1935, while walking a corridor in the towering state capitol he had built in 1931.

Long's death did not, however, restore high society's political control or produce government officials much more to its liking. New Orleans judge Richard Leche became governor, observing, "When I took the oath of office, I didn't take any vows of poverty." Good as his word, Leche conducted his administration with such venality that he was forced to resign after being indicted in 1939 and spent time in the penitentiary, being briefly succeeded in office by his lieutenant governor, Long's younger brother Earl. Walmsley's successor as mayor of New Orleans was an old friend of Huey Long named Robert Maestri, who, starting out as a supplier of various goods to the bordellos of Storyville, had amassed a large fortune. When Long was fighting off the impeachment threat in 1929, he told Maestri he wanted to argue his case in a series of circulars distributed statewide, but did not have the forty thousand dollars needed to pay for them. Brother Earl should travel to New Orleans the next day and would find the money waiting for him, Maestri replied. The white elite was not best pleased to be living under a mayor of Italian extraction.

Worse was the prospect that Earl Long might be elected to the governship he had inherited on Leche's resignation. A group of New Orleans's richest men gathered in Esmond Phelps's law office one day in 1939 and resolved to devote as much money and energy as were necessary to see that that did not happen. Jews and Gentiles united in the cause, for the prejudices of Carnival aristocrats did not spill over from the secret rites of the old-line krewes into the practical world. Thus Phelps and Monte Lemann, a famously brilliant Jewish lawyer, became joint leaders of the campaign to elect Sam Jones as governor. Jones, a lawyer from Lake Charles, started the campaign from a position of great obscurity, but the New Orleans committee helped raise large amounts of money and trumpeted the need for reform in state government. Long was defeated; Jones took office in 1940 and proceeded to correct many of the worst abuses that Huey Long had introduced. That Jones was indebted to the better class of people in New Orleans was under-scored when a member of the committee that had supported Jones's campaign, Charles Fenner, was made king of Carnival in 1941.

Around the time that the committee to elect Sam Jones was holding its first meetings, Perry Young, who had continued to turn out Carnival pamphlets since the debacle of *The Mistick Krewe*, published *The History of Mardi Gras and Carnival in New Orleans*. This was Young's last effort—he died in 1939—and encapsulates attitudes that subsequent generations of old-line maskers wish had never been committed to print. Young, evidently impressed with the liberal spirit of the Carnival season, noted that black maskers actually trod the same streets as "other shades that generally hold aloof from niggers." Young nevertheless had what he evidently thought were kind words for the black men hired by the old-line krewes:

> In the white parades no element is more essential, or more sin-cerely part and parcel, than the thousand or fifteen hundred black torch-bearers and muleherds, white-shrouded, cowled, that dance before the cars, between them, alongside, toiling, but dancing. They think that they belong and they earn the affilia-tion. A dollar apiece they get, or a dollar and a half, their way is long, the asphalt hard, the blazing torches hot and heavy—but they dance. Not for the dollar and a half—they do it for being part of the parade, a part that can't be done without, a part that cook and chambermaid, scrub-woman and black mammy, ad-mire as much as madame on the Avenue admires the masks that might be son and heir, lord and master, or fine and chosen true love.
>
> At the balls of society, who is more important in the dress-ing room? And who is blacker? At each masquerade are 50 or 100 or 150 of those humble servants buttoning lords, princes, clowns, barcarols, beasts, into the right costumes; pulling tights and breeches over old, fat, hairy, skinny, carnival legs; dripping

coffees, mixing drinks, shaving unshorn—looking through the peepholes at last to see the things that most white folks never get to see. What do these boys know of carnival? Very much more than you'll read in this book.

Young also echoed from the inside what visitors had been saying about the city for generations: "New Orleans hasn't the flamboyant culture of the eastern cities. It isn't booky, doesn't write books, doesn't read many. Its manners are easy, unaffected. Its English is faulty, its French nearly gone. But if it does not flaunt learnedness, it has an understanding of classic myth, of history, legend, romance, of opera, music, art, that would be hard to find in another population."

Young made no mention of the Square Deal Association, but was more inclined to hark back to the glory days when the Sicilians were massacred in 1891, which, he thought, spoke volumes about the character of the krewemen:

These men, practiced together in faith and loyalty, have done many things noble and fine that have naught to do with carnival except in their sworn comradeship. The sixty men, for instance, who, with shouldered arms, and undisguised, marched from Clay Statue to Parish Prison and exterminated the Mafia gang, were not the Mistick Krewe of Comus—but put your finger on the man of them who was not its member. They were Catholic, Protestant, Creole, Anglo Saxon, who read to the world possibly the most salutary lesson in Americanism that ever has been pronounced.

Americanism, or at least Young's brand of it, made no apologies for its anti-Semitism. Certainly, Young noted, Jews were excluded from all the elite nonparading organizations as well as from Comus, Momus and Proteus, but then they just didn't fit in. "The papers named a Jew as member of the first Momus Reception Committee," Young wrote, "not a Jew to be ashamed of, but the fact is denied now." Young thought it unlikely many Jews would want to go to Carnival feasts where pork or "souse, chitlings, fatty-bread, all of them unkoshered" might be served. "Bless the Jews," he concluded, "we couldn't be gentiles without them." Hermes, a businessmen's krewe that rolled for the first time on the night of the Friday before Mardi Gras in 1937, faithfully followed the old-line model except that it was even less inclined than Rex to hew to anti-Semitic custom. "It is understood that a king of Hermes was a Jew," Young noted, leaving his readers to draw their own conclusions.

As for black people, Young noted that they went masking on the same streets as whites, "mingling without race murders." Some of the old-line krewemen, however, were a bit much even for Young. The 1940 calendar, he noted, included "resuscitation of the old Carnival German by old carnival gentlemen of the old school; limit 100; price, $200 and a pedigree; objects and purposes, to outsnoot the snooty—and now *we* won't get invited." The German soon disappeared again, this time for good, and all Carnival celebrations were called off when the United States entered World War II. When the Japanese attacked Pearl Harbor, Esmond Phelps was preparing to reign as Comus on February 17, 1942. *Times-Picayune* readers, however, were confronted with the traditional notice:

To Ye Mistick Krewe—

Greetings!

Whereas, War has cast its gloom over our happy homes and care usurped the place where joy is wont to hold its sway. Now, therefore, do I deeply sympathizing with the general anxiety, deem it proper to withhold your Annual Festival in this goodly Crescent City and by this proclamation do command no assemblage of the

—Mistick Krewe—

Given under my hand this, the 14th day of December, 1941.

Comus

CHAPTER TEN

Krewes Come
Marching Home Again

The end of World War II found Esmond Phelps with a great deal on his plate. Socially, he was at the epicenter as Comus of 1946. Politically, he was in the thick of things, plotting the overthrow of the despised Mayor Maestri, who had elevated graft to a level that disgusted even the long-suffering inhabitants of New Orleans. The Mafia controlled much of the city's commerce, while prostitution and gambling flourished openly. Among the servicemen returning from the war who concluded that their efforts on behalf of foreign democracies merited a better version at home was deLesseps "Chep" Morrison, a dedicated anti-Longite, who, as a state representative before the war, had played a leading role in Sam Jones's gubernatorial campaign. Morrison had joined the army in 1942, won several medals for bravery in Europe and risen to the rank of colonel. Though born in the country town of New Roads, he was well accepted in New Orleans society, becoming a member of the Elves of Oberon. When the committee that had helped Jones win the governorship was revived and expanded, Morrison was the obvious candidate to support for mayor, and he eagerly accepted the offer. Jones himself campaigned hard for Morrison, and once again Jew and Gentile united in the name of reform. Among the new Anglo-Saxon members was Darwin Fenner, soon to become captain of Rex, whose father Charles had played a prominent role in the campaign to elect Sam

Jones. Jewish adherents included Edith Stern, whose father was Julius Rosenwald of Sears Roebuck, and her husband, Edgar. The Sterns, noted philanthropists and owners of New Orleans's first television station, had a habit of leaving town at Carnival to spare their Gentile friends the embarrassment associated with the season's mandatory ostracism.

Promising to rid the city of corruption, Morrison, with his youthful good looks and energy, seemed like a breath of fresh air. His campaign took off when his supporters, in order to draw attention to the deterioration of city services during Maestri's administration, fanned out at night, placing "Elect Morrison" signs in potholes and atop piles of garbage the sanitation department had failed to pick up. The next day city crews would scour the city, collecting the garbage, fixing the streets and removing the signs. Citizens quickly realized that all they had to do to get their own garbage picked up, or the streets in their neighborhood repaired, was to call Morrison headquarters and request a few signs. That was the end of Maestri's political career, and the old-line men could, for the first time in many years, view the political scene with satisfaction.

They were, however, annoyed with the black men who carried the flambeaux for their parades and who went on strike in 1946 seeking a raise from two dollars to five dollars. The demand was refused, and that year's night parades were unilluminated, although the flambeau-carriers did secure a more modest raise in time to resume their duties the next Mardi Gras, when another group of strikers, picketing a building in the central business district, donned masks and costumes for the occasion.

If the flambeau-carriers were back at work, things were not so rosy for the mule minders, known as "monkeyshines." The Carnival mules were borrowed from the city sanitation department, which was now switching to tractors and forcing the krewes to follow suit, so that monkeyshines disappeared from Carnival altogether around 1950. At the same time, new white

Flambeau bearers line up before the start of a parade. Photo courtesy of the Times-Picayune.

parading krewes were being formed apace, while prominent black citizens had Carnival get-togethers in such organizations as Your Friends midday dance, the Jug Buddies afternoon party and the Gaylords breakfast dance.

With Morrison's victory in the mayoral election, the Long faction seemed to have been finally defeated, and there was nothing to fear from the governor's mansion, now occupied by the country singer and songwriter Jimmie Davis, who succeeded Sam Jones in 1944. At least the mansion was occupied by Davis when he wasn't off in Hollywood making inferior movies. Davis, who was absent for three hundred days during his four years in office, once made a movie about a country singer who was elected governor of Louisiana, and the best known of his compositions, "You Are My Sunshine," was named state song. Davis did, however, dramatically increase spending on health, education and drainage, and, unlike his two predecessors, left a large budget surplus.

Louisiana voters, though they may suffer periodic fits of reformist zeal, have a limited tolerance for good government. The Jones and Davis administrations had committed the cardinal sin of Louisiana politics and left the voters somewhat bored, while Earl Long, as he put it, had "plenty of snap left in my garters." The prospect that the Long machine might be resurrected naturally filled the New Orleans ruling caste with horror, and Morrison threw all his weight behind Sam Jones's effort to regain the governorship. Morrison was by now something of a national figure, having been lionized in such magazines as *Time* and *Reader's Digest* for his whirlwind performance as mayor. New roads and overpasses appeared everywhere, city services were delivered with an efficiency rarely encountered in New Orleans government, and business at the port picked up dramatically thanks to Morrison's promotional efforts. His administration was, in fact, driven by patronage much as Maestri's had been, but he was more discreet, and neither the press nor the public doubted that he was a knight in shining armor. Morrison alleged that Long was on the take from the Mafia, as, indeed, later FBI investigations indicated was the case, but he couldn't make the charge stick. Long was, if anything, a more gifted demagogue than his brother Huey had been, and he set about exploiting rural distrust of New Orleans with harangues that were by turns devastating and hilarious. Long stumped the state for sixteen hours a day, with sound trucks moving ahead from town to town announcing his imminent arrival. He would jump out of his car, handing money to the local children and turkeys, hams, watermelons and beer to the adults. He wore shoes with holes in the soles, baggy trousers held up by suspenders, and cheap, gaudy shirts as he delivered a speech, without notes, emphasizing that he was the only candidate who could identify with the problems of poor country folk. In fact, his family was, by the standards of Winn Parish, fairly well off, but Long gave a masterful display as an earthy son of the soil taking on the pretentious and privileged classes. Jones he dismissed as "an educated fool, high-hat Sam, the high society kid who pumps perfume under his arm." Morrison, whose first name Long insisted on pronouncing "Dellasoups," was "smoother than a peeled onion." Long managed to impugn the integrity of another candidate in that governor's race, Judge Robert Kennon, by making fun of his extremely prominent ears. "Judge Kennon's got the best ears around," Long said. "He can stand in a courthouse in Ville Platte and hear a dollar bill drop in Opelousas."

For the first time in the twentieth century, the black vote had become a factor in Louisiana elections, thanks to a 1944 federal ruling that the whites-only Democratic primaries were unconstitutional. When that decision was handed down, 1,029 blacks were registered to vote in Louisiana; by 1948 the number had risen to 22,576. Long, when tossing coins to children on the campaign trail, had a rule: "a quarter for the white kids, a nickel for the niggers." Long won the election with some ease, and set about punishing Morrison by sponsoring legislation that reduced his mayoral powers and the city's tax revenues. It was a vindictive display that earned Long considerable obloquy in the national press. *Time*, for instance, observed: "Earl has aped his brother with the beetle-browed assiduousness of a vaudeville baboon learning to roller skate." When a delegation of prominent citizens went to Baton Rouge to complain about Long's anti-New Orleans campaign, he refused to see them, but had an aide write, in a letter to Esmond Phelps at the *Times-Picayune*: "Your little boy blue pretty boy deLesseps (debutante's delight) Morrison says he wants political peace, plus a bigger piece of taxes to spend and entertain Mr. Luce of Time magazine at the city's expense so they will write articles telling the nation how great little Cheppie is and how terrible

Governor Long is. Oh, give deLesseps more taxes to be a big shot, but don't give Governor Long anything to keep his promises to the people."

While Long's onslaught almost brought New Orleans to its knees, it was increasingly recognized, throughout the country and beyond, as the place to be during the Carnival season. Zulu pulled off a coup in 1949 when Louis Armstrong, then at the height of his powers as the greatest jazz trumpeter of them all, agreed to be its king notwithstanding the repugnance that black celebrities felt for the segregated South. Armstrong did indeed know what it means to miss New Orleans, where he was born in 1900, though not on the Fourth of July, as he claimed, but on August 4. Armstrong witnessed the early Zulu parades, learned to play the bugle as an inmate of the municipal Colored Waifs' Home and left for Chicago when the first opportunity to make the big time came along in 1922.

The year after Armstrong's visit, old-line Carnival was in a state of high excitement as it awaited the arrival of the most socially eminent guests to grace the season since the grand duke Alexis in 1872. The former King Edward VIII of England, now the Duke of Windsor, and his American-born Duchess, Wallis Simpson, decided they wanted to see Mardi Gras and asked some friends in New Orleans for an invitation. The Windsors' grasp of Carnival court conventions was not what it might have been, however, for the people they approached were Jewish. Informed that they would need the good offices of some Gentiles, the Windsors made the necessary contacts and duly appeared alongside Queen Mary Brooks Soule to watch the Rex parade from the balcony of the Boston Club. The Windsors returned Rex Reuben Brown's salute with considerably more warmth than the grand duke had managed at the inaugural parade and then slipped away for cocktails at the house where Confederate general Pierre Beauregard had lived in the French Quarter. After dinner at Antoine's, the Windsors were escorted to the municipal auditorium, where the Comus and Rex balls were in full swing, and an awkward question of etiquette arose. Tradition demands that gentlemen bow, and ladies curtsy, when presented to Carnival royalty, but whether a former king of England and his lady could be expected to knuckle under, nobody knew. In any event the duke and duchess paid Rex and Comus the usual honors, and the duchess remarked that it was "fabulous" and "such fun" to be in the company of three kings at the same time. A more un-American occasion could hardly be imagined, for, if a foreign title will get you into a Comus ball, service to the Republic may not. Bess and Harry Truman once came to town for Mardi Gras, but could not wangle an invitation to Comus; neither, later on, could Joan and Teddy Kennedy.

When Morrison won a lopsided victory over a Long-backed candidate in the New Orleans mayoral election of 1950, a more conciliatory mood set in. Long quickly restored the revenues he had taken away two years earlier, expanded the powers of the mayor and shepherded a bill through the legislature that gave New Orleans home rule. As subsequent events were to prove, however, he hated Morrison, and all he stood for, with undiminished passion. Stepping down after one term as governor in 1952, as the state constitution obliged him to, Long campaigned nonstop to get his job back when his successor, Kennon, completed his four years. Morrison was still enormously popular in New Orleans, the face of which he had changed dramatically with huge public works projects, including a new airport and a new bridge over the Mississippi. He was quite the man about town, too, hobnobbing with the Gabor sisters and other glamorous show-business types.

He was ubiquitous during the Carnival season, turning out for balls and parades galore. The parades, however, had become relatively drab, and the huge papier-mâché figures that had dominated earlier Carnivals had scarcely been seen since before

World War II. Rex captain Darwin Fenner decided to import some fresh ideas from Europe, and dispatched a young float painter named Blaine Kern to research Carnival floats there. Thus Carnival floats, having been designed and built in New Orleans since Comus's "Origin of Species" presentation in 1873, were once again imported as they had been in the early days. This time, however, they came not from France but from Italy and then Spain—outlandish figures in papier-mâché and, later, fiberglass. The European trips were the foundation of a flourishing business for Kern, who took to calling himself "Mr. Mardi Gras" and renting out floats of standard design that could be adapted to almost any theme.

Morrison decided to run for governor in 1955, encouraged by letters and telegrams from country politicians and a visit from two men with five thousand dollars each for his campaign fund. They were, in fact, all working for Long, who relished nothing more than the prospect of enticing the highfalutin mayor into the election campaign. "I'd rather beat Morrison than eat any blackberry or huckleberry pie my mother ever made," he explained. "Oh, how I'm praying for that stump-wormer to get in there. I want him to roll up them cuffs and get out that old little tuppy [toupee] and pull down them shades and make himself up. He's the easiest man to make a nut of I've ever seen in my life." Another candidate, the handsome Francis Grevemberg, Long noted, "looks better without makeup than Dellasoups 'Storytelling' Morrison does with it." Long, with a million dollars to spend on his campaign, half of it contributed by mobsters Carlos Marcello and Frank Costello, won a resounding victory.

The election returns galvanized the segregationists, who were already in a state of high dudgeon over the U. S. Supreme Court decision in the *Brown* v. *Topeka Board of Education* case two years earlier, which struck down the "separate but equal" doctrine in public education. Now it turned out that Long had

Comus raises his goblet during the parade of 1955. Photo courtesy of the Times-Picayune.

won, in part, because of his appeal to black voters, who numbered 161,410 and accounted for 15 percent of the total registered. Two-thirds of them went for Long, and the implications were obvious and alarming. Blacks had gradually increased their political participation since the whites-only primary was thrown out in 1944, and could now even affect the outcome of an election unless stern measures were taken. The man for the hour was state senator Willie Rainach, one of the most rabid racists in Louisiana public life, whose own home parish had more black residents than white. Rainach was chairman of a

joint legislative committee established just after the Brown decision "to maintain segregation of the races in all phases of our
life in accordance with the customs, traditions and law of our
state." Long promptly cut the committee's budget on taking
office, and he remained a staunch advocate of black voting
rights for the rest of his life. To Long, Rainach was a "little pin-
headed nut."

The legislative committee was not, however, the only string
to Rainach's bow, for he had also organized the Association of
Citizens' Councils of Louisiana, which was dedicated to purg-
ing black voters from the rolls by means of the understanding
clause adopted at the constitutional convention of 1921 but
held in abeyance ever since. The Association put out a pamphlet in 1956 entitled *Voter Qualification Laws in Louisiana—the
Key to Victory in the Segregation Struggle*, which was distributed
at state-sponsored meetings for registrars of voters and other
public officials. The Association's counsel, William Shaw, distributed twenty-five test cards to each of the registrars, while
Rainach reminded them that, when blacks voted during Reconstruction, the public schools had been integrated. A return
of that evil could be expected if blacks were allowed to vote in
large numbers. Rainach, as one registrar put it, "wanted me to
pull those hard cards on colored people." Blacks began to disappear from the rolls in large numbers, while white registration was barely affected.

While Rainach was conducting his voter purges, President
Eisenhower appointed John Minor Wisdom, the quintessential
New Orleans aristocrat, to the Fifth Circuit Court of Appeals
in 1957. Wisdom had grown up in the Carnival tradition and
was a member of the Rex court in 1929, the year of Comus's
alleged anti-Semitic snub. He lived in a splendid antebellum
mansion in the Garden District, and, in the year of his appointment to the federal bench, had demonstrated sufficient
stamina to ride in Comus, Momus, Proteus and Rex. He be-

longed to all the exclusive clubs, and was, for a time, president
of the Louisiana. Out of disgust with Huey Long in the 1930s
he had joined the Republican Party, an affiliation which his father, the White Leaguer and Liberty Place veteran Mortimer
Wisdom, could never have foreseen. For all the racist and violent strands in the history of the Carnival elite, John Minor
Wisdom emerged as one of the most instrumental forces in dismantling the apparatus of segregation in the southern states.
Although Wisdom took the bench three years after the *Brown*
case had been settled, it had had hardly any discernible effect,
for there was a catch in the Supreme Court's order—integration was to proceed with "all deliberate speed," which southern
officials had interpreted as a pretext for doing nothing. A handful of black children was admitted to white schools, but segregated public education was still the norm, as were such petty
indignities as separate drinking fountains and bus station waiting rooms for whites and blacks. Blacks were, for the most
part, denied the right to vote by the understanding clause. "In
those days," Wisdom once recalled, "blacks could not go to good
restaurants, they could not go to good hotels. There was a silent policy that they could not cross Rampart Street on Canal.
They had no swimming pools, no wading pools." Blacks were
discouraged from walking down Canal Street below Rampart
Street, because that was where all the leading stores were. In
fact, blacks were sometimes allowed to buy clothes in the Canal
Street stores, but could not try them on first, since no white
person would want to touch them afterwards.

The impetus for change came from Wisdom and three other
fifth circuit judges of liberal bent—Warren Jones of Texas, El-
bert Tuttle of Georgia and Richard Taylor Rives of Alabama.
Wisdom emerged as the intellectual dynamo of the group, writing scholarly and forthright opinions that established the principle of equality in public accommodations once and for all.
Almost his first act as a judge was to vacate a death sentence on

U.S. Fifth Circuit Court of Appeals Judge John Minor Wisdom,
son of a Battle of Liberty Place veteran and author of groundbreaking
civil-rights decisions, impersonates Andrew Jackson in 1990. The occasion was
a re-enactment of Jackson's return to New Orleans in 1840 to celebrate the
25th anniversary of his victory over the British. Photo by Darlene Hingle Olivo.

grounds that blacks had been excluded from the jury, as they had been from every jury in New Orleans since Reconstruction. Mayor Morrison, meanwhile, had managed to build up a reputation as a moderate in racial matters, although he had the press and public of the time hornswoggled; he was more than happy to exploit segregationist sentiment for his own political advancement, whereas his old enemy Earl Long took a principled stand against it. Each emerged in his true colors in 1959, when Morrison wrote to Leander Perez, the political boss of St. Bernard Parish and the only public official in Louisiana who might claim to hate blacks more than Rainach. "I am making substantial and rather definite plans to make the race for governor," Morrison informed Perez. "I would appreciate your support in getting Rainach, Trist and Howard to back me. With a united front, I am sure we can defeat Earl Long and return good government to Louisiana." In the end Rainach himself ran for governor with the support of Perez and the other ardent segregationists Morrison had named—Sheriff Nicholas Trist of St. Bernard Parish and Mayor W. L. Howard of Monroe. First, though, came the legislative session of 1959 and a series of furious clashes between Long and Rainach. That session attracted huge publicity nationwide, most of it tending to portray Long as a buffoon, droning on incoherently for hours, smoking cigarettes. Long was, indeed, a sick man at the time— he was committed to a mental institution shortly afterwards— and his demeanor was so bizarre, his mode of expression so earthy, that press accounts failed to note that he was the good guy in this debate. "You got to recognize that niggers is human beings," he told Rainach. "I plead with you in all candor. I'm a candidate for governor. If it hurts me, it will just have to hurt." Long's plans to run for governor, of course, depended on his finding a way around the constitutional prohibition on consecutive terms. The rumor was that he planned to resign before the end of his term, so that he would not be the incumbent when the election was held. In the event, he ran for lieutenant governor unsuccessfully, while Morrison ran first in the gubernatorial primary and a resurrected Jimmie Davis second. Long continued to deride Morrison, whose dapper appearance he contrasted with his own pea-patch clothing: "I see Dellasoups has been elected one of the ten best-dressed men in America," he said on the stump one day. "He has fifty-dollar neckties and four-hundred-dollar suits. Put a four-hundred-dollar suit on Uncle Earl—look like socks on a rooster." In the runoff, the segregationists decided that Morrison was too headstrong, and threw their support behind the more malleable Davis, who prevailed. Long ran for Congress and won, but dropped dead before he could take his seat. He may not have quite matched his brother Huey in malevolent brilliance, but Earl Long is remembered as at least his equal in Louisiana's peculiar style of demagoguery. Morrison, despite three attempts, always came up short in gubernatorial elections because he never got the hang of country politics, of finding ways to win the support of conflicting constituencies. Long was the master, explaining, "I know how to play craps. I know how to get in and out of Baptist churches and bet on horses." He knew how to be discreet, too: "Don't write anything you can phone. Don't phone anything you can talk face-to-face. Don't talk anything you can smile. Don't smile anything you can wink. And don't wink anything you can nod."

Davis took office only days before a deadline imposed by federal judge Skelly Wright for the Orleans Parish School Board to submit an integration plan. The Rainach faction called on Davis to fulfill his campaign to block integration, while the local school board defied Judge Wright, closed down the schools and asked Davis and the legislature to take over its responsibilities. The state appointed a committee, headed by state representative Pappy Triche, to take over the system and resist all attempts at integration. Triche, who was later to make public apologies for his role, managed to stave off the inevitable until

Krewes Come Marching Home Again

November while the legislature passed several laws asserting that the state, not Judge Wright, had authority over public education. Neither Morrison nor his society friends were inclined to become involved. The establishment remained silent, while Morrison only once suggested that the schools should reopen, made no attempt to lobby for compliance with the federal court order and frequently stated his own preference for racial segregation. Integration, when the state finally capitulated, came only on a token scale, with three black students transferring to one white school and one to another. Almost all the white children were withdrawn from the two schools, and the next day Rainach urged a crowd of five thousand white people to "bring the courts to their knees." Perez adjured them: "Don't wait for your daughter to be raped by these Congolese. Don't wait until the burr-heads are forced into your schools. Do something about it now." A mob marched to the school board office, where it was repelled with high-pressure hoses, and Morrison went on television to deplore violence and to reassure the public that the police department "has not and is not enforcing the federal court order relative to school integration." His concern, Morrison said, was that the disorder might damage "the image of New Orleans as a thriving center of commerce and industry." The result was further riots, albeit brief and with no deaths, although several were injured and about 250, mostly blacks, were arrested. The police did, in fact, turn out in force to supervise the first tentative steps towards integration of the public schools, although they connived at many acts of harassment. Still, though there was plenty of racial hatred in the air, public school integration arrived in New Orleans with less violence than was the case in other southern cities. There was enough of it, nevertheless, to slow down the city's economy, and the social and civic elite, led by a group of Carnival types that included Harry McCall and Darwin Fenner, finally bestirred itself with a radio, television and advertising campaign. The public gradually came to accept the token integration of its public schools and to acquiesce in the demands of Avery Alexander, Carl Galmon and other activists that blacks be allowed at lunch counters and other public places. Morrison resigned as mayor in 1961 on his appointment by President Kennedy as ambassador to the Organization of American States, and he died in a plane crash three years later. In the racist climate of the time, Zulu's burlesque tradition made many black citizens of New Orleans uneasy, and membership in the krewe dropped to eighty in 1961 after an advertisement in the *Times-Picayune* urged a boycott of the parade in 1961 and averred: "Zulu does not represent the Negro; rather it represents a warped picture of the Negro painted by segregationists and used by them to discriminate against us."

Morrison's replacement, Victor Schiro, was a bird of a much different feather, being not only of Sicilian descent but habitually displaying a propensity to malapropism and mangled syntax that would offend the ear of any old-line kreweman. In one of his most memorable pronouncements, during a hurricane scare, Schiro adjured citizens: "Don't believe any false rumors unless they come from City Hall." This was not a mayor the upper class could, or would want to, call its own.

Over at the court of appeals John Minor Wisdom was in the middle of a burst of judicial activity that struck deep into the fastidious heart of his class. In 1962 he wrote the famous opinion ordering the University of Mississippi to admit its first black student, James Meredith. "The case was tried below and argued here in the eerie atmosphere of never-never land," Wisdom wrote. However, "a full review of the record leads the court inescapably to the conclusion that from the moment the defendants discovered Meredith was a Negro, they engaged in a carefully calculated campaign of delay, harassment and masterly inactivity." Meredith, surrounded by federal marshals, walked onto the campus in one of the tensest and most violent scenes of the civil rights era. The next year, Wisdom tackled the voter registration law that Rainach had hoped would eventually lead to the disfranchisement of all blacks. Rainach's campaign had already had a great impact, Wisdom noted, and in twenty-one parishes where the interpretation tests had been administered only 8.6 percent of black adults remained on the rolls, compared with 66.1 percent of whites. Blacks had been purged wholesale, while whites had been left alone. Wisdom concluded, "A wall stands in Louisiana between registered voters and unregistered, eligible Negro voters. We hold: this wall, built to bar Negroes from access to the franchise, must come down."

Thanks to the ingenuity of local school boards and state legislatures in circumventing the Supreme Court order in the *Brown* case, the public schools of the southern states remained largely segregated. In Louisiana, Mississippi and Alabama, only 1 percent of black children attended school with whites in 1965, when Wisdom's court decided that the answer was affirmative action and busing. "The only school desegregation plan that meets constitutional standards is one that works," he wrote in an opinion that year. "The clock has ticked the last tick for tokenism and delay in the name of 'deliberate speed.'" The next year Wisdom's daughter was queen of Comus.

The whole time he was writing the opinions asserting the principle of equality in public accommodations, Wisdom would regularly be seen trotting off at lunchtime to the Louisiana Club for martinis and bridge just like any well-established member of New Orleans's white male elite. Although his judicial activism was hardly calculated to appeal to the other members, as several of them noted, upper-class solidarity was proof against any philosophical differences, and Wisdom has always said that his work never cost him a friend in clubland. The redneck element was not so forgiving, however, and Wisdom, who had a listed telephone number throughout the civil rights era, received frequent abusive calls in the middle of the night. Two of his dogs were poisoned and rattlesnakes tossed into his yard. He sees no contradiction between his championship of public integration and his membership in the most racially exclusive private organizations to be found anywhere, asserting that under the First Amendment "you can found a club for little green men, or for redheaded people only, if you want to."

In 1994 the federal appeals court building was named after Wisdom, who, at the age of eighty-nine, was still working there daily as a senior judge. Directly across the street from the courthouse is Lafayette Square, dominated by the same statue of Henry Clay that stood on Canal Street when Wisdom's father and the rest of the White Leaguers gathered around it before the Battle of Liberty Place in 1874. Wisdom, though slightly deaf and walking with a cane, remained as clear of eye and intellect as ever, and his short, slight figure could still be seen entering one or other of the gentlemen's clubs at lunchtime. He complained good-humoredly that everybody thought of him as a civil rights judge and paid no attention to his work in admiralty law and other fields, which he thought just as significant. He was something of a literary scholar, too, with a particularly acute appreciation of Shakespeare and Marlowe. When he was eighty-eight, Wisdom spent his summer break at festivals in Stratford-upon-Avon and Stratford, Ontario, and altogether showed no sign of any loss of intellectual curiosity or appetite for work as his ninetieth birthday approached. That a member of the Carnival class should turn out to possess a great legal mind is not, perhaps, surprising. But it required a preternatural deftness of touch for Wisdom to use that mind in the cause of civil rights without weakening the bond between himself and his fellow sons of cloistered privilege.

Around the time that Wisdom's daughter was queen of Comus, business and professional men not bred to high society were losing patience with what they regarded as the dull conservatism of Carnival. Rex had introduced Carnival doubloons in 1960, and pretty soon every krewe in town was throwing them, but that about exhausted the old line's powers of invention in that era. The season's appeal to tourists had evidently waned, too, for the hotels were little more than half full. The weekend before Mardi Gras was particularly desolate, with no parade on Saturday night or on Sunday. A young advertising salesman named Ed Muniz filled the Saturday night void in 1967 with the new krewe of Endymion, which started with 155 men on 16 borrowed floats from an unfashionable part of the city near the fairgrounds racetrack. The first Endymion was Jewish, the theme was the decidedly un-Comus-like "Take Me Out to the Ballgame," and riders determined to be more generous with throws than any other krewe, minting a hundred thousand gold-colored doubloons bearing the likeness of Babe Ruth. Endymion followed the old-line lead with a masked ball after the parade. By naming the krewe after the eternally young shepherd of Greek mythology, Muniz not only maintained the tradition of Carnival nomenclature but honored a horse on which he had just won a lot of money at the fairgrounds. In its second year, the krewe, with a respect for Huey Long not encountered uptown, decided to adapt his "Every Man a King" slogan to Carnival and henceforth to select the member who would impersonate Endymion by drawing lots.

Another group of business and professional men, also convinced that New Orleans had become an inhospitable place to outsiders during the events, decided to liven up the season. One evening in 1968, hoping to give the local economy more of a Carnival fillip, they met at the Garden District home of Adelaide Brennan, a member of one of New Orleans's best-known restaurant families, to form a new krewe that would apply for a permit to parade on the open Sunday night. The idea was to stage the mother of all parades, with bigger floats and more riders throwing more beads and doubloons than had ever been seen before. The affair would culminate, not with a ball at the municipal auditorium, but with a dinner-dance, open to all members and guests, at the city-owned convention center, the Rivergate. The krewe did follow convention by naming itself after a mythological god, but the choice was one that old-line Carnival was bound to take as an insult. The new krewe was called Bacchus, an appropriate choice since he was the Greek god of wine but a tactless one insofar as he was also the father of Comus. The krewe organizers resolved to invite a national celebrity to reign each year as Bacchus. The krewe rolled for the first time in 1969, the same year that Hughes Walmsley, son of the redoubtable Sylvester, was Rex. The masses, however, crammed the parade route to see Bacchus, in the person of Danny Kaye, defy all the old-line rules. For one thing, Bacchus I was a practicing Jew. Comus, Momus and Proteus, moreover, had courtiers to attend them, whereas Kaye used his own hands to heap huge quantities of throws on the crowds as the parade moved down Canal Street and past the Boston Club, where the reviewing stand on the sidewalk was empty and all the lights inside were dimmed. It was the same story for the next three men to reign as Bacchus—Raymond Burr, Jim Nabors and Phil Harris—but the establishment's curiosity overcame its snobbery in 1973, when the lights burned in honor of Bob Hope. It was more than the competitive spirit of Ed Muniz could endure, and he decided to outdo Bacchus with bigger parades and more showbiz stars riding in the parade and also performing afterwards at what he called an extravaganza, first in the Rivergate, later in the Superdome. In 1974 Doc Severinson of the *Tonight Show* became Endymion's first celebrity rider, and performed after the parade at the Rivergate along with Stan Kenton, Sam Butera and Frankie Mann.

With Morrison's departure from the mayor's office, the social establishment retreated further from the political struggles of the real world in favor of the more tasteful competition for preferment in the Carnival courts. One old-liner, Charles Smither, did sit in the state legislature for a spell in the 1960s, however, and the social establishment was not finished yet in mayoral politics, reasserting itself in the election of 1970 when one of its own, Ben C. Toledano, was a candidate. Toledano did not get the endorsement of high society, however, which opted for a state representative named Moon Landrieu, an erstwhile protégé of Chep Morrison but not by any means a man bred to the purple. Toledano, on the other hand, really was what many people in New Orleans pretend to be—a descendant of eighteenth-century Creole aristocrats. Louisiana genealogies include among Toledano's paternal forebears Louis XIV of France as well as early French and Spanish colonists. Toledano's mother was Beecye Casanas, the queen of Rex allegedly snubbed by Comus in 1929. Although his mother never confirmed the story to him, Toledano says he "would have been surprised if that hadn't happened to a little Jewish girl." Toledano says his establishment friends told him in 1970 that they had decided to support Landrieu because of his demonstrated knack for dealing with black people. "We need a buffer between us and the niggers" is how Toledano recalls the point being made. Landrieu, rolling in campaign money raised at the Boston Club, duly won the election, but remained beyond the pale socially, even though some of his upper-class sponsors tried to have him accepted. When someone took Landrieu backstage at the Comus ball, however, krewemen were incensed at the intrusion and one of them took a swing at him.

Louisiana's attempts to bring precision to the intractable problems of racial classification brought forth a new state statute in 1970 that, on its face, represented a slightly more liberal approach, superseding the ancient rule established by Louisiana courts that anyone with a "traceable amount" of black blood was officially a Negro. The legislature decreed that, henceforth, "In signifying race, a person having one-thirty-second or less of

Negro blood shall not be deemed, described or designated by any public official in the state of Louisiana as 'colored,' a 'mulatto,' a 'black,' a 'Negro,' a 'griffe,' an 'Afro-American,' a 'quadroon,' a 'mestizzo,' a 'colored person' or a 'person of color.'" Local government in New Orleans, and elsewhere, employed clerks responsible for altering birth certificates where people with more than a thirty-second admixture of black blood tried to pass themselves off as white. Appearances, of course, were no help to the clerks if, say, a citizen was black in the eyes of the law because only fifteen of his sixteen great-great-grandparents were Caucasian.

Since Landrieu, who was the last white mayor of New Orleans, public office has been generally left to people conspicuously short of social credentials. When the authentic voice of uptown was once again heard in the corridors of power, with Peggy Wilson's election to the council in 1984, it certainly came through loud and clear. But demographic trends had altered the face of city government and, for the most part, that voice might as well have been crying in the wilderness. Uptown money still had a role to play, and sometimes a decisive one, in elections for public office and even, on occasion and through the judicious use of clandestine persuasion, on some aspects of public policy. As the progress of Dorothy Mae Taylor's desegregation ordinance was to demonstrate, the Carnival elite was not quite a spent force politically, but it most assuredly no longer ran the city. Indeed, so far as most people were concerned, it was no longer even the leading force in Carnival itself.

The rise and gradual decline of the old-line krewes pretty well mirrored the fortunes of New Orleans itself. Comus was born as an unparalleled spectacle in a vibrant city that was the commercial queen of the South. When he disappeared from the streets, New Orleans had become a faded dowager trying desperately to regain her lost prestige while the taste of Carnival paradegoers had switched to the razzle-dazzle offered by a welter of upstart krewes. Yet, to connoisseurs of traditional Carnival, the few years before the withdrawal of the old-line krewes marked a return to the standards of yesteryear after a succession of parades that, if not exactly dull, fell somewhat short of the golden age.

By the mid-1970s, if float designers for the old-line krewes were a little short of flair, the social cachet of membership was undiminished. The code of silence was as rigid as ever, too, although Momus of 1974 was put under considerable pressure to break it. Shortly after he was wheeled out of the den to begin the parade, strapped firmly to his throne, the float caught fire. The flames spread while Momus struggled vainly with his buckles until a krewe lieutenant rode up in the nick of time and freed him. Firemen and police officers swarmed around the scene, and the near-victim was approached for purposes of an official report.

"What is your name, sir?"

"Momus."

"Your real name?"

"Momus."

The God of Mirth and Ridicule would not budge, although those who heard the exchanges say the frustrated officers of the law threatened arrest before finally leaving, still wondering who was that masked man.

The fire of 1974 caused more excitement than anything Momus had been doing lately with his parades, which were distinctly milksop in comparison with the early satirical efforts that had culminated in the mock flames of his Reconstruction-era "Dream of Hades." The uproar over that effort was so intense that Momus had given up political lampooning ever since. Now, however, the centennial of "Hades" was approaching, and

several members of the krewe felt that the time was ripe for a
return to the more robust commentary of yore. The Momus
captain approached Henri Schindler, most scholarly of New
Orleans Carnival historians, and asked whether he could come
up with some parade ideas that would "get us run out of town."
Schindler duly produced plans for a parade of floats poking fun
at various politicians and scandals. The face of the mayor, Moon
Landrieu, appeared in a huge blue crescent on a float named, of
course, "Blue Moon," dapper Louisiana governor Edwin Edwards was transformed into a dandy named "Breau Bummel,"
and a short-load scam in the grain industry was memorialized
as "Measure for Measure." The parade, as Momus tradition demanded, consisted of a mere fifteen floats, just enough to create
what Schindler called a "rolling cartoon" hitting the most egre-
gious local miscreants. Possibly the most keenly felt was the
float entitled "Wrecking Ball," which carried a gigantic image
of developer Louis Roussel, who had just razed the St. Charles
Hotel and replaced it with an office building. This was not the
same St. Charles Hotel so famed for opulence before and after
the Civil War; that one burned down in 1894. The replacement,
however, which featured a huge and ornate lobby, was a worthy
one, and many of the richer crowd thought Roussel a vandal.

With Momus reestablished in his proper role as the wiseacre
of Carnival, Schindler turned his attention to restoring Comus
to its classical tradition so that the last parade of the season
would pass in a succession of bold images and striking colors.
Like Momus, Comus and Proteus always kept their parades
short, at seventeen and twenty floats respectively, with few of
the marching bands and other distractions that so extended
some of the newer parades that they could take two hours or
more to pass. Watching an old-line parade was a brief pleasure,
but, to connoisseurs, the image of Comus rolling through the
streets stayed in the mind's eye. It was the greatest thrill of the
season, especially before the city council banned major parades

from the French Quarter in 1972 and Comus had to find another route to his ball at the municipal auditorium.

If the old-line krewes were as meticulous as ever in preserving their racial and social purity, the state legislature finally recognized in 1983 that statutory attempts to define the race of each citizen were futile and anachronistic. The absurdity of the one-thirty-second law was underscored when Susie Phipps, a fair-skinned woman who thought herself Caucasian, ordered a copy of her birth certificate and found to her astonishment that she was classified as black. She filed suit to change that, but the law stipulated birth certificates could be changed only if there was "no room for doubt" that they were wrong. A New Orleans judge ruled that Phipps, whose forebears, according to state attorneys, included a slave named Margarita, had failed to meet that standard. Although the legislature promptly repealed the statute, the effect was not retroactive; Phipps lost on appeal and remained black by law.

Comus, to the dwindling band of Carnival traditionalists, was reborn in his former splendor in 1988 when Schindler, after several years in a subsidiary role, was given full control of float design and construction. Rex, meanwhile, appointed him art director. Whether or not old-line krewes achieved wit or grace, however, was a matter of indifference to most parade-goers and to business and professional people excluded from the finest social circles. The last hurrah, before the Dorothy Mae Taylor ordinance drove the Mistick Krewe from the streets, was the 1991 parade, to which Schindler gave what he regarded as a theme long overdue in the hot and sticky environs of New Orleans—"Entomological Empire." It was not, perhaps, the theme Comus would have chosen had he known this was his valediction, for he would surely have preferred to depart with a flourish of English literature.

Schindler's timing could hardly have been more unfortunate; he was realizing his long-cherished ambition and starting to direct Carnival back to its classic roots just when the public taste had become too debased to notice and when angry forces were gathering to strike at the supremacist heart of the old line and force it into a modern, egalitarian mold.

Even before the U. S. Supreme Court upheld New York City's "facial" right to regulate private clubs in 1988, two New Orleans attorneys had approached the ACLU's Bill Quigley with a proposal that a lawsuit be filed challenging the right of segregated societies to parade on public streets and hold balls in public buildings. One of those attorneys was none other than Ben C. Toledano; the other was Joseph Bernstein, who had grown up with the uptown elite and felt the sting of its anti-Semitism. The assault on old-line Carnival was not, however, simply a matter of personal pique. Both Toledano and Bernstein argued passionately that New Orleans had been relegated to an economic backwater because businessmen, Jew and Gentile, black and white, had no desire to live where society shunned them and devoted its time and energy to debutante seasons, Carnival balls and ersatz royal courts. Toledano had been a famous traitor to the Carnival fraternity since January 1971, when, in the course of a speech delivered in Birmingham, Alabama, he averred, "Mardi Gras is probably one of the most depleting and wasteful things we have in New Orleans. In what other city do the men sit down and plan costumes, themes, color schemes and plumage? We in New Orleans do not clutter our minds with information; we are not an intellectual city. If you would look for intellectual activity, you would have to look for it in the Jewish community. They are the angels who support our cultural activities."

The obvious paradox here is that old-line Carnival parades frequently were cluttered with information and with obscure literary and classical allusions that did not suggest an aversion to intellectual pursuits. Visitors to New Orleans, moreover, had been commenting on its philistinism long before Comus's first,

ostentatiously erudite, parade. Still, there was no denying that
New Orleans was hardly a mecca for anyone seeking mental
stimulation, or that closed Carnival societies did tend to produce a self-absorbed and unadventurous cast of mind. The cultural effect was unfortunate, but the implications for the city's
social and economic life were disastrous. All those impressive
statistics about the money Carnival brought to the city meant
nothing compared to the cost of rejecting new people and ideas
and stifling the entrepreneurial spirit. New Orleans, at the end
of World War II, had every opportunity, as one of the world's
great seaports, to join in the bonanza that brought spectacular
progress to other parts of the United States. The first Morrison
administration developed an airport that was a natural gateway
to Central and South America. The establishment's Whitney
Bank was then the biggest in the South. Louisiana had an abun-
dance of minerals, and some of the most prolific fisheries and
fur trapping in the country. But Mardi Gras was back, and
New Orleans lapsed into its familiar torpor; a golden opportunity to reverse decades of decline was lost. The city's bankers
remained conservative to the point of timidity, and the oil
and gas companies went to Texas banks for loans. The airport,
hemmed in by swamps and Lake Pontchartrain, grew hardly at
all while national and international airlines sought out other
southern cities as hubs and New Orleans assumed it would be
futile to compete. Had Houston been so easily defeated by ge-
ography, its ship channel would probably never have been dug
to create a deep-water port that rivalled New Orleans itself.
New Orleans might have benefitted from the kind of new
blood that had helped its heady development before the Civil
War, but later generations were even more comfortable and hostile to outsiders than the Creoles of old. The mentality of the
closed and secret society suffused the city, which was determined to keep its distance from the land of opportunity. As
Toledano puts it, "Bankers lent money to two groups, those who

didn't need it and those who were fellow club members, persons of their own class"; in most instances the two groups were actually the same. Lawyers had their services engaged not by virtue of their talents but because of their associations, their social standings. So it was with insurance and financial services, a daisy chain of "our class."

Professional basketball and major league baseball teams, for instance, do not play in New Orleans, which Bernstein and others attribute partly to the narrow-mindedness, racism and anti-Semitism that hobble all commercial enterprise. New Orleans's pride is that it is unlike any other American city, which is also its undoing. Nobody takes a gloomier view of the city's prospects, or regards the social system with more disgust, than Toledano, now running a small law practice on the Mississippi Gulf Coast. Toledano finds the run-down condition of New Orleans so depressing that he visits only rarely and when he has no choice. "The old system worked much too well," he says. "In its intense efforts to keep people out, it cut off the supply of life to the community and now only mutilates the dead."

Toledano and Bernstein were still toying with the idea of filing suit when Dorothy Mae Taylor confided that it would be unnecessary, because she was reviving her plan to impose integration through council ordinance and would call a public hearing. Accordingly, the nervous old-line krewemen flocked to the city hall basement in December of 1991.

CHAPTER ELEVEN

Miserable Krewes

When the old-line krewemen filed out of the council meeting on passage of the desegregation ordinance in 1991, they could not have felt any gloomier if they had just lost the Civil War all over again. This, certainly, was not the peaceful and lily-white future envisaged by their defeated Confederate forebears. Several of them vowed that, rather than submit to meddling from city hall, they would abandon their parades and restrict their Carnival activities to private balls and parties. Within days the krewe of Hermes decided to call off its 1992 parade, but this was not regarded as a major blow to the season. Hermes was an all-white-male krewe, respectable but not top-drawer, and, having been around only since 1937, was still something of a parvenu. High society, meanwhile, was busy preparing for Christmas and New Year's festivities before the serious social whirl began on Twelfth Night, when the Revelers would crown as queen whichever debutante received the slice containing the traditional golden bean. At the first opportunity, however, the old parading krewes would have to meet and consider their response to the Taylor ordinance.

As soon as the ordinance passed, Comus officials told Schindler to suspend his preparations for the 1992 parade. Schindler had been toiling nightly in the krewe's den, one-third of a huge uptown warehouse owned jointly with Momus and Proteus, on a series of fantastic figures to illustrate the theme "Enchantments and Metamorphoses." It was a typical Comus effort, full of allusions to mythological characters that would escape almost every curbside spectator. Exquisitely fashioned, large-scale papier-mâché figures, including a few copied from the famous 1873 "Missing Links" effort, lined the warehouse aisles or stood on floats. The effect, with the glitter of gold leaf and the unnatural luster of theatrical paints, was dazzling, although everything would look much more subdued in a parade moving through the streets at night. Flambeaux lay scattered around century-old chassis in a scene that trumpeted the old line's distance from the everyday life of a modern American city.

Taylor was now the most hated public official in the city. It became a truism of white conversation that she was more of a racist and dictator than any old-line krewe captain and that she was prepared to destroy Mardi Gras out of pure ill nature and envy. She was mercilessly lampooned. T-shirts appeared all over the city bearing her picture and the legend "The Wench Who Stole Mardi Gras." She became the butt of the disk jockeys, while krewemen used their fax machines to distribute ribald cartoons on the ordinance. She was identified most often as "Queen of Rex," which struck the debutante class as very droll indeed. If Taylor was offended, she didn't show it.

The Knights of Momus, as they styled themselves, were doubly vulnerable to the ordinance because they also constituted the membership of the Louisiana Club, possibly the most exclusive in the city. Three days after Twelfth Night the members of Momus convened in their den to consider a response, but there was never any doubt about the outcome. The Knights' feelings were hurt. "You don't go where you're not wanted" was how several members summed up the consensus. The possibility that hoi polloi might not appreciate the nameless, masked men atop the Momus floats for their various contributions to the civic weal had not occurred to most of them.

Now, several Momus members asserted at the den meeting, parading would no longer be safe. In recent years, they had noticed a small, but militant, group of protesters in the parade crowds. The ordinance could only heighten racial tensions and expose krewe members to the threat of violence. Nobody suggested that the danger could be averted by changing the policy that restricted membership to upper-class white men. There was, in fact, no evidence that anyone planned to attack the krewes in mid-parade. It had never happened and, indeed, so many policemen congregated along the parade routes that assault would probably have been foolhardy. Given the high emotions of the Carnival debate, the possibility that someone in the crowd might try to inflict some bodily harm to a rider could not be ruled out—it never could—but the more honest members of the krewe conceded that the safety issue was a subterfuge. The Knights of Momus just did not wish to be forced into an association with blacks and would not sacrifice what they believed were their First Amendment rights for the sake of a parade. On January 11, a terse announcement was released: "Momus, son of Night, God of Mockery and Ridicule, regretfully and respectfully informs his friends, supporters and his public that he will not parade the streets of New Orleans on the Thursday evening before Shrove Tuesday, 1992, as he has customarily since 1872."

The loss, to connoisseurs of Carnival tradition, was a grievous one. Momus strove for a classy parade every year and, in common with the other old liners, would never dream of skimping on expenses by recycling and redecorating last year's floats, as was the practice with the newer and poorer krewes. Class, in Momus's case, did not mean any great visual splendor but an attempt to revive the wit and political satire for which the krewe was known in its earliest days. Momus had become a rolling commentary on current events. Its 1991 parade, for in-

stance, was entitled "Momus Brews a Toxic Brew," and featured floats with environmental and political themes. One, entitled "Iraq of Lamb," depicted the lamb of Kuwait about to be
basted with a barrel of oil, while another, "DuKKKe Soup,"
had David Duke in Klan robes being boiled in a pot by his political enemies—not, perhaps, the subtlest of sallies, but worth
a guffaw from a Carnival crowd. The cancelled Momus parade
was to have featured a float showing Taylor, a shovel in her
hand, next to a coffin labelled "Mardi Gras, 1992."

Since many members of Momus belonged to other old-line
krewes, the possibility of further cancellations had city officials
scurrying. Councilwoman Clarkson said she thought the krewes
had been "rudely treated" and wouldn't blame others for following Momus's lead, but added, somewhat unconvincingly,
that she hoped they wouldn't. Councilman Giarrusso and Mayor
Barthelemy both issued statements urging the krewes not to
act precipitately but to wait for the blue ribbon committee to
do its work. At Comus's den, the entreaties fell on deaf ears,
and the parade was cancelled January 15. "Comus finds Himself and His Mistick Krewe in a quandary as to whether or not
their annual parade will be either appreciated or indeed welcomed," the official statement explained. The same day, Rex
and twenty-two other krewes announced that they would go
ahead as normal for 1992. An obviously relieved Councilwoman Taylor took time out from a ceremony commemorating
the birthday of Martin Luther King, Jr., to praise those krewe
officials who were "really concerned about this city."

Four more krewes decided to go ahead with their parades,
but Proteus still hadn't taken a position. Anyone who thought
the furor might be dying down was quickly disabused. Public opinion polls commissioned by the news media found
that most citizens, black and white, opposed interference with
Mardi Gras and believed that forced integration was an inva-

sion of privacy. It was the same story in every one of the city's councilmanic districts, while both Taylor and Barthelemy had forfeited much of their popularity among all racial groups since setting their sights on Carnival. The blue ribbon committee, meanwhile, began working at frenetic speed. Half its members were appointed by the mayor and city council and half by the Mardi Gras coordinating committee; its makeup was hardly representative of the city's demographics. Bassich and Charbonnet were both on it, and white members outnumbered blacks two to one. The city council had contrived to entrust review of its ordinance to an overwhelmingly hostile crowd.

The political fallout had clearly rattled some members of the city council, though not Taylor, who dismissed the public opinion polls by observing, "If you would have polled the slaves during slavery, they would have liked the way it was. They didn't know any other way." Other council members, however, did not have such strong nerves. They began to consider ways of diluting the ordinance, which set a maximum sentence of five months in jail and a three-hundred-dollar fine for krewe and luncheon club officers convicted in municipal court of flouting Human Relations Commission desegregation orders. Clarkson first proposed eliminating jail terms and then, gathering steam, called on her fellow council members to exempt Carnival krewes from the ordinance or to repeal it. Giarrusso also announced that he favored exempting the krewes, as did a subcommittee of the blue ribbon committee. Wilson and Clarkson threatened to launch a petition to force a referendum on the issue if the council refused to go along. The ordinance also required krewes, as of Ash Wednesday, 1993, to prove to the commission that they did not discriminate before they could obtain parade licenses. Councilman Lambert Boissiere now proposed that it be amended to shift the burden of proof away from the krewes and require the commission to deny permits only after investigating complaints. All members of the council, except for Taylor, reported a barrage of phone calls opposing attempts to change Mardi Gras. Wilson took more calls than anyone else and found the issue had raised the temperature of city politics to an unprecedented level. For the first time in her political career, constituents were complaining about "niggers."

These developments put the city's black ministers in a fire-and-brimstone mood. They were a powerful political influence in the city, and did not hesitate to promote their agenda from the pulpit. Baptist pastor Zebadee Bridges, thundering veteran of civil rights campaigns, led the charge when thirty-five preachers summoned the press and issued a statement denouncing, and threatening, council members who might be tempted to backpedal. "If they reverse the vote, they'll hear from us at the polls. The black vote in this city is strong enough to elect anybody and if they want to be elected in this city, they're going to have to get the black vote," Bridges said. The burden of the ministers' statement was straightforward enough: "Discrimination based on race, creed or gender is plainly and simply wrong."

Less than two weeks earlier, Barthelemy had named the members of the blue ribbon committee on Carnival, and stressed that they were not to tamper with the antidiscrimination spirit of the ordinance. The committee's deadline was the end of 1992, but Barthelemy said he hoped that a report could be produced by the end of the summer.

The committee did much better than that. Its chairwoman, Joyce Eaves, was there ready to pass on the committee's recommendations when the city council met on February 6. Eaves, a black public relations consultant, who also chaired the Mardi Gras coordinating committee in conjunction with Bassich, briskly told the council that the committee had decided the krewes should not have to bear the burden of proving they did not discriminate in order to obtain city licenses. Jail terms should be removed. The committee had discussed exempting krewes from the ordinance altogether but had not made a decision.

Now Barthelemy strode to the podium to address the council. He was not widely credited with either courage or intellectual prowess, and nobody was shocked to find he had changed his tune considerably since unequivocally endorsing the ordinance in December. He said, "I want to commend the excellent work done by the blue ribbon committee. We need to end discrimination but we need to uphold the principle of cultural diversity." He went on, growing limper, "Heated discussions in recent weeks have threatened to divide the city against itself. The task before us is to get everyone to calm down—the city and the krewes. Let's have a happy Mardi Gras."

The white krewemen weren't much in evidence this time, although Harry McCall, who never missed a chance to champion the cause of the elite, was there to tell the council that he still hated the ordinance but thought the amendments improved it considerably. Schindler also turned up to argue against dismantling the traditions of Carnival, but found Taylor inclined to impugn his motives. As Schindler paused in his address to the council, Taylor pounced to remind everyone that he had a financial stake in the old-line krewes. "Are you a floatbuilder?"

Schindler, with a shrug and a half-smile, replied, "I was."

The most emotional testimony came from blacks scarred by past humiliations and anxious to secure a fairer deal for succeeding generations. "I was a caddy at Metairie Country Club but never played golf. I racked pins at Mid-City Bowling Lanes but never got to play until I graduated from college. I never had a record as a juvenile, but I was arrested when I got off the bus to take part in the lunch counter sit-in on Canal Street during the civil rights campaign," Harold Fontenette said. Attorney Henry Julien recalled that city government provided little recreation for blacks when he was growing up, adding, "I never learned to swim." Another black opponent of any dilution to the ordinance, who did not give his name, noted that "Ms. Clarkson's pet statement is that it is wrong to put krewe captains in jail while murderers are on the street. Crime is only a symptom of the problem, which is that white America has refused to let blacks into the economic mainstream." A wan and slender white man with long, stringy hair, Brad Ott, a member of one of the informal, satirical krewes that have taken to parading around the French Quarter in recent years, found the old-line night parades offensive. The black men hired to carry the flambeaux, he said, "look like lawn jockeys."

They were all whistling in the wind, for Taylor now stood alone on the council. She was determined to go down fighting, however, and she found in Julien a kindred spirit to inveigh against the appeasers. Taylor derided the proposal to shift the burden of proof away from the krewes as impractical. "When Momus made its announcement, it was just signed 'Momus.' Nobody knows who these people are. How do you know who to complain about if you don't require proof of nondiscrimination to get licenses?"

"Right," said Julien. "You have to get invited to join. If you're not invited, how can you prove discrimination?" Julien was no more inclined than Taylor to believe the public opinion polls. "Blacks are taught—I know I was taught—if asked how you feel about white folks, to say, 'I feel fine.'" But it was clear that Julien had long since unlearned that lesson. "We put vagrants and alcoholics in jail. Why not the rich and powerful?"

Taylor weighed in to complain that the removal of jail terms would constitute preferential treatment for krewe officials. "Five months in jail is the standard penalty for violating municipal ordinances. If you're drunk in public, if you sell tickets to a sports event for more than their face value, if you ride your bike too fast in Audubon Park, five months is the maximum. We keep hearing about putting krewe captains in jail, but the ordinance leaves penalties to the discretion of judges. This is just the same maximum sentence you get for any municipal violation. Is the unauthorized use of moveables a greater offense than racism?"

She added that Carnival float riders were already subject to five months in jail if, instead of throwing doubloons, beads and trinkets to the crowd, they resorted to more formidable missiles. "We have the prohibited-throws ordinance. They were already covered by this." Singleton obviously felt guilty about deserting the desegregation cause, but made it clear he was going to do so nevertheless, saying, "I am not happy with this, but we have to make the best we can of the circumstances. We need to enjoy Carnival without the tensions we have experienced in the last few weeks." Wilson saw no need for further discussion—"Let's vote and put this to bed"—but Taylor needed to register one last protest. She was miffed that the committee had acted so quickly that there had been no "time for public and council contributions" to its deliberations. But, most of all, she was offended because she thought her colleagues had abandoned principle. "It is unfair to play favorites with one class of people. To say take out criminal penalties because these are krewe captains makes no sense to me. This is right and just. Mardi Gras should be open to all."

Her colleagues voted to adopt the amendments that diluted the ordinance, and the council broke for lunch. Joe Giarrusso and Peggy Wilson did not return after the recess, and Johnny Jackson asked if he could change his vote. When his colleagues refused, Jackson left in a huff and the meeting came to an end for want of a quorum.

Five days later, Bassich summoned the members of Proteus

to the krewe den and announced that, in view of the changes made to the ordinance, the krewe's executive board had recommended that the 1992 parade go ahead. Members voted overwhelmingly to do so, and cheered heartily. Bassich then announced the decision to a crowd of reporters outside the den by sliding back a metal door to reveal the king's float draped with a banner declaring "Proteus Rides in '92." Comus and Momus remained adamant that they had done parading forever. Indeed, Comus went further, announcing that, not only would there be no parade, but that uncertainties over the effect of the Taylor ordinance made it necessary to cancel television coverage of the meeting of the courts. If the gesture was meant to make the citizenry feel deprived, it backfired, since most people found the spectacle absurd and stultifying. A dedicated minority did tune in every Mardi Gras night to watch the posturing of their social betters, but what had been a fascinating glimpse of a forbidden world when the cameras were first admitted in 1953 now came across as a drab sideshow.

At the next meeting of the council, Jackson managed to have the desegregation ordinance brought up for reconsideration over the strong objections of Wilson and Clarkson. Jackson apologized to anyone inconvenienced by his abrupt departure of the previous week, but pointed out that he was not the only offender. "Councilwoman Wilson was here, too, but left to go"—he paused for a few seconds—"to a Mardi Gras ball." Wilson insisted that the ordinance could not be reconsidered if Barthelemy had signed it into law, and repeatedly asked council clerk, Emma Williams, if he had done so. "The clerk does not have the ordinance," Taylor snapped. Wilson continued to press Williams, whereupon Taylor exploded, "I've answered for her. I am chairing the meeting."

Clarkson threw up her hands. "This is insane." As it turned out, none of the discussion made any difference, since, when the vote was taken, Jackson was the only one to change sides. "I just want to get on with the meeting and leave this insanity behind," Clarkson said. Taylor leaned forward to her microphone. "We never had the insanity until you got on the c uncil. We never heard the word 'insanity' until you got here."

Mardi Gras went off without any mishap in the city, although a couple of racial clashes were reported in the suburbs. A black brass band from a New Orleans high school marching in a parade in Slidell was attacked by a white mob yelling, "Go back to nigger land," and "You're not from New Orleans; you're from Africa." Taylor's patience finally ran out when the Krewe of Okeanos, parading ten days before Mardi Gras, displayed her picture with the red circle and diagonal slash that signify "No." She fired off a letter to the Mardi Gras coordinating committee complaining that Okeanos had violated an ordinance that prohibits electioneering during parades. No action was taken. A few white street maskers expressed their displeasure at the desegregation ordinance by carrying signs with such racist legends as "I has a dream." Another read "Someone stinks in City Council."

To most people in New Orleans the Carnival season culminating on March 3 seemed much the same as usual. Local bakeries did their usual brisk business in king cakes, sticky confections containing not a golden bean but a tiny plastic baby. (King cakes, together with beads, doubloons and other seasonal items are nowadays advertised on the Internet and mailed to distant Carnival devotees, while, in New Orleans, modern workplace custom requires the recipient of the baby to buy the next cake.) On the streets parade after parade moved through huge, noisy crowds of locals and tourists yelling "Throw me something, mister" to the float riders. Most people hung strings of beads they caught around their necks. Here and there young women bared their breasts to attract throws. Children, many perched atop ladders, strained to snatch gewgaws from the air, while their elders drank beer and ate po-boys. Down in the French Quarter maskers roamed the packed streets, and bare flesh was, as usual, a common sight. The barrooms were packed to the rafters. But the difference was certainly noticeable on the Thursday before Shrove Tuesday at Gallier Hall, where guests at the mayor's annual Mardi Gras ball had always walked outside to take their seats on the reviewing stand when Momus approached. Barthelemy had decided not to reschedule the ball to an evening when another parade was due to pass, although many of his guests felt the occasion greatly reduced.

Mardi Gras morning found Wilson, dressed as an equestrian, strolling down St. Charles Avenue, the oak-lined principal uptown thoroughfare. Taylor was a few blocks away, watching the parades with her grandchildren. Other council members went masking and watched the parades pass Gallier Hall that morning. The morning went off pretty well as usual, beginning with Zulu, who, in keeping with tradition, hauled up in a boat at 6:30 A.M. and led his parade of grass-skirted subjects distributing coconuts to selected spectators, for these are the season's most coveted street prize. Weeks in advance, the men of Zulu haul sacks of coconuts from the city's French Market, shave off the hair and apply an undercoat of gold paint. Wives, sisters and girlfriends paint faces on them, adding a Z and the year of the parade, and finish them off with a sprinkle of multicolored glitter. Rex followed immediately after Zulu, pausing to toast his queen, though not at the traditional spot outside the Boston Club. Now Her Majesty awaited her sovereign at the Intercontinental Hotel.

If Mardi Gras morning left nothing to be desired, the same could not be said of the night without Comus. To the connoisseurs of Carnival the loss of Comus and Momus meant a further drop in the season's already diminished intellectual and aesthetic stock. For some, Mardi Gras night would never be the

*Mardi Gras Indian Spy Boy Thomas Dean of the Seminoles, Mardi Gras 1992.
Photo by Norman J. Berteaux/Times-Picayune.*

same without the understated elegance of Comus, and the bigger, gaudier, plastic-ridden floats of modern vintage were scant consolation.

Taylor thought the changes to Mardi Gras were by no means enough, and, though she had been beaten back to some extent,

233

she was not finished yet. Come Lent, she was determined to put some teeth back into the desegregation ordinance. Wilson was equally determined to scuttle the whole initiative.

City workers were busy removing the usual tons of trash left on the streets by paradegoers when Ash Wednesday of 1992 dawned, and Peggy Wilson arose, ready to join battle once again with Dorothy Mae Taylor.

Wilson was born a Henican, one of the most familiar names in the uptown pantheon, and was married to a prominent Republican lawyer who, so long as George Bush remained in the White House, had hopes of a federal judgeship. While Ronald Reagan was president, Gordon Wilson had resigned from the Boston and Louisiana clubs to preempt allegations of racial prejudice during U. S. Senate hearings should he be nominated. Peggy Wilson, representing the only district in New Orleans with a majority of white voters, planned to ask her colleagues on the city council, at their meeting the next day, March 5, to repeal the desegregation ordinance. She was also to suggest that the council call a referendum on the question of whether city government should be barred from regulating Carnival krewes altogether. Wilson cheerfully conceded she had no chance of success with either measure, but she had thwarted the will of the council majority before by getting up the petition to force the referendum limiting councilmanic terms. She was confident she could do the same again with the Carnival ordinance, and Clarkson was ready to help. The telephone calls from outraged constituents were still coming, and Wilson had by now logged several hundred. Never before had she encountered such passion from the public on any council ordinance.

Taylor appeared at the council meeting looking as unrattled and determined as ever. Even her detractors conceded that there was much to admire in the way she stuck to her guns. Giarrusso was not present, leaving Taylor at one extreme of the

debate, Wilson and Clarkson at the other, and Boissiere, Singleton and Jackson ruing the day they had ever decided to fool
with Mardi Gras. Wilson introduced her ordinance calling for a
November referendum, claiming that the opinion polls and the
barrage of letters and phone calls to members of the council
proved that the citizenry was anxious to be heard. "We have an
opportunity to completely defuse the issue, to abide by the
wishes of the public." When Boissiere suggested that the council refer the question to the blue ribbon committee, Wilson delivered her expected threat: "To the credit of our citizens, we've
had a successful and peaceful Carnival season. It's now time to
give those citizens a chance to decide the issue. If the council
won't call a referendum, we will proceed with a petition drive,
as of today." Singleton, visibly offended, reminded Wilson that
the council had voted unanimously to establish the committee
she now intended to bypass. "Are we at the point where we're
going to do everything by referendum? We all agreed to the
process. Now every time we meet, someone wants to change it.
There's been tension, from lots of different sides, and now we
seem to be prolonging it beyond the point where it's necessary.
We ought to conduct our affairs in a more dignified manner."

But neither Taylor nor Wilson was in the mood to conceal
animosity for the sake of greater dignity or anything else.
Taylor even tried to suggest that Wilson, having voted at the
earlier meeting for the watered-down version of the desegregation ordinance, was now wilting. "If the political pressures, the
surveys and the polls caused some people to step back and
change their position, that's their right to do so," Taylor said,
her voice heavy with disgust, "but this issue was aired loud and
long enough for any intelligent person to understand what
they were voting on." Wilson was not about to let anyone ac-
cuse her of temporizing on this of all issues. "Everybody knows
we voted for the compromise because it was better than the al-

ternative. Everybody knows we voted for the lesser of two evils. Perhaps it's because we're less intelligent than the rest of the council, but you'll just have to live with our limitations."

Further debate was pointless, because it was obvious that most of the council wanted to buy time by tabling Wilson's referendum ordinance and referring it to the committee. Wilson withdrew her second ordinance, exempting krewes altogether, when her colleagues gave the blue ribbon committee sixty days to come up with its recommendations. They were just asking for trouble. The committee's performance thus far hardly suggested it would seek more effective ways to enforce desegregation, while political analysts were confident Wilson could collect the ten thousand signatures she needed on her petition.

When the committee met the following Monday, several of its members made no secret of their desire to gut the desegregation ordinance even further. One of its members, Charles Andrews, captain of the white Krewe of Sparta, threatened that his and other parades for 1993 would be cancelled if uncertainty over the reach of the ordinance were to persist. Diane Buras, captain of the mixed-gender but predominantly female Krewe of Pandora, spoke for several other members of the committee when she urged that Carnival organizations should not be covered by any public accommodations law: "If they are going to legislate our social life, you really have a serious problem." Bryan Wagner, a prominent Republican and Wilson's predecessor on the city council, announced that the committee would once again work at breakneck speed and prepare a revised ordinance for council consideration by April 27. Over the next few weeks, the committee went through the motions of public hearings, at which a majority of speakers, including that year's Rex, B. Temple Brown, urged that the krewes be left alone. Brown, owner of a dairy-products firm, thought that integration would come naturally and could be entrusted to "the new generation coming up." Barthelemy, meanwhile, was doing all he could to mollify the krewes without amending them out of the desegregation ordinance. He was desperate to avoid a referendum, and complained to aides that he was being distracted from the other problems that beset New Orleans, such as rampant crime, unemployment, and illiteracy, which made the integration of Carnival krewes seem of minor import. Members of his administration held a series of meetings with Carnival bigwigs and came up with the idea that krewes should be spared investigation by the Human Relations Commission if they would just pledge in writing not to discriminate.

Wilson was charging ahead with her petition and had collected sixty-five hundred signatures before March was out. Her success alarmed not just the political class but also the business establishment, which included many leading lights of Carnival. If, as now seemed certain, the Taylor ordinance was to be defanged, the city's top executives saw no point in holding a referendum that could stir up racial hostilities, scare off tourists and otherwise disrupt the city's already sick economy. On March 30, therefore, Wilson was invited to the office of Robert Howson, chairman of the board at McDermott Inc. and head of the New Orleans Business Council.

Wilson knew she was going to be asked to abandon her petition drive. Several local plutocrats, including John Charbonnet, former Rex and owner of a construction company, had already asked her to do so, but when she walked into Howson's office she was confronted by twenty of the most powerful men in the city. The group included, in addition to Charbonnet, four former Rexes—lawyer George Denegre, shipping executive Erik Johnsen, awning manufacturer Brooke Duncan and coffee-company owner Boatner Reily. The honor of being named Rex had for years been reserved for prominent citizens with a background of civic and philanthropic work, whereas in the other old-line krewes social position and breeding remained the principal criteria. This was not, therefore, a change of heart by Carnival traditionalists so much as a pragmatic move by businessmen with interests to protect. Oil, insurance and banking company presidents were there, together with two of New Orleans's most successful black businessmen, real estate broker Jim Thorns and banker Alden McDonald. The only politician in the group, also black, was Ken Carter, one of the city's seven elected property tax assessors and a close friend of city councilman Jim Singleton. It was, for Wilson, an intimidating confrontation, but if the men thought that Wilson would buckle under or yield to entreaty, they were in for a surprise. They took turns pointing out that the Carnival issue had already created a highly charged atmosphere in the city and that a referendum could only arouse further hostilities and lead to a "bloodbath." If the referendum succeeded, and the council's powers were circumscribed, moreover, protracted litigation was sure to ensue. Carnival of 1993 might well be in jeopardy if the city were to be dragged down into racial conflict. Every man in the room wanted Wilson to call off her petition drive, or not to turn in the signatures she collected for authentification by the registrar of voters. She refused point-blank, telling the men that the petition drive now had a life of its own and involved so many people that she was powerless to stop it. Not to turn in the signatures would be a breach of faith with the people. She added that she was tired of being threatened with a "bloodbath" every time a dispute with racial connotations arose. It was an insult to black people, she said, to suggest that they would riot if they lost a political argument. Most of them were on her side, in any case. She would be willing to consider whatever the blue ribbon committee recommended, but was making no commitments. With that, the room went silent and she took her leave.

The blue ribbon committee was still considering whether to

recommend to the council that the krewes be exempted from city regulation, but it finally stopped short, although only just. A couple of weeks before its self-imposed deadline, the committee, after lengthy consultation with Barthelemy aides, came up with its draft of an amended ordinance that was ludicrously feeble, purporting to promote integration in the krewes but providing no means of enforcement whatsoever. Abandoned altogether was the idea of prohibiting gender discrimination or exclusion of homosexuals. This, however, was not a contentious issue within the Carnival fraternity, since almost everybody preferred single-sex krewes. Various krewemen at the blue ribbon committee hearings had pointed out the practical problems of, say, admitting women to a krewe of dedicated beer drinkers who would be miffed to find the port-o-lets on the floats occupied for lengthy periods during the parades. Homosexuals had established their own flamboyant parades, and were not pushing to be admitted to the ranks of the straight krewes.

The committee had approached its supposed task of promoting racial integration with a rare cynicism. It proposed that, in order to secure parade permits, krewes would need merely to produce a letter certifying that they had no written discrimination policies. In the event of a complaint against a krewe for alleged discrimination, a similar letter would be regarded as proof of innocence and the Human Relations Commission would be barred from investigating. No krewe, of course, had ever reduced its segregation policies to writing; there was no need to do so, when everyone knew the score.

Black leaders were incensed, and council members clearly had to restore some semblance of teeth to the law. When the council convened May 7, therefore, the city attorney's office had drafted a couple of further amendments requiring the krewes to declare by affidavit that they had no discrimination policies, written or unwritten, and would give equal consideration to all potential members. Even here, though, the requirement was not absolute since the krewes were to seek integration "pursuant to their own by-laws." In old-line krewes, where admission was by invitation and any nominee could be blackballed without explanation, this seemed to leave a loophole for the bigots. Krewe officers would be under pressure to be truthful, however, since the affidavit requirement would leave them liable to prosecution for perjury if they weren't.

Taylor opened proceedings with a brief tongue-lashing for Eaves and the chairman of her civil rights subcommittee, Earl Jackson, a leading player in black Creole Carnival circles. "I feel because you were so heavily weighted with people who favored continuing discrimination, you could not give us proper consideration," Taylor observed as she dismissed them. Before a vote was taken on the latest version of the ordinance, the usual speakers were wheeled out to make their views known. The mayor began proceedings with his familiar impersonation of a Creole Pangloss: "We have reached a historic announcement to end the heated debate and divisive argument of recent weeks. We have shown that we of the government process, we of different ethnic backgounds, can resolve a very difficult issue. We hope that Mardi Gras will be open and everyone can participate. Mardi Gras of 1993 will be an integrated Mardi Gras."

Charbonnet took a similar line, although making it clear that he wanted the krewes to take the credit for any liberalization of Carnival and wanted the council to adopt the ordinance as the blue ribbon committee had drafted it. "Rex supports the recommendations of the committee. I believe in 1993 there will be significant integration by the krewes and I believe Rex will be one of them. We have a statement signed by several, but not all, the parading krewes pledging that we will seek to become racially and ethnically inclusive in membership. This is a free and voluntary decision made not because of the force of law but because krewes recognize it is good for the city—for the public good." Charbonnet paused lest anyone should fail to

catch that he had just quoted the Rex motto, *Pro Bono Publico.*
He continued, "Let us put this to rest so that we can plan for
the 1993 Mardi Gras. It would serve no good purpose to proceed with more amendments. I also suggest that those well-
intentioned people who signed the petition for a referendum
let the blue ribbon committee do its work so that we can see if
Mardi Gras can survive without the intrusion of government
directing it."

Taylor looked grim. "I was waiting for the statement coming from the representatives of the krewes."

"I believe you will see in the 1993 Mardi Gras significant integration of the krewes."

"Wasn't there supposed to be a statement read aloud?"

Charbonnet could not wriggle out of it. That morning he
had been closeted across the hall from the council chamber with
Barthelemy, assessor Ken Carter and a couple of mayoral aides
to hammer out a statement pledging to end discrimination.
Taylor had insisted on reviewing and approving it before she
would vote for any further dilution of her ordinance, and now
she wanted from the krewes a public acknowledgment of their
sins. In fact, only five krewes joined Rex in endorsing the statement, which hardly amounted to a dramatic mea culpa. The
krewes did, however, promise, "beginning in 1993, to seek to
become racially and ethnically inclusive in their membership
policies and not to discriminate on the basis of race, color, creed
or religion." Among those not signing was the Zulu Social Aid
and Pleasure Club. Its secretary, Philip Baptiste, pointed out
that the parades sponsored by his organization had for years
accepted white riders. Zulu believed the council should have
stuck with the ordinance as Taylor first introduced it.

Baptiste's manner had been of the mildest, but there was no
such restraint from the next opponent of any concessions to the
segregationists. The tall and beefy figure of Carl Galmon, now
in his fifties, gray-haired but as fiercely devoted to civil rights

as ever, advanced to the microphone, identified himself as spokesman for an organization called the Louisiana Committee against Apartheid, and unleashed his fury. "This is nothing but a sham. If you were serious, you would have maintained the original ordinance.

"If you want a sham, the first thing you do is appoint a sham committee. Not one person on this committee has ever been involved in civil rights. Nobody on this committee has ever supported us in our struggle. Rex came out of the Boston Club which was organized in 1841 by slave owners and slave traders. How can you expect them to do anything about the discrimination they have been practicing for a hundred years? They didn't change in 1964, when the Civil Rights Act was passed, so why should they change now because of some ordinance? Two percent of the population owns 60 percent of the business in New Orleans. Tourism is totally controlled by whites. If you're not making any money off Carnival, what are you worried about?" Galmon held up pictures of what he said were forty martyrs in the civil rights cause. "Blacks have died so that we could have a black-majority council, could elect blacks to the council. If they had wimped out and sold out like I see you doing today, it would never have happened. We don't need Uncle Toms on the committee voting to keep the status quo."

Galmon's words stung nobody more than Ben Edwards, one of the committee's black minority and Taylor's appointee. Edwards said he and others had ensured there were not enough votes on the committee to exempt krewes from the ordinance, but he had joined the rest in recommending the amendments submitted to the council. He now regretted it deeply. "After further consideration, I recognize that the compromise is not in the best interests of the city. We failed to address the mayor's charge not to interfere with the nondiscrimination spirit of the ordinance. We were given 330 days to do what was right and create opportunities for everyone. We took 71 days to do otherwise."

Eddie Jordan, speaking for the Martinet Society, a black lawyers' organization, urged the council to stick with the ordinance as originally passed, and a few others did the same before Harry McCall strode up to restate his freedom-of-association case. "I urge you to adopt the amendments, to amend the ordinance entirely. It is fatally flawed constitutionally." In the squabble over Carnival, the gentlemen's luncheon clubs had not been mentioned that day, and they remained as public accommodations within the definitions spelled out in the ordinance. This, McCall told the council, would not be allowed to stand. "Clubs are like an extension of home. I am almost certain you will be facing litigation."

If McCall's congenital arrogance had not already irritated the council majority, his next remark was an open invitation to Taylor's wrath. "I heard Mrs. Taylor ask whether closed-membership policies violate the Fourteenth Amendment, but she asked the wrong question. The right question is whether this ordinance violates the First Amendment rights of the members." He was about to sit down when Taylor stopped him in his tracks, her voice rising to a screech: "Just one minute, Mr. McCall. Don't you tell me what question to ask. We don't need y'all to tell us what to think anymore. I asked what I wanted to know." McCall attempted a response but was ordered to keep silent.

As if the meeting had not become rancorous enough, Henry Julien now stepped forward to say his piece. "It's absurd when someone is accused of wrongdoing and they can be declared not guilty by simply saying they didn't do it. What would our legal system be like if a woman accused a man of rape and the judge declared him not guilty just because he said he didn't do it? With this ordinance, you have insulted the accuser." He

grew menacing. "We're going to check the names of the signatories to the petition. They'll hear from us. We're going to
bring this debate to you, to your neighborhoods and churches.
This is a symbol. This is our Rodney King. The ordinance is
not a compromise; it is a capitulation."

Bryan Wagner was practically whining as he attempted a response. "I have sat here while people have trashed our committee, a committee that worked hard to produce these suggested
amendments. Don't mess with what we did. It was fine the way
it was." There was no chance of that, and Singleton promptly
announced that he would support the ordinance with the affidavit requirement. "The krewes say, 'Trust me.' Well, I'm going to trust you this time. I must say if we'd spend as much
time on the recreation department or on crime as we have on
Carnival, the city would be in better shape." Boissiere, too, observed that the council would be better occupied tackling the
city's chronic social problems than endlessly debating Carnival,
which earned him a reproachful glance from Taylor.

Whatever the council did might not ultimately make much
difference, Wilson pointed out. "We're going to give the angry
and frustrated a voice. We have twenty thousand signatures.
We will hear from them when we hold a referendum." As for
those who wanted her to scuttle the petition drive, she said, "I
can't see what is wrong with the democratic process." Clarkson,
however, had concluded that the time had come to bury the issue. "My district is a microcosm of this community, with all
races and creeds represented, and 80 percent of those people favor compromise. Otherwise the city will die under the threat."

It was time for Taylor to wind up the debate, and the room
fell silent. In addition to her disappointment with the blue ribbon committee, she was now angry with those who suggested
the Carnival row was distracting the council from more pressing concerns. "Don't tell me about housing and education. I've

worked in those areas all my life, and I've always heard white people say, 'We want to keep the niggers in their place.' All my life I have stood up for truth and justice.

"This has been a personal battle for me. For the first time, the business community and the kings and queens of Carnival admitted that discrimination existed in their ranks and publicly pledged to end it. Is Dorothy Mae Taylor satisfied with this compromise? No. Will this be the first step to ending racism and discrimination in Carnival? I think so. My head has been bloodied, but it is yet unbowed." The vote in favor of the ordinance was unanimous.

CHAPTER TWELVE

Guess Who's Coming to Rex

The New Orleans Registrar of Voters had verified more than the required ten thousand signatures on Peggy Wilson's petition by early August 1992, and she announced that she expected an election to be called the next January on the proposition that the city charter be amended to prevent the council from "regulating the internal policies" of Carnival krewes. It was widely assumed in New Orleans that the city council had no choice but to put the Wilson proposition on the ballot. Dorothy Mae Taylor, however, had other ideas. She sought advice from city attorney Bill Aaron, who obliged with an opinion that the petition was "either meaningless or unconstitutional," and that the council could therefore refuse to sanction an election. If the intent were to circumvent antidiscrimination measures, the proposition would be unconstitutional, Aaron said. But it could also be rejected as too vague. "I think what you have is an attempt of sleight-of-hand. It intentionally does not mention the word discrimination. It doesn't really say anything." If the council didn't go along with Aaron's opinion, Taylor had another trick up her sleeve. She had prepared a second proposal to amend the city charter, this one confirming the council's right to enforce desegregation. The council, by majority vote, could call a referendum on the Taylor proposition and put it on the same ballot as Wilson's. If both should pass, the

Taylor version would take precedence as the more specific one, Aaron advised.

City hall announced that krewes would have to file affidavits renouncing discrimination before the end of August if they were to receive parade permits for the next Mardi Gras. The announcement took all the krewes by surprise, since everyone had been under the impression that the ordinance would not take effect for another year. That had, indeed, been the original intention, but when the blue ribbon committee came back earlier than expected with its recommendations, the grace period was dropped.

Whatever hopes there might be of an eventual return to the unregulated days of yore, the Proteus board of directors needed to make a prompt decision on whether to abide by the affidavit requirement. There was never much doubt what they would do; the risk of being prosecuted for perjury was not one they were inclined to take and the thought of being bossed around by city hall functionaries—black ones at that—gave most of them the heebie-jeebies. A brief announcement was handed out to the media: Proteus would parade no more. "The fun and excitement are gone." Erroll Laborde, a local journalist and Carnival aficionado, who distributed the Proteus announcement, said of the ordinance, "Ultimately it was a political document, and it was a question of who's enforcing it and how it's being interpreted." The rest of the city's parading krewes, however, swore the required oath.

Classic Carnival was all but gone from the streets. Proteus, like Comus and Momus, had insisted on doing things the traditional way, with old wooden carriages and papier-mâché displays rather than the chassis and fiberglass used by the newer krewes. Old-line themes were always built into float superstructures; Comus, Momus and Proteus would never have stooped to the painted-on figures of their upstart imitators. The connoisseurs now found an eloquent spokesman in Henri

Schindler, Comus's float builder, to express their grief and rage. Schindler, at a dinner party one night, was bemoaning the fate of the old-line parades to Jim Amoss, editor of the New Orleans *Times-Picayune,* who suggested he write a guest column on the subject. Schindler produced an impassioned piece, which appeared September 4 and read in part:

> There are times when ignorance becomes sadistic. Councilwoman Dorothy Mae Taylor's Carnival ordinance has brought such a time to the people of New Orleans. Ham-fisted politics, venomous rhetoric and an inability to comprehend the truly fabulous textures of New Orleans or of Carnival have taken a horrific toll. The people of New Orleans may never again see a torchlight procession by the Mistick Krewe of Comus, the Knights of Momus or the Krewe of Proteus. In a festival that has continued to grow and has mushroomed during the last 25 years in every way but artistry, Comus, Momus and Proteus retained their magic. They infused the celebration with mystery, with pomp and bombast, with wit, gesture and timing. For 135 years Comus beckoned with his cup, the great symbol of transformation, the life-blood of the season. In his wake came the one float in all of Carnival that no one rode, the golden title car announcing on a gilded banner the subject of the procession. For Comus the choice was usually from mythology or nature, and for generations we were witness to scenes of the gods and demigods, of enchanted beasts and temples and bowers of antiquity. The last float of Comus was the last float of Carnival, and as it disappeared into the glowing fog it had created, we were reminded that dull reality and ashes would soon again be ours.
>
> Momus, Son of Night and God of Ridicule, for decades was the first parade of the season. While he was eventually preceded by scores of younger krewes, Momus marked for many the first real taste of vintage Carnival. He was, behind his mask, our first glimpse of the inscrutable—no stage beard and rouge for Momus! Momus was the great wit of Carnival.

To many eyes, the most beautiful float of Carnival was the No. 1 car of Proteus. Seated on his throne of oversized jewels in a quivering gold and pink scallop, Proteus riding the waves was one of the great apparitions of the season and also served as harbinger that Mardi Gras itself was only hours away.

Schindler concluded with a broadside at Taylor: "The divisiveness and bitterness of the last nine months are not forgotten—nor the inquisitorial tone and self-righteous cries of racism from one who has become its most frequent political practitioner."

Taylor was not impressed. When the city council met on September 17 to decide the fate of the Wilson petition, the old animosities surfaced once again. "Mardi Gras krewes are social organizations. This is a civil rights issue," Wilson began. Asked repeatedly to explain what effect her proposition would have on the council's powers, Wilson refused to answer, saying only that it didn't matter what the proposition meant, because the council was legally required to put it on the ballot. Taylor didn't agree, saying, as she picked up her copy of the ordinance that would have called a referendum, "Dress it up in costumes and call it tradition, but we know what it is. We are being asked as lawmakers to be lawbreakers. The only thing this ordinance is good for is this." With that, she tore it to pieces. Wilson and Clarkson were the only council members to vote yes on the ordinance, and the referendum was killed. "My job," Wilson explained, "was to bring this forward and try to put it on the ballot, and if the city attorney and council choose not to do that, they have to answer to the public." Given that the rulers of Carnival were themselves fearful of racial disorder should the issue come to a public vote, Wilson's statement seemed to amount to capitulation. She was, however, by no means finished yet.

A few days later, Rex issued a press release, datelined "The summer palace of Rex, the king of Carnival," confirming that he was indeed making some effort to mend his ways. How were the mighty fallen. In the old days, Rex would have issued a proclamation, yet now he was faxing a release to the press. The wording had little of the old-time flourish either:

Greetings to all. We eagerly await February 22nd when we will arrive in New Orleans for our Mardi Gras parade. Much has occurred about Carnival and its traditions since our last visit and we hope these discussions have ended. Now is the time to accentuate the positive and eliminate the negative. Continued repetition of differences and attempts to tarnish Carnival traditions do no good for our fair city or its people but only serve the individual aims of those who persist in these attempts. Recently a number of persons from many walks of life and varied background have joined our loyal following and all have expressed the same views. We will continue our cherished tradition of Carnival secrecy regarding our members and we wish all those planning for Mardi Gras 1993 great success. Pro bono publico.

This, of course, was Rex's way of announcing that black men had been invited to join the club. In fact, only three had been deemed acceptable: surgeon Henry Braden III, Norman Francis, president of Xavier University, and Charles Teamer, vice president of Dillard University. The anointing of Teamer and Francis was a reminder that, though the city council might be intent on desegregating Mardi Gras, Louisiana had still not managed to do the same for its higher education system. The students and faculty at both Xavier and Dillard are almost all black. Xavier, in fact, preens itself on being the only black Catholic university in the United States. Braden and Teamer became members of Rex, but Francis refused, explaining that he already had his hands full with professional and family obligations.

The white male luncheon clubs, the original targets of the Taylor ordinance, seemed to have been forgotten in the fuss over Mardi Gras. Just before Christmas of 1992, Earl Taylor, director of the Human Relations Commission, told the press that no complaints had been lodged against the clubs' membership policies, and Harry McCall said, "They are going to function as they have in the past. I think the attitude is that this is none of the city's business." Many people, in any case, suspected that the city had no more tedious an experience to offer than lunch with superannuated white males obsessed with status and debuts. Bob Tucker, one of the most successful black businessmen in New Orleans, said, "The whole notion of seeking to integrate areas where we are not wanted peaked in the civil rights era. I don't know of any black who has at the top of his list to become part of a battering ram to get into the Boston Club or the Pickwick Club." Evidently, he did not know Clarence Hunt.

According to a discrimination complaint Hunt filed with the Human Relations Commission on New Year's Eve, 1992, he was a businessman in San Francisco with plans to open an office in New Orleans. He had called "several private clubs" twice—the second time only three days earlier—identified himself as a black man and requested membership application forms, but had received no response. There is, of course, no such thing as an application form to join any of the exclusive luncheon clubs. One has to be invited, and nobody gauche enough to seek membership could ever be admitted. The Human Relations Commission did not notify the clubs that a complaint had been lodged against them, but encouraged Hunt to generate some documentation to support his case. Accordingly, on January 20, 1993, he repeated his request for application forms in letters to the Boston, Pickwick, Stratford and Louisiana clubs. With what appeared to be studied crassness, Hunt explained that he wanted to join the clubs so that he could have a place to entertain his business clients. He added that he was African American.

The Pickwick ignored Hunt's letter, but the others responded with varying degrees of condescension. All stressed that they were private, purely social organizations with no obligation to disclose information to outsiders. Louisiana Club president Cyril Geary suggested that Hunt join one of the city's lesser clubs which "admit non-New Orleans residents to membership, encourage the conduct of business, allow members to bring guests and can well serve the needs mentioned in your letter." Who, if anyone, put Hunt up to approaching the clubs was the subject of considerable speculation in the city, but nobody was saying. Hunt, a native of New Orleans, maintained he was just trying to prepare the ground for his return home.

While the clubs were mulling over Hunt's provoking letter, three citizens of New Orleans filed a federal suit alleging that the council's refusal to put Wilson's proposed charter change on the ballot had deprived them of their voting rights. Nobody doubted that the plaintiffs were in cahoots with Wilson, who, indeed, toyed with the idea of having her husband represent them in court. Gordon Wilson, however, decided that he was too busy to take on the case.

The krewes still clung to the belief that, if the court ruled in Wilson's favor, a referendum would restore their right to operate without any interference from city hall. The Human Relations Commission, however, was intent on invading the citadels of white privilege, informing the clubs, five days before Mardi Gras, that it had received a discrimination complaint from Hunt and would conduct an investigation. For all the conflict and acrimony of the preceding year, however, Carnival remained as segregated as ever, except at Rex. Even there, most of the men riding the floats on February 23, 1993, were unaware of the masked black men in their midst, and few could name both of their new companions.

Now that Rex was left as the last of the old-line krewes, he took over Comus's favorite subject, but the effort was, by the erudite standards of yore, a little gauche. The title alone, "Royal

British Scribes," was proof enough of that, for "scribe" was hardly an adequate term for any of the honorees, none of them was royal, and one, Jonathan Swift, was Irish, while another, Beowulf, was an Anglo-Saxon epic poem. Edward Hancock would never have been so sloppy. The other "scribes" honored with a float in the Rex parade of 1993 were Wells, Shakespeare, Milton, Lewis Carroll, Coleridge, Spenser, Blake, Stevenson, Chaucer, Sir Thomas More, Wordsworth, Beatrix Potter, Walter Scott, Kipling, Conan Doyle, Dickens, Tennyson and the Brontë sisters.

Over at Tulane University, bastion of political correctness, the beef against Rex was not that the parade was clumsily titled but that its theme defied the spirit of the Taylor ordinance by perpetuating "white patriarchal traditions." One published analysis complained that the British authors were all white, which Rex might fairly have pointed out was hardly his fault. The two floats honoring female writers caused outrage, too. The Brontës' float carried a replica of a parsonage, which, to most spectators, seemed fair enough, since the sisters lived most of their lives in one. To campus deconstructionists, however, it suggested that Rex endorsed "the containment of nineteenth-century women." Rex's gloss on the works of Beatrix Potter was no less sinister, for he did not scruple to enlist Flopsy, Mopsy, Cottontail and Peter in the cause of subjugating women and minorities. In the story, the rabbits' mother warns them to "stay out of Mr. McGregor's garden, reminding them that their father's intrusion into that private space resulted in his untimely death." The implications are obvious, at least at Tulane: "The float performance, then, signals the restrictive space assigned to women and minorities as well as the authority of white patriarchy to assign them."

The other floats were just as incorrect. Kipling's *Kim*, for instance, is an attempt to justify the suppression of colored people, while the "misogynistic" Sherlock Holmes has a bad case of "scientific and intellectual elitism," attributes which, however objectionable they may be on modern campuses, would probably be all right so far as a detective's clients were concerned. Spenser's *Faerie Queen* becomes a celebration of "male victory over female sexual, creative and moral authority," and altogether Rex emerges as devilishly clever in his "use of aesthetics to define [his] elitism" and communicate to the cognoscenti his displeasure with the Taylor ordinance. He would also have needed to be clairvoyant, since Schindler had designed all the floats two months before the ordinance was introduced. Rex thought he was just putting on a Mardi Gras parade.

Nobody in New Orleans was more distressed by the demise of the three old-line Carnival krewes than Schindler, who staged a spectacular demonstration of grief when he reigned in 1993

King Sarcophagus (Henri Schindler) reads a proclamation mourning the loss of Comus, Momus, and Proteus at the doors of the Boston Club, Mardi Gras, 1993. Photo by Michael P. Smith.

over the seventh annual Carnival procession of the Krewe du Vieux, a marching club specializing in pointed social commentary, chaos and carousing. Schindler, who styled himself King Sarcophagus I, rode a funeral float of his own design through the French Quarter, accompanied by subjects in black robes, veils and masks. The procession moved onto Canal Street and came to a halt outside the Boston Club, where a large wreath was removed from the front of the float and placed at the doorstep. Sarcophagus addressed the throng: "We have not come to the Boston Club this evening to mourn the gods. They are immortal. We have come to mourn the interruption of our traditions and to honor this club's 150 years of Carnival merriment and ritual." Sarcophagus then read a proclamation, issued by Comus, Momus and Proteus and written in an evocative, antique style reminiscent of a nineteenth-century Rex decree:

> We cousins, God of the Sea, God of Laughter and Ridicule, the son of the Goddess Night and the Sorcerer, born of Bacchus and Circe, greet you this Shrovetide. By this proclamation we command the Krewe of Proteus, the Knights of Momus and the Mistick Krewe of Comus to stay this year their street pageants, and by it we exhort each of you to enjoy nevertheless a festive Carnival season.
>
> Seven of your generations in this goodly Crescent City have known us only through our rides on avenue and street. So near to crossing with us into yet a third century, old as the oaks they travelled under, our parade cars wait now at rest and our flambeaux know neither fuel nor flame. Wooden wheels which rode the cobbles to the shouts of your great, great grandfathers might turn not again, and the torches which lit their laughing faces might nevermore reappear, but, citizens, be certain, our societies will endure.
>
> So, let the celebration that we sired proceed apace. Go forward, New Orleanians, with carefree abandon and Carnival gladness unabated. Adieu, fair city, until the coming of some

happy day when the Furies are done and the Fates call us to ride again to greet you.

Proteus

Momus

Comus

Schindler added a postscript: "Now, we Sarcophagus and our loyal subjects, say to the junta in power at City Hall, sucking the lifeblood of our Carnival and our city: your days are numbered.

"To our future leaders who would restore harmony and joy to this city, we cry out: Bring back Momus! Bring back Proteus! Bring back Comus!"

Two days after Mardi Gras, the Boston, Stratford and Louisiana clubs filed federal lawsuits to block the Human Rights Commission investigation as a violation of their constitutional rights to privacy, freedom of association and freedom of assembly. The Pickwick Club soon afterwards followed suit. Clarence Hunt, who owned a business supplying temporary office personnel, described the suits as "obviously frivolous and retaliatory." The clubs were "trying to take the high moral ground but there is no way you can legally support an institution of segregation." He was quoted in the newspaper as saying that he intended to use the clubs to make business contacts, which brought several of the members close to apoplexy. That was simply not done and, besides, who could imagine that fourth- and fifth-generation members of New Orleans's finest clubs, the last word in taste and distinction, would want to rub shoulders with a man like Hunt?

CHAPTER THIRTEEN

The Second Battle of Liberty Place

ajor Hearsey a century earlier had acidly wondered whether someone might so take leave of his senses as to chuck the Liberty Monument into the river. That was not what Carl Galmon proposed. He wanted to "take that sucker out in the Atlantic Ocean and dump it." He had another suggestion for it, too. "Let David Duke take it and put it in his front yard," he told the city council on March 18, 1993, during a hearing on Dorothy Mae Taylor's latest stab at the white establishment, an ordinance that would clear the way for the monument's removal. Duke, sitting with a small group of his supporters in the chamber, smirked as Galmon said his piece: "The so-called Liberty Monument had nothing to do with liberty. It had everything to do with white supremacy. The White League was a bunch of terrorists and we should not erect monuments to terrorists." Galmon was in his normal state of fury and still had the appearance of a man who would happily exchange blows in the civil rights cause. He was solidly built, with something of an athletic bearing that testified to his days as a professional baseball player thirty years earlier. Galmon always maintained that he could have made the major leagues had his career not been interrupted by the draft when he was playing for a Boston Red Sox farm team. The Liberty Monument had been a thorn in Galmon's side for the whole of his life. A favorite rallying point for the archsegregationist Dixiecrats in the 1940s, it had, in more recent times, become a magnet for klansmen and neo-Nazis, and Duke had delivered many a rabble-rousing speech in its shadow.

After his strong showing in elections for the U. S. Senate and the Louisiana governorship, Duke barely caused a ripple when he ran for president in 1992, and he now seemed washed up politically. He had gone to the well once too often, and, besides, political pollsters suspected that many of his votes came, not from true disciples of his racist ideology, but from a frustrated middle class seeking to register its disgust with the political establishment.

Three weeks after Mardi Gras 1993, however, Dorothy Mae Taylor was handing Duke an opportunity to return to the limelight he craved. Taylor wanted the Liberty Monument removed from public display as a symbol of white supremacy. Duke, at least in his public pronouncements, insisted the Battle of Liberty Place had nothing to do with racism but was a heroic effort to resist despotism and injustice. Taylor was more inclined to view it as an attempt to deprive blacks of the legitimate gains they had made during Reconstruction. The motives of the combatants in 1874 were the subject of endless debate throughout the city, but there was little point in denying that the monument was a racist symbol. If it were not already (the United Daughters of the Confederacy laid wreaths at its side every September 14), Duke had made it so when he adopted Liberty Place as the habitual setting for his demagoguery. The Liberty Monument Commission, with the city council's approval, moreover, had added these words to the plinth in 1932: "United States troops took over the state government and reinstated the usurpers but the national election November 1876 recognized white supremacy and gave us back our state." Only the names of the White Leaguers killed in the battle were listed on the monument, which most black citizens were delighted to see removed from public view when it was put in storage to make room for improvements to Canal Street in November of 1989.

Federal historic preservation officials told Barthelemy that the monument would have to be reerected when street construction was complete, and he signed an agreement to do so at or near its original site by May 1, 1991. He blew that deadline and another on September 1 and then asked the curator of the state museum if he would take the monument off the city's hands. State officials nixed that idea and, in December 1991, a Duke supporter named Francis Shubert filed a federal lawsuit to compel the city to put the monument back on the street. Shubert, who operated a pharmacy uptown on Prytania Street, just a few blocks from John Pope's old place, said it was a desire to preserve historical relics, rather than racism, that drove him to file the suit, which claimed that so long as the monument remained in storage he would "continue to suffer extreme hardship and irreparable injury in that he has ancestors who were involved in the Battle of Liberty Place." Although that seemed to overstate the plaintiff's trauma somewhat, Barthelemy also came under pressure from federal officials in Washington to keep his end of the bargain, and in September 1992 he told federal judge A. J. McNamara that he would settle the suit by putting the monument back on the street by January 20, 1993. As usual, he missed the deadline, but the Liberty Monument did finally reappear on February 10, 1993, although on a much less conspicuous site than the original one. It was now placed behind the Aquarium of the Americas, a block off Canal Street. The white-supremacist inscription added in 1932 had been removed and replaced by a plaque that bore the names of the Metropolitan Police officers killed in the battle as well as a little homily: "A conflict of the past that should teach us lessons for the future." In fact, the list of slain Metropolitans, identified through research conducted by Tulane history professor Judith Schafer, was a reminder that the races were less polarized during Reconstruction than some members of the city council assumed. Most of the dead were white, three of them, not surprisingly given the temper of the times, Irish. James McManus, who was shot down by his own commander, General Badger, in an attempt to stop the retreat, was born in America, but Michael O'Keefe and John Kennedy, an officer in the Confederate army, immigrated from Ireland.

A federal court in New York handed down a decision on February 26, 1991, that seemed to carry a lesson for the city council and the Carnival krewes. The Ancient Order of Hibernians, having been denied a permit for its annual St. Patrick's Day parade because it refused to include the Irish Lesbian and Gay Organization, sued the city, claiming that its First Amendment rights had been violated. The court agreed, finding that "a parade is by its nature a pristine form of speech" and therefore constitutionally protected. The message to be conveyed by the parade was to be determined by the organizers, not by the state or city. The Hibernians, moreover, had a right to associate, or not to associate, with whomever they pleased. The implications of the ruling were obvious to the old-line krewes, but no lawsuit was forthcoming in New Orleans. Krewemen still reasoned that there was no point in parading where they were not wanted, although all the evidence suggested that, whatever the views of the council, most of the citizenry was firmly opposed to changing Mardi Gras. There was also a practical obstacle to litigation, since no krewe member would be in a position to testify without breaking his vow of secrecy. Comus himself would have had to be sworn under his real name, and that was unthinkable.

The cosmetic changes to the Liberty Monument were not enough to erase the overarching insult, so far as Taylor was concerned, and she was as implacable as she had been during the row over segregated Carnival krewes. Duke appointed himself head of the campaign to preserve what he claimed was a vital part of the city's history, and several of his associates were now calling themselves the Friends of the Liberty Monument. They arranged a rededication ceremony for March 7. Meanwhile, someone ripped out one of four small columns in the monument, and a prominent member of Duke's circle, a paralegal named Hope Lubrano, filed a complaint with the city police department and tried, unsuccessfully, to get the FBI to investigate.

On the day of the rededication ceremony, Duke and about fifty others were gathered at the foot of the monument, ringed by police officers and waving American, Louisiana and Confederate flags, when state representative Avery Alexander, now eighty-two years old but still full of the passion he had brought to decades of civil rights campaigning, appeared at the head of forty black protesters intent on disruption. Shouting "down with white supremacy," the protesters tried to force their way through police lines but were held back. "Racism must go," they chanted. "Jesse Jackson must go," the Duke crowd responded. While the rededication ceremony continued with prayers and speeches, the black protesters tried again to push their way through the cordon, and press photographers and television cameramen got pictures of white reserve officer Jeffrey Galpin putting a chokehold on Alexander. The scene evoked memories of thirty years before when Alexander, demanding service for black people at a food counter in a city hall basement, was dragged away by police and up the stairs, his prone body bumping on each one as it ascended to the ground floor.

Four black protesters, including an enraged Henry Julien, were led away in handcuffs from the Liberty Monument rededication, whereupon Lubrano complained that the black protesters "had no respect for what this is all about." (Lubrano was evidently unaware that the white elite who built the monument didn't have much more time for people whose names ended in vowels than they did for blacks.) "If they want a Black His-

Veteran civil rights activist, the Rev. Avery Alexander, is restrained by police during a protest at the rededication of the Liberty Monument in 1993. Part of the monument can be seen in the background, where a David Duke supporter holds a Confederate battle flag. Photo by Kathy Anderson/Times-Picayune.

tory Month, fine," Lubrano said, "but respect American history. That's what this is all about—liberty. We all have the freedom of speech." Duke, a bodyguard by his side, was thinking of the Bill of Rights, too, and said, "We may be a minority in this city, but I tell you, we still have rights. We still have the right to assemble. This ceremony is dedicated to those who died to protect those rights." Alexander replied: "The monument is a symbol of humiliation for black people all over this country. We can't tolerate it. I'm out here because I'm opposed to racism. I'm opposed to slavery. I'm opposed to persecution."

This was not the first attempt to get rid of the monument. Black citizens had gathered around it to protest from time to time over the past twenty years; in 1981 Dutch Morial, New Orleans's first black mayor, ordered its removal, which, the city council decided, was beyond his authority. The council, which at that time had only two black members, Barthelemy and Singleton, adopted an ordinance requiring the monument to be left in place, and Morial acquiesced. Morial, who died in 1990, was a trailblazer in the civil rights movement, the first black graduate of the Louisiana State University law school, the first black assistant United States attorney in Louisiana, the first black state legislator since Reconstruction and the first black appeals court judge in New Orleans. He was that familiar type in New Orleans, black in law but not in appearance. His father, a cigar maker named Walter Morial, was such a light-skinned Creole that he passed himself off as a white man. Dutch Morial, though he was never a *passe blanc,* as those who cross racial lines are known in New Orleans, was no swarthier than many an Aryan just returned from the ski slopes. Amid all the hoopla over Morial's election to the state legislature, a veteran member, looking around on the first day of the session, loudly enquired, "Where's the nigger?" Morial was standing in plain view a few yards away.

Having lost the battle to remove the Liberty Monument, Morial decided that it was, at least, within his power to block the view. He therefore ordered the parks commission to plant ligustrum bushes all around it, where they stayed until its temporary removal in 1989.

The press pictures of the sainted Alexander in a chokehold led to the suspension of Galpin from the police department and provoked a chorus of protest. The state legislature's black caucus called for a police department investigation of brutality in its ranks, and student leaders of three predominantly black universities, Southern University–New Orleans, Dillard and Xavier, denounced what they said was excessive force used against Alexander. "This man is the father of the civil rights movement, not only in New Orleans but Louisiana and the

South," one of their spokesmen said. "You hit our father. It's not morally right." A lively debate was assured when the public hearing on Taylor's latest ordinance began on March 18.

The ordinance would empower the council to order the removal of any statue or monument that honored "ideologies which are in conflict with the requirements of equal protection for citizens." The council would also have the right to take down any monument that attracted vandals, provoked conflict or was otherwise deemed a "nuisance." The Carnival elite was nowhere to be seen this time, although not because they were indifferent to the fate of the Liberty Monument. Now that Duke had contrived to make himself the leading opponent of Taylor's ordinance, the respectable classes were wary about espousing the cause publicly. In the clubs and the fashionable uptown residences, however, people seethed at the prospect of the monument's removal. Taylor, it was everywhere said, was trying to rewrite history and destroy what was, for better or worse, a significant relic of the city's past. What would be next? Would Taylor tear down the statues of Robert E. Lee, Pierre Beauregard, Jefferson Davis and anyone else who did not meet with her approval? That the defense of the city's heritage was now in the hands of a man like Duke added to the widespread sense of frustration.

The audience at the public hearing was mostly black, and animated by such violent passions that the council had brought in several policemen to keep the peace. Alexander led the charge, telling the council, "We feel that this monument constitutes a slap in the face to every fair-minded white and every black citizen in this community. We call upon the city of New Orleans to remove this albatross from around our necks." Galmon was one of dozens of other speakers who echoed those sentiments, while members of the Duke faction, when their turn came to speak, seemed to go out of their way to antagonize the majority. Lubrano addressed the black members of the audience as "you people," while another Duke follower, an ex-cop named Kenny Knight, objecting to interruptions from the Alexander faction, told Taylor, "I wish you would control this circus." Lubrano, Knight and Duke himself all praised the police for the "restraint" they had shown at the rededication ceremony. "One of the worst offenders that day was the good Reverend Alexander," Duke said. "He crashed through the crowds and jumped on a police officer's back." Duke added that he would urge the federal government to cut off all financial aid to New Orleans if the monument were removed.

Walter Ross, a black supporter of Alexander's, started to say his piece to the council but changed his mind and suddenly lunged towards Duke, who was sitting in the front row. The police got between the two men and led Ross out of the room, while the meeting degenerated into a racial slanging match. The council referred Taylor's ordinance to the city attorney for review, and, amid loud and repeated cries of "Go home, David Duke," the meeting broke up. Three days later someone spray-painted the city's statue of Martin Luther King, Jr., white.

Taylor's public monuments ordinance was on the agenda for the city council meeting of April 16, 1993. The day before, Judge McNamara had ordered the city to pay the twenty-seven-thousand-dollar legal bill Francis Shubert had run up in bringing his lawsuit to force reerection of the Liberty Monument, and Giarrusso, Clarkson and Wilson now urged Taylor to defer her crusade so that they could concentrate on other business. She would have none of it. "It couldn't help but trick my mind back to the mid-sixties, when every time we as African-American people would stand up to gain respect and dignity, we'd hear, 'It's not the time, it's time to wait, it's time to defer.' I say you're wrong, wrong, wrong for even attempting to delay this matter any further than this day. Either decide that you're for it or decide that you're against it." The audience, save the Duke contingent, applauded. The familiar arguments from both sides of the controversy were trotted out again. Avery Alexander told the council that there was no place in the city for any monument that "promoted violence and killing, and demeans and denigrates one group while extolling another," while Kenny Knight promised to fight the ordinance all the way to the U. S. Supreme Court. Hope Lubrano added that, if the Liberty Monument were to be removed, so should the Martin Luther King, Jr., statue, which was "offensive to the white community." Giarrusso and Clarkson voted against the ordinance, but Wilson joined the others in passing it. It required the Human Relations Commission to investigate and hold hearings to identify offensive monuments, and to make recommendations to the city council. Once the monument issue was out of the way, the council went on to approve a lease for a casino on Canal Street. With the state on the verge of issuing permits for gambling riverboats in the Mississippi, Lake Pontchartrain and a few suburban bayous, the way, according to the Barthelemy administration, was clear for a bonanza that would snatch the city from financial ruin.

The Human Relations Commission was weighing the pros and cons of the Liberty Monument on June 15, 1993, when David Duke got up and denounced the campaign to remove it as "a Nazi-like act." A startled Rabbi Edward Cohn, who was chairing the meeting, had the wary air of a man who was not quite sure whether he was the victim of a practical joke or whether he had misheard. "Were you," he asked after a few seconds' silence, "condemning acts of Nazism?" He stared incredulously as Duke replied, "I freely condemn Nazism. Nazis are the ones that try to change history. The monument is part of our history and should be preserved." Otherwise, there were no surprises from either side. The commission in June recommended that the monument be removed from the street and a place found for it in a museum, a solution that had already been proposed by others, notably Tulane history professor Lawrence Powell in a *Times-Picayune* op-ed column. The commission concluded: "Subsequent generations have erased the laws of segregation that were part and parcel of the Liberty Monument's generation. The stone obelisk that remains a visible symbol of their handiwork should enjoy no greater immunity than the laws themselves."

Judge McNamara ruled on July 9 that carnival krewes were not entitled to immunity either, at least not by virtue of a referendum on Wilson's proposed change to the city charter. The city council was within its rights to refuse to put the proposition on the ballot, McNamara decided, because its wording was so imprecise that it would have "absolutely no effect on the legislative or regulatory power of the city." Five days later, to nobody's surprise, the city council voted to remove the Liberty Monument from the street, with Giarrusso casting the lone dissenting vote because, he said, of fears that it could cost the city federal money unless historic preservation authorities concurred. He also suggested it was a bad precedent to buckle under to pressure from demonstrators who had threatened to destroy the monument. In a move to preempt an expected lawsuit from the Friends of the Liberty Monument, hours after the council vote city attorneys filed suit in state court asking for a declaratory judgment that it was within its rights.

This was a busy time for the city attorneys, who were preparing their defense against the lawsuit filed by the luncheon clubs and taking depositions from several of their members and officers, including a few with family names identified with the social elite for a century and more. Charles Janvier III and Peyton Llewellyn Early Bruns, for instance, were vice presidents of the white elite's favorite bank, the Whitney, and had never worked anywhere else. Walter Flower III had an investment counseling business. Janvier belonged to the Boston, the Stratford and the Louisiana, Bruns just to the Boston, and Flower to the Boston, the Pickwick and the Stratford. The clubs tried to maintain the cherished secrecy of the elite, but were turned down when they filed a motion seeking to have hearings held in camera. The decision meant that the public would get its first glimpse into the arcana not only of the clubs but of the krewes. Not only were all members of the Stratford transformed into High Priests of Mithras for the annual ball, and members of the Louisiana into the Knights of Momus, but there was also considerable overlapping among the other clubs and krewes.

In his deposition, Bruns, aged forty-eight, was asked how he had become a member of the Boston Club. "God, how did I become a member? Daddy put me up. I know Daddy was a member. And at the time, I think, as I say, I was the youngest member. I was the youngest member at one time, so Daddy must have put me up very early because I was very young, because we have limited, you know, membership, you know that the numbers are limited. And I guess Daddy realized we had a lot of friends in my group, made sure I got in, the early group friends."

Other depositions were more coherent, but the picture that emerged was of a plutocracy so deeply suspicious of outsiders that it had become ossified. None of the clubs allowed members to bring guests living in the New Orleans area; indeed, the Louisiana Club did not allow male guests at all. Women were admitted only on special occasions, in particular during the Carnival season when the debutante daughters and granddaughters of club members paraded in their finery. The Pickwick Club, though it no longer had any formal connection with the Mistick Krewe, always held a Mardi Gras reception "where we have the queen and the maids, along with their mothers, grace the club room for that evening from about five to seven," testified its president, former Rex Erik Johnsen.

The four clubs all operated along the same lines, drawing

new members from the ranks of family and close friends. Nobody proposed for membership was informed, unless his nomination survived a complicated screening process, described by John Combe, president of the 330–member Stratford Club: "Three or more members propose an individual for membership to the club. In making that proposal, they are telling the membership that they are vouching for the man's character, his honesty, his personal integrity and that he will be compatible with the existing membership. At that point, additional members who know the individual candidate are encouraged to sign the proposal as endorsers, also further verifying those same characteristics of the individual. The name is then submitted to a membership committee for further screening. Then the applicant's name is taken to the board for further consideration and screening. After that, assuming that the candidate passes through those qualifications, his name is submitted to the general membership for their consideration. If three or more members decline to authorize his membership for whatever reason—the reasons are unstated—then the candidate is not invited to join the club."

In the circumstances, there was obviously little chance that anyone but Gentiles of north European extraction would be anointed, and club officers in their depositions made only the feeblest efforts to deny it. As Kennedy Gilly, vice president of the Boston and a member of the Louisiana, explained, "It's not that we discriminate against any body or group, but we are very partial to our own." He conceded that he did not know if anyone of African descent had been admitted, but added, "I haven't traced the genealogy of any or all of our members, and, under the Louisiana law at the time, any traceable mixture of Negro blood would make someone in law a Negro or a colored, whatever the term used in the civil code is. But I certainly haven't traced anybody's genealogy back to Adam and Eve to

determine whether there's any traceable admixture." George
Mayer, president of the Boston and a member of the Louisiana,
when asked whether there were any black members, also pro-
tested that it was impossible to tell. "Unless you have the genealogy of individuals going back many, many years, there just
isn't any way." That this was a disingenuous argument was
apparent as the city's attorney, Bruce Naccari, continued his
examination:

Q. Have you ever made a judgment about the race of a person
whom you did not know and about whom you did not know
the genealogy?
A. No.
Q. Well, I'm momentarily at a loss because I find that ex-
tremely unusual. I'm having to reformulate my questioning.
Are there any black employees of the Boston Club?
A. Yes.
Q. How do you know that they are black?
A. They are colored.

Mayer used the lack of genealogical data to evade the question of whether the clubs had any Jewish members, although
he admitted he did not know of any. As for members with
Italian surnames, Mayer said, "I can name a name that may or
may not be. I'm not sure." Johnsen, however, made some claim
for diversity at the Pickwick. After admitting that he did not
know if the club had any Jews or men of African descent in its
ranks, he was asked if anyone "of Italian, Sicilian or other
Mediterranean descent" had been proposed for membership. "I
would say yes. I don't know specifically the day, but I know in
years that they have had a number of various descents. We have
had Mexican members, and we have had other similar types,
and also Mediterranean descent members." Johnsen overlooked
the most remarkable exception to the rule that Italians are unwelcome in New Orleans high society, for Gus Miceli, an im-

migrant from Palermo who died twenty years earlier, had been not only accepted but elected president of the Pickwick Club and written its official history.

Every club officer and member insisted that the clubs lived up to the bylaws that defined their roles as purely social, literary and intellectual. Indeed, the formal name of the Louisiana Club is the Louisiana Debating and Literary Society. Six clubmen, however, testified that their dues and expenses had been paid by their employer, the Whitney Bank, where the clubs maintained accounts and, in some cases, had made mortgage loans. Otherwise, the city's attorneys got nowhere in their attempts to prove that people joined the clubs for business advantage and that it was therefore unfair to exclude women and entire ethnic groups. Evidence was overwhelming that no member of the clubs would ever dare to open a briefcase or negotiate a deal at the large tables where they gathered for lunch and cards. That the bonds forged between members would inevitably lead to some kind of business links on the outside, however, stood to reason. The clubs nevertheless filed a motion asking for a summary judgment that they were private organizations immune from investigation by the Human Relations Commission. That motion was filed September 13, one day before the anniversary of the Battle of Liberty Place, which passed off without any of the violent scenes that had attended the rededication ceremony. The Duke crowd had gathered to celebrate the anniversary Sunday, September 12, but no protesters showed up. Alexander explained that the council vote to remove the monument made further confrontation pointless.

Barthelemy, meanwhile, was working on a plan to ease the city's financial woes by selling T-shirts, caps, canvas bags and aprons bearing a trademarked Carnival insignia. He also wanted to recruit sponsors who would pay for the privilege of providing official Mardi Gras credit cards, beer, soft drinks, film and other products. Barthelemy arranged for a marketing company to put on a presentation explaining his brainwave to the city's committee of krewe captains, who were uniformly unreceptive. Committee chairman Beau Bassich told Barthelemy that the proposal had been flatly rejected as "the first step towards commercialization," with promises that some of the revenues would be shared with the krewes cutting no ice. Since the krewes paid for the parades and other events, the city's legal right to license Mardi Gras products was also questionable, several of the captains pointed out. Lambert Boissiere, a candidate in the upcoming election to replace his friend Barthelemy, did his best to gainsay the traditionalists, observing, "Some people say leave Mardi Gras like it is, but if we left everything like it is, we might still have slavery." French Quarter merchants added their voices to the protest, since they feared that an official line of T-shirts and other gimcrackery would reduce demand for the unofficial products on which a substantial proportion of their business depended. The deal, in fact, was even worse than anyone realized, for the mayor had signed a contract that envisaged corporate sponsorship of parades, which was forbidden by city ordinance. Half the revenues would go to the marketing company, which had only recently been incorporated and by a close friend of Barthelemy's at that. New Orleans was clearly not ready for the commercialization of Mardi Gras, at least not on the terms proposed by Mayor Barthelemy, and the idea was quietly shelved.

Judge McNamara was in no hurry to rule on the luncheon clubs' motion for summary judgment while, in state court, the litigation over the Liberty Monument was also consigned to limbo. The case was allotted to Yada Magee, a black judge of the civil district court, who had been elected several years before as a protégé of then-mayor Morial. A favorite butt of the Duke crowd, Magee was seriously overweight, and, according to the unanimous opinion of attorneys who practiced before her, no great shakes as a legal scholar or jurist. In her first election campaign she had claimed the endorsement of God. Magee's great virtue, however, was a keen sense of fairness, and it was not particularly surprising when a hearing, scheduled for December 4, was postponed because she had decided to withdraw from the case. Magee told the assembled litigants that she had participated in a protest against the monument on the hundredth anniversary of the Battle of Liberty Place in 1974. "I could not in good conscience sign a judgment that would allow the monument to stay," she said. "I would quit my job first." As the city got ready for the Carnival season of 1994, therefore, the disputes that had poisoned race relations in the city were all bogged down in litigation, while Peggy Wilson considered whether to appeal McNamara's ruling on her proposed charter amendment. She was also wondering whether her crusade had been too aggressive for some of the establishment. That, certainly, was one possible explanation for the fact that her husband had been blackballed at the clubs. Once Bill Clinton was elected president, a couple of Gordon Wilson's friends, now that his chances of a federal judgeship had disappeared, put him up for reelection to the clubs he had quit to improve his chances of confirmation. Enough members objected, however, to keep him out, although, of course, the objectors were not required to say why or to identify themselves.

The city was barely back to normal after the excesses of Carnival when, on March 10, McNamara handed down his decision on the clubs' suit against the city and rocked all parties back on their heels. He issued a permanent injunction prohibiting government investigation of complaints against any of the clubs because "each plaintiff club has clearly demonstrated that it is a private club located at the most intimate end of the qualitative continuum of personal relationships." The clubs, McNamara ruled, "have a First Amendment right to enter into and maintain certain intimate human relationships without undue state intrusion and a right not to have their private affairs made public by the government." The clubmen's jubilation was mixed with astonishment at their total victory, because, as many of them observed, it was rare indeed for the courts to uphold the constitutional rights of the wealthy and the privileged. Barthelemy, with only a few weeks left in office, talked things over with incoming mayor Marc Morial, who agreed to appeal McNamara's order as soon as he took office. Morial explained that, with such fundamental principles at stake, he felt morally obliged to do so. The case went to the U. S. Fifth Circuit Court of Appeals, where the senior and most revered member was none other than John Minor Wisdom, although he, of course, played no part in the deliberations. McNamara's ruling was upheld, and the city appealed to the U. S. Supreme Court, which, in June of 1995, refused to take up the case, causing Morial to issue a statement welcoming the fact that "the contours of the city's regulatory powers" had been defined.

Schindler's fond wish that Comus, Proteus and Momus might one day return to the streets, meanwhile, seemed unlikely to be fulfilled any time soon. The old-line krewemen were right when they complained that the public did not appreciate their efforts. Comus may always have been above the heads of the masses, but that only enhanced the awe he excited in the old-line's halcyon days. When Carnival went lowbrow, public loyalty shifted away from Comus and his kin long before there was any talk of integration. While krewemen thought their parades were a splendid and uplifting gift to the citizens, the supposed beneficiaries, regardless of class, creed or color, began to feel patronized.

Carnival in general, but the old-line krewes in particular, began also to draw the wrath of the religious right, which was incensed by Rex's continued use of a huge papier-mâché Boeuf Gras atop a float, surrounded by krewemen dressed as butchers and carrying carving knives. A church pamphlet, entitled *The*

Crowds yelling for throws at the "superkrewe" Endymion parade of 1994.
*Photo by Kim D. Johnson/*Times-Picayune.

Spirit of Mardi Gras and published in New Orleans, explained the symbolism, adjuring readers to remember that "Baal, the ancient Canaanite god (who once almost supplanted true worship in Israel) was represented as a bull!" There was plenty more evidence that the "spirit of idolatry" informs Mardi Gras: "This is readily seen in the history of the holiday, which is richly steeped in Egyptian, Grecian and Roman fertility rites, and the lewdness, revellings, drunkenness and nudity that characterize them. As we have already observed, the very same spirit prevails today! Undoubtedly, the idolatrous spirit of the celebration is exposed for all to see in noting that the titles of the carnival parades are named in honor of the very same ancient pagan gods that the Holy Scriptures condemn." The pamphlet also notes, accurately, that homosexuals "strut like peacocks through the French Quarter, staging their own parades and costume contests." It is also hard to take issue with the assertion that Mardi Gras is "one huge drunken orgy of sin, and New Orleans just loves it!" The strange notion that the old-line krewes are the genuine votaries of heathen deities can also be encountered among the Mardi Gras Indians, whose own customs are not notably pious. When the New Orleans gangs met delegations from Louisiana's native tribes in the summer of 1994, and participated in religious rituals on the site of Congo Square, members boasted of their own spiritual superiority to krewemen who would honor false gods.

CHAPTER FOURTEEN

The Biter Bit

P rints that circulated in Europe during Carnival season when Louisiana was a wild colonial outpost showed fish flying and pupils beating their teachers. In Napoleonic times, urchins were depicted leading parades through the streets of Paris. On Comus's appearance in New Orleans, however, the traditional conceit of a world turned upside down was nowhere in sight. Otherwise, Confederate krewemen, at their most whimsical, might have conjured up a black, female government official publicly rebuking a scion of the New Orleans aristocracy. That would have been a stretch comparable to the old European cartoon that showed a king walking alongside a peasant on horseback.

Dorothy Mae Taylor was proof enough to the old-line krewes of today that the world had been turned on its ears, and no joke. They complained, to a large extent correctly, that they were the victims of a racist animus, and left it to others to savor the irony.

The old-line view of Carnival—that it was an uplifting experience for which people on the streets should be grateful to their benefactors—had not changed since Comus first took to the streets. The absence of the subversive tradition at the dawn of modern Carnival in New Orleans is not surprising, for the original members of Comus must have had too many doubts about the stability of the antebellum social hierarchy to mock it. At the time terrorism was rampant, as the Know-Nothings struggled to keep the huge immigrant population in check. Role-reversal fantasies, moreover, would have been less likely to amuse the white elite than to fuel the fears of murder and rebellion to which slave-owning societies are naturally prone.

Certainly, Europe was no stranger to oppression when the establishment there tolerated, or even encouraged, the lèse-majesté implied by images of a topsy-turvy world. It was not unknown for the joke to turn sour, turning Carnival celebrations into bloody revolt, but, on the whole, the peasantry, having vented its frustrations and resentments, appears to have been content to tug the forelock for the rest of the year.

Whatever insecurities beset Comus just before the Civil War were present in spades during the Unionist occupation and Reconstruction, even as new Carnival societies were established. The krewes showed that they were quite capable of mordant subversive jokes at the expense of the federals and their local supporters, but that merely underscored the purported superiority of the elite white men in New Orleans. The old-line krewes never did develop a taste for laughing at themselves, in part because of a stuffy conviction that they were the living relics of more gracious and refined times and in part because New Orleans has always been too rowdy for patriarchs to rest easy.

The krewes have played a big part in perpetuating the myth that the South sustained a great civilization until it was destroyed by Yankee vandals. The Confederate caissons, which bore Comus floats until the last parade in 1991, sit ready to be wheeled out again should he ever reappear in public.

There is no sign that Comus, Proteus or Momus have a mind to return to the fray, although now that Dorothy Mae Taylor has departed from public office, her campaign to desegregate the krewes and the clubs is remembered as a disaster for New Orleans and Carnival, which many people regard as the same thing.

If the old-line krewes drew their members from the better class of people who set the tone for modern New Orleans, not the least of their contributions was to give racism a respectable face. It is not necessary to judge the architects of modern Carnival by the standards of today to brand them bigots. Indeed, given the atrocities some of them committed, that would be to let them off lightly. Krewemen who were surprised to find that Taylor and her allies hated all they stood for were just plain dumb.

Just as dumb was the proposition, familiar everywhere in recent years and trotted out ad nauseam during the Carnival controversy, that black people, having long been victimized by racism, should never be accused of it. In truth, certain members of the city council took such a palpably racist delight in the discomfiture of the old-line krewes that whatever the ordinance was designed to accomplish in the cause of civil rights became secondary. That, perhaps, is human nature, but anyone promoting the ideal of a "color-blind society" would have been laughed out of court in New Orleans that year.

The racial tensions stirred up whenever government sets out to enforce integration have naturally receded lately, but not because there is a new spirit of reconciliation abroad. Quite the reverse is true, with the white elite more isolated than ever at its balls and luncheon clubs. The Taylor ordinance never lived up to its billing as a natural progression in the civil rights struggle; it produced little more than angry posturing in a futile cause.

The cause was futile for reasons that are both depressing and encouraging. The dark side is that nobody in New Orleans needed the O. J. Simpson trial to demonstrate that the races live in mutual distrust and incomprehension. If the problems of America's urban wastelands are to be solved, it must be accomplished, on the evidence of the Carnival row, without a tolerant spirit or even civilized public discourse, which seems like a tall order.

On the other hand, those who believe America is being undermined by intrusive government and the forces of political correctness will be cheered by the refusal of the clubs and krewes to toe a multicultural line. Although the progressives do not doubt that they have a monopoly on virtue, the krewes and the clubs regarded themselves as the defenders not of bigotry but of principle. Indeed, if the cause of liberty was advanced by the Carnival conflict, it was thanks to the clubs, which, in their litigation against the city of New Orleans, struck a blow for the First Amendment that should encourage politicians everywhere to stick to their proper sphere.

There is no question that Carnival in New Orleans is the poorer for the loss of its old-line parades—victims of racism from within and without—and of politicians intent on legislating a proper mindset. Comus and his kin will return either when they climb down and admit black people or when the city council swallows its principles and allows segregation back on the public streets. Or when fish fly over Jackson Square.

CHAPTER ONE

This is firsthand reportage of the city council meeting, augmented by interviews with public officials, krewe members, civil rights activists and others on both sides of the debate. Municipal Ordinance No. 14,984 of 1991 is the only written source.

CHAPTER TWO

Acts and Deliberations of the Cabildo, in the Louisiana collection of the New Orleans public library, contains the first record, dated January 19, 1781, of a Carnival season in the city. Descriptions of Mardi Gras before that can be found in such books as Perry Young's *Carnival and Mardi Gras in New Orleans* (New Orleans: Harmanson's, 1939) and Robert Tallant's *Mardi Gras, The Way It Was* (Garden City, N.Y.: Doubleday, 1948) but no sources are cited. Likewise, the Marquis de Vaudreuil's position as the colonial father of the elegant Carnival ball cannot be substantiated, although Bennett H. Wall, ed., *Louisiana, a History* (Arlington Heights, Ill.: Forum Press, 1984) notes that "some sources" believe it. Bill Barron's *The Vaudreuil Papers: A Calendar and Index of the Personal and Private Records of Pierre de Rigaud de Vaudreuil* (New Orleans: Polyanthus, 1975), however, offers those sources no comfort. Charles Gayarre, *The History of Louisiana* (New Orleans: F. F. Hansell & Bro. Ltd., 1903) asserts, but does not document, that "long after (Vaudreuil) departed, old people were fond of talking of the exquisitely refined manners, the magnificent balls, the splendidly uniformed troops, the high-born young officers, and many other things they had seen in the days of the Great Marquis." Demographic information is taken from Louisiana censuses, general histories and specialized studies such as

Arnold R. Hirsch and Joseph Logsdon, eds., *Creole New Orleans, Race and Americanization* (Baton Rouge: Louisiana State University Press, 1992) and Gwendolyn Midlo Hall, "Africans in Colonial Louisiana," *Cultural Vistas* 3, no. 4 (winter 1992). Newspapers, in particular the *Daily Picayune*, the *Crescent*, the *True Delta*, *The Bee*, the *Courier* and the *Commercial Bulletin* are the most comprehensive source of information on nineteenth-century Carnival and on the social and political context in New Orleans. Antebellum travelers who published their impressions of New Orleans and Mardi Gras include J. H. Ingraham, *The South West by a Yankee* (New York: Harper & Bros., 1835); James Silk Buckingham, *Slave States of America* (London: Fisher, Son & Co., 1842); Louis Tasistro, *Random Shots and Southern Breezes* (New York: Harper & Bros., 1842); Sir Charles Lyell, *A Second Visit to the United States of North America* (London: J. Murray, 1849); and Henry Murray, *Lands of the Slave and Free* (London: J. W. Parker, 1855). Disparaging remarks about New Orleans and its unbookish ways come from Robert Gibbes Barnwell, ed., *The New Orleans Book* (New Orleans: Robert Gibbes Barnwell, 1851) and Aubrey Starke, "Richard Henry Wilde and the Establishment of the University of Louisiana," *Louisiana Historical Quarterly* 17 (October 1934). Judith Schafer, "New Orleans Slavery in 1850 as Seen in Advertisements," *Journal of Southern History* 47, no. 1 (1981) notes the white complexions of many supposed Negroes.

The antebellum interaction between Americans and Creoles of European stock is documented by Joseph G. Tregle, Jr., in *Hirsch and Logsdon*. The migration of the elite from the central city is examined in Frederick Starr's *Southern Comfort: The Garden District of New Orleans, 1800–1900* (Cambridge, Mass.: MIT Press, 1989). Among the buildings featured is John Pope's place, although his role in Mardi Gras is not mentioned. New Orleans's fascination with the dance is demonstrated in R. Randall Couch's "The Public Masked Balls of Antebellum New Orleans: A Custom of Masque Outside the Mardi Gras Tradition," *Louisiana History* 35 (fall 1994). Robert C. Reinders, *End of an Era, New Orleans 1850–1860* (Gretna, La.: Pelican, 1964) provides a detailed account of the condition of New Orleans at the time of Comus's emergence. The early years of modern Carnival are covered in J. Curtis Waldo's *History of the Carnival at New Orleans from 1857 to 1882* (New Orleans: Graham, 1882); Perry Young's *The Mistick Krewe, Chronicles of Comus and his Kin* (New Orleans: Carnival Press, 1931); *Diamond Jubilee,* a booklet privately published by Comus in 1931; and Arthur LaCour's *New Orleans Masquerade* (New Orleans: LaCour, Inc., 1957). Collateral information is supplied by Stuart Landry, *History of the Boston Club* (Gretna, La.: Pelican, 1938) and Augusto Miceli, *History of the Pickwick Club* (New Orleans: Pickwick Press, 1964). The quotations from *Comus, a Maske Presented at Ludlow Castle in 1634* are taken from *The Poetical Works of Milton,* ed. Helen Darbyshire (London: Oxford University Press, 1958).

CHAPTER THREE

The Carnival fraternity's Civil War exploits are traced through newspaper accounts, Landry and Miceli, and the comparison of club membership lists with Arthur W. Bergeron's *Guide to Louisiana Confederate Military Units 1861–1865* (Baton Rouge: Louisiana State University Press, 1989). Harry Hays's campaigns are covered in Terry L. Jones's "The Louisiana Tigers," *Civil War, Magazine of the Civil War Society* 11, no. 5 (September–October 1993). The saga of the *Pioneer* is recounted in Thomas M. Czekanski's "The Confederate Submarine on Jackson Square," *Cultural Vistas* 5, no. 3 (fall 1994). Accounts of Benjamin Butler's sojourn in New Orleans include James Parton's *General Butler in New Orleans* (New York: Mason Brothers, 1864), "Rule of the Beast," *Newsletter of Louisiana Historical Association's Memorial Hall Foundation* (January 1994) and Gerard Patterson's "The Beast of New Orleans," *Civil War Times Illustrated* (May–June 1993). Other sources include John Blassingame, *Black New Orleans, 1860– 1880* (Chicago: University of Chicago Press, 1973); Mary Boykin Chesnut, *A Diary from Dixie,* Ben Ames Williams, ed. (Boston: Harvard University Press, 1949); and William Howard Russell, *My Diary North and South* (Boston: Harper & Bros., 1863). Whitelaw Reid's Civil War reports are collected in James G. Smart, ed., *A Radical View: The Agate Dispatches of Whitelaw Reid* (Memphis: Memphis State University Press, 1976). The Civil War cartoon of Butler is among the memorabilia at the Confederate Museum in New Orleans.

CHAPTER FOUR

In addition to newspaper accounts, the atrocities that occurred in the aftermath of the Civil War are catalogued in *Riots in New Orleans in 1866,* Congressional Select Committee Report, 1867; Emily Hazen Reed's *Life of A. P. Dostie* (New York: William P. Tomlinson, 1868) and *Ku Klux Conspiracy,* Congressional Select Committee Report, 1872. Joe Gray Taylor's *Louisiana Reconstructed, 1863–1877* (Baton Rouge: Louisiana State University Press, 1974) is the definitive work on the general history of the period, while the United States Fifth Circuit Court of Appeals ruling in *Louisiana v. United States,* 1963, written by John Minor Wisdom, gives an overview of racial strife from Louisiana's foundation. Miriam G. Reeves, *The Governors of Louisiana* (Gretna, La.: Pelican, 1972) is helpful in the political context. *Carpet-Bag Misrule in Louisiana* (New Orleans: Louisiana State Museum, 1939) illustrates the unreconstructed supremacism of white New Orleans generations later. Charles Dufour, *If Ever I Cease to Love* (New Orleans: The School of Design, 1970) provides an exhaustive history of Rex parades and balls. The Comus Origin of Species booklet and Charles Darwin's letter to the krewe captain are in the Tulane University Mardi Gras collection.

CHAPTER FIVE

Newspapers, in this chapter and henceforward, provide firsthand accounts with sufficient detail to offset their frequent political bias. Later accounts of the Battle of Liberty Place that were consulted include Judith Schafer's "The Battle of Liberty Place: A Matter of Historical Perception," transcript of a lecture given to the Louisiana Historical Society, New Orleans, October 13, 1992, and Stuart Landry's *The Battle of Liberty Place* (Gretna, La.: Pelican, 1955). The role of the krewemen and club is traced by means of the *Roster of the White League* (New Orleans: 1977). The account of the White League's invasion of the integrated school is taken from George Washington Cable's story "The Haunted House" in *Strange, True Stories of Louisiana* (New York: C. Scribner's Sons, 1889).

CHAPTER SIX

The Lafcadio Hearn quotation is from "The Dawn of the Carnival," *New Orleans Item* (February 2, 1880). The Henry Hearsey story has been put together largely through his own writings, although John Wilde's *Afternoon Story, a Century of the States-Item* (Baton Rouge: Louisiana State University Press, 1976) provides perspective. Visitors' impressions are from Ernst von Hesse Wartegg, *Travels on the Lower Mississippi* (Leipzig: Verlag von Carl Reisner, 1881), and from George Sala, *America Revisited* (London: Vizetelly & Co., 1883). Tulane's Amistad Research Center and Hogan Jazz Archive contain exhibits on the Mardi Gras Indians, whose best chronicler is Michael P. Smith, *Spirit World: Pattern in the Expressive*

Folk Culture of Afro-American New Orleans (New Orleans: New Orleans Urban Folklife Society, 1984) and *Mardi Gras Indians* (Gretna, La.: Pelican, 1994). Authoritative source on the red-light district is Al Rose's *Storyville* (Tuscaloosa: University of Alabama Press, 1974). Where the Comus of a particular year is identified, in this and subsequent chapters, the source is a list maintained by a krewe member but not, of course, published.

CHAPTER SEVEN

Contemporary accounts, including newspaper advertisements inciting the lynching, are bolstered by "The New Orleans Mafia Incident," *Louisiana Historical Quarterly* 20 (October 1937) and Thomas Dabney, *100 Great Years: The Story of the Times-Picayune from its Founding to 1940* (Baton Rouge: Louisiana State University Press, 1944).

CHAPTER EIGHT

The United States Supreme Court epochal ruling in *Plessy v. Ferguson* came on May 18, 1896. William Ivy Hair, *Carnival of Fury, Robert Charles and the New Orleans Race Riot of 1900* (Baton Rouge: Louisiana State University Press, 1976) retells the last big story of Major Hearsey's career. Information on the long-ago popularity of the German is drawn from Vaughn L. Glasgow, "The Mystery of the Carnival German," *Cultural Vistas* 4, no. 4 (winter 1993). The "Letter from President Theodore Roosevelt to John Parker" is in the possession of the Parker family.

CHAPTER NINE

Flyers distributed in uptown New Orleans urging support for the attempt to displace Huey Long are to be found in private collections in the city, and a few old-timers still remember the incident. T. Harry Williams's *Huey Long* (New York:

Knopf, 1969) is a comprehensive biography, although Carnival types tend to regard it as something of a whitewash. Carnival developments between the wars are traced through newspapers and other sources mentioned above.

CHAPTER TEN

The spirit of Earl Long has been captured in several books, including A. J. Liebling's *The Earl of Louisiana* (New York: Simon & Schuster, 1961), and Michael Kurtz's and Morgan D. Peoples's *The Saga of Uncle Earl and Louisiana Politics* (Baton Rouge: Louisiana State University Press, 1990). Judge Wisdom's career is summarized in Gregory Roberts's "Judge John Minor Wisdom," *Dixie Magazine* (New Orleans: August 21, 1983). The newer "superkrewes" are the subject of Myron Tassin's *Bacchus* (Gretna, La.: Pelican, 1975) and Arthur Hardy's *Silver Memories, Twenty-Five Years of Endymion* (New Orleans: Arthur Hardy Enterprises, 1991).

CHAPTER ELEVEN

This is entirely the result of firsthand reporting on hearings, committee reports and amendments to the desegregation ordinance and of interviews with interested parties.

CHAPTER TWELVE

This chapter also largely consists of firsthand reporting. The consolidated case of the *Louisiana, Stratford, Boston and Pickwick Clubs v. City of New Orleans* in the United States District Court, Eastern District of Louisiana, was numbered 93–658. Henri Schindler's *Times-Picayune* column was titled "The Gods Depart" and appeared September 4, 1992.

CHAPTER THIRTEEN

This is also mostly firsthand reporting. Clubmen's quotations are from depositions given in the litigation against the city.

The Liberty Monument controversy was also summarized, and a solution proposed, in Larry Powell's "A Concrete Symbol," *Southern Exposure* 18, no. 1 (spring 1990). The anti-Carnival fundamentalist pamphlet, Russell K. Tardo, Faithful Word Publications, is undated.

CHAPTER FOURTEEN

The European Carnival tradition of imagining society turned upside down is examined in Peter Burke's *Popular Culture in Early Modern Europe* (New York: New York University Press, 1978) and quoted in Samuel Kinser's *Carnival American Style: Mardi Gras at New Orleans and Mobile* (Chicago: University of Chicago Press, 1990). The examples cited in this chapter are taken from Burke.

Index

Index

Index

Index

Index

Semmes, Thomas, 160
Severinson, Doc, 212
Seymour, Horatio, 87
Shakespeare, William, 254
Shakspeare, New Orleans Mayor
 Joseph, 137, 145, 148, 150, 152,
 160, 178
Shakspeare, Nita, 160
Shaw, F., Jr., 44
Shaw, William, 202
Shenandoah Valley, 84
Sheridan, General Philip, 80, 81,
 84, 94, 120, 121, 126
Sherman, General William
 Tecumseh, 126
Shiloh, Battle of, 60, 95
Ship Island, 60
Shreveport Times (newspaper), 122,
 125
Shubert, Francis, 261, 267
Sicilian Protection Fund, 149
Sider, J. A., 160
Silvain, opera performed in 1796,
 30
Simpson, O. J., 281
Singer Sewing Machines, 99
Singleton, New Orleans City
 Councilman James, 21, 23, 229,
 235, 238, 265
Slave uprising of 1811, 33, 67
Smarter Set (musical), 168
Smither, Charles, 213
Soule, Mary Brooks, 198
Soulie, George, 102, 103, 131
Southern University, New Orleans,
 265
Southward, Marian, 73
Sparta, Krewe of, 236
Spenser, Edmund, 90, 254, 255

Spotsylvania, Battle of, 77
Square Deal Association, 175, 187,
 191
Standard Oil Company, 179
Stanley, Henry Morton, 42
Stauffer, William, 165
Stern, Edith, 194
Stern, Edgar, 194
Stevenson, Robert Louis, 254
Stith, New Orleans Mayor Gerard,
 51
Story, Sidney, 159
Story, William, 168
Storyville, 159, 167, 169, 170,
 173, 189
Stratford Club, 157, 252, 257, 269,
 270, 271
Supreme Court of Louisiana, 40,
 118, 170, 182
Supreme Court of the United
 States, 16, 173
Swamp, the, area of New Orleans,
 42, 43
Sykes, Troisville, 138

Taft, William Howard, 165
Taylor, New Orleans City Council
 member Dorothy Mae, 3, 4, 14,
 15, 16, 17, 20, 22, 23, 24, 25,
 26, 97, 214, 217, 220, 222, 224,
 225, 226, 227, 228, 229, 231,
 232, 233, 234, 235, 240, 241,
 243, 244, 245, 247, 250, 254,
 255, 259, 266, 267, 279, 280,
 281
Taylor, Earl, 251
Teamer, Charles, 251
Tennyson, Alfred, Lord, 254
Thompson, Lydia, 96, 99, 100

Index